Practicing Basic Skills in Reading

Ray Beck, Ed.D., Peggy Anderson, Ph.D.,
and A. Denise Conrad, Ed.D.

Sopris West®
EDUCATIONAL SERVICES

A Cambium Learning® Company

BOSTON, MA • LONGMONT, CO

12 11 10 09 08 5 4 3 2 1

ISBN-13: 978-1-60218-506-7
ISBN-10: 1-60218-506-9

Printed in the United States of America
Published and Distributed by

Sopris West®
EDUCATIONAL SERVICES

A Cambium Learning® Company

4093 Specialty Place ▪ Longmont, Colorado 80504 ▪ (303) 651-2829
www.sopriswest.com

165999/0237/05-08

About the Authors

Ray Beck, Ed.D., is currently a consultant for Sopris West Educational Services, where he trains and consults in the development and dissemination of both positive discipline and fluency programs. As a school psychologist and former Director of Special Education in Great Falls, Montana, Beck directed the development of two U.S. Department of Education-validated programs, *Project RIDE* (Responding to Individual Differences in Education) and *Basic Skill Builders*. Beck conducts training and/or workshops on three Sopris West publications: *RIDE, Basic Skill Builders,* and *One-Minute Academic Functional Assessment: Can't Do It ... or Won't Do It?*

A. Denise Conrad, Ed.D., recently retired as Director of Special Education in Great Falls, Montana, has past experience as a teacher and administrator in both general and special education. In addition, Conrad has been providing consultation, workshop, and university-level training to educators and other professionals throughout the United States and Canada since 1973. A primary focus of her work has been training educators to provide effective educational programs and services to children and adolescents with various types of disabilities. Conrad has developed numerous classroom curricula and teacher training materials. She is a codeveloper of the *Basic Skill Builders* Program, and she most recently coauthored *Cool Kids: A Proactive Approach to Social Responsibility.*

Peggy Anderson, Ph.D., recently retired as the Superintendent of Schools in Frenchtown, Montana, was an elementary principal for 14 years in Florida and Montana prior to becoming the Superintendent of Schools. An educator for the past 36 years, Anderson has been an elementary classroom teacher, a special education resource room teacher, and the coordinator of the U.S. Department of Education Validated Project "Basic Skill Builders Precision Teaching." She has been a trainer in both *Basic Skill Builders* and *Project RIDE* and is coauthor of the *Basic Skill Builders Handbook*. Anderson brings her experience from both the regular education classroom and her work with special education students to her training with administrators, teachers, parents, and para-educators. She assists districts as they incorporate *Basic Skill Builders* into their current curriculum.

Contents

**Small print fluency skill sheets recommended for use only by older students.*

Phonemic Awareness—Phoneme Isolation

Grades K–2; Intervention Grade 3 and Above

Skill Sheets 7–16 contain single and multisyllabic words related to a specific topic.

Phonemic Awareness—Phoneme Segmentation

Grades K–2; Intervention Grade 3 and Above

Reading Isolated Sounds

Grades K–2; Intervention Grade 3 and Above

Blending/Reading Isolated Decodable Nonsense Words

Grades K–2; Intervention Grade 3 and Above

Blending/Reading Isolated Decodable Real Words

Grades K–2; Intervention Grade 3 and Above

**Small print fluency skill sheets recommended for use only by older students.*

Reading High Frequency Sight Words

Dolch Words by Level

Grades K–3

Dolch Words by List

Grades K–3, Intervention Grade 3 and Above

**Small print fluency skill sheets recommended for use only by older students.*

General High Frequency Words (Coordinated With *Basic Skill Builders Spelling*)

Intervention Grade 2 and Above

**Small print fluency skill sheets recommended for use only by older students.*

Beginning Reading—Isolated Words and Sentences

Grades K–2

Reading Passages

K–7; Intervention Grades 3–12

Appendix

Note: As detailed in the following table, Pre-First and Second Grade reading passages from Alan Hofmeister's *Iseesam Series* are reproduced with permission from Reading for All Learners, 131 N. 1175 W., Ste. 5, Logan, UT 84321. E-mail: read@iseesam.com.

Grade Level	Book	Pages Used	Word Count
Pre-First			
0.1	Set 1-1	all	38
0.2	Set 1-3	all	38
0.3	Set 1-5	all	46
0.4	Set 1-7	all	54
0.5	Set 1-9	all	70
0.6	Set 1-11	all	74
0.7	Set 1-13	all	58
0.8	Set 1-15	all	64
0.9	Set 1-24	all	96
10	Set 1-27	all	79
Second Grade			
2.1	Sam Set 5-1	9–11	189
2.2	Set 5-3	5–7	206
2.3	Set 5-5	17–19	185
2.4	Set 5-7	5–7	240
2.5	Set 5-9	29–31	211
2.6	Set 5-11	5–7	252
2.7	Set 5-13	5–7	198
2.8	Set 6-1	5–7	222
2.9	Set 6-3	13–15	219
2.101	Set 6-5	5–7	240
2.11	Set 6-7	15–17	219
2.12	Set 6-9	5–8	201
2.13	Set 6-11	5–7	204
2.14	Set 6-13	15–17	226
2.15	Set 7-1	13–15	219
2.16	Set 7-3	5–7	198
2.17	Set 7-5	5–7	203
2.18	Set 7-5	17–20	224
2.19	Set 7-9	15–17	211
2.2	Set 7-11	18–20	207

The remaining reading passages are adapted from Susan Ebbers' *Power Readers*, published by Sopris West Educational Services, and selections from the *Nonfiction Bookbag*, also published by Sopris West.

Introduction

An individual is considered fluent in a skill, whether it is athletic, music, art, or academic, when he or she is able to demonstrate the skill accurately and perform it quickly. Educators often equate fluency with words like: "automatic," "without thinking," "flows," "can do it quickly," "comfort," "smooth," and "competent." To become fluent, students need first to be taught the skill and then provided multiple opportunities to practice it.

Becoming fluent means there is a higher probability that the student will retain the skill over time, that the skill can be applied to higher-level tasks, that the student will be less distracted, and that the skill will be generalized across settings. It is important to remember that fluency comes after the student has been "taught" the skill. Without appropriate instruction, including modeling and guided practice, independent practice will have little, if any impact. Our motto is: TEACH FIRST, then practice.

The full One-Minute Fluency Builders series is a collection of over 1,500 basic skill sheets that focus on math, reading, grammar, spelling, and handwriting, as well as other content areas. These are accompanied by a set of classroom procedures and a monitoring process that, when combined, significantly increase the chances of students in regular and special settings becoming comfortable and competent in everyday skills.

Once a student has been taught a skill, five steps guide the process for fluency building:

I. Selecting the Skill and Fluency Sheet(s)
II. Providing Practice Opportunities
III. Monitoring and Charting Progress
IV. Making Data-Based Decisions
V. Refining, Reviewing, and Selecting the Next Skill to Practice

Questions to consider in the process:

- What specific skill will be practiced and which Fluency Sheet(s) can be used to facilitate the practice activity?
- How will the goal be set and what is an appropriate goal for my students?
- How will practice opportunities be structured during the school day?
- What kind of chart or graph will be used to keep track of the data?
- What are the guidelines for making data-based decisions?
- What is the next step—do we move on, continue, or step back?

The Reading Fluency Sheets contain fluency sheets for both primary and intermediate or more advanced skills. In each skill sequence, the Fluency Sheets are organized from easy to more difficult. Keep in mind it is *not* necessary that a student complete or demonstrate fluency on each sheet in the entire sequence. Part of the process, (Step 1), is to select the Fluency Sheet that best fits your reading curriculum and the needs of your particular student(s).

Step I. Selecting the Skill and the Fluency Sheet(s)

When selecting a reading skill on which to work, first decide the general skill you want to address, such as oral reading of isolated words. Fluency Sheets are available in a variety of reading skill areas, including:

- Saying letter names
- Phonemic Awareness—beginning and ending sounds
- Phonemic Awareness—word segmentation

- Saying isolated consonant and/or vowel sounds
- Reading decodable words—nonsense words or real words
- Reading high frequency sight words
- Reading phrases or sentences

After deciding the general skill you want to address, e.g., reading isolated decodable words, determine the specific skill or difficulty level at which to start, e.g., consonant-vowel-consonant words with the short "a" sound.

In selecting skills to practice and monitor, you will want to match the skill sheet selected to the curriculum or other assessment materials being used on a regular basis in the classroom. Fluency Sheets can be used in conjunction with any commercial basal reading program. If the reading program is one which is highly skill-based, such as *Read Well* (Sprick, et al., 2006–2009), the teacher can easily use the in-program assessments as a basis for selecting which skill to target. For example, if the *Read Well* unit test indicates the student is struggling with recognizing and saying isolated letter sounds, the teacher can select an appropriate Fluency Sheet such as See to Say Reading Isolated Sounds: Consonant Sounds and Digraphs (page 113).

The teacher might instead use other assessment information already available to aid in selecting a starting point. For example, many teachers and schools may use assessment programs such as Dynamic Indicators of Basic Early Literacy Skills (DIBELS) (Good & Kaminski, 2003), assessing the performance of all students several times a year and some students every few weeks. However, the teacher may use the Fluency Sheets to provide *daily* practice and measurement on those skills identified as needs through the DIBELS assessments. For example, the DIBELS Nonsense Word Fluency test assesses a student's ability to blend letter sounds together to form "words." Any of the Blending/Reading Isolated Decodable Nonsense Words or Blending/Reading Isolated Decodable Real Words Fluency Sheets might be used on a daily basis to help the student increase fluency in this area.

If the student and teacher can only use the One-Minute Fluency Builders process for a few minutes each day, they may choose to work on only one skill strand at a time. If this is their decision, it is highly recommended that they focus on the global skill of orally reading passages or prose. While some beginning level sentence reading sheets are available in the One-Minute Fluency Builders materials, the teacher may need to develop additional fluency sheets based on the classroom reader being used by the student. To develop oral passage reading sheets:

- Select a passage from each story or selection in the student's grade level text.
  - Choose passages of consistent difficulty and readability.
  - Avoid passages with unique dialogue, many unusual proper nouns, etc.
- Each passage should be long enough so that students cannot completely read the entire passage within the one-minute timing. Passages for students in second grade and beyond will need to have 150–200 or even more words on each sheet.
- Type the passage using a print or font familiar to students. Put a cumulative count of the number of words read at the end of each row so that the listener can easily track how many words per minute the student has read without having to go back and count each word.
- Make at least two copies of the sheet—one for the student and one for the teacher or listener.

While many teachers may choose to practice and measure only one reading skill at a time, it is possible to address several different reading tool skills each day if the fluency building session is a little longer. For example, the student might complete four different one-minute timings:

1. Saying isolated sounds
2. Using blending skills to orally read a list of consonant-vowel-consonant (CVC) words
3. Orally reading a list of high frequency sight words
4. Orally reading words in context, such as a first grade level story

Fluency Sheets can be used to reinforce a skill that the teacher is currently teaching in the classroom; or they can be used as practice to increase fluency on skills that have been previously taught but ones on which the student has not yet developed fluency. Reading high frequency sight words, for example, may be a new skill for a first grader. The teacher selects Fluency

Sheets that are tied to the classroom curriculum as one way to practice a skill as it is being introduced and taught by the teacher. Reading high frequency sight words is not a new skill for a third grader, but rather a review activity. Some student(s) may have developed accuracy, but are not yet fluent in this skill. In other words, sight words are not automatically recognized, easily retrieved, nor used for more complex reading tasks. To assist in building fluency a teacher would select a Fluency Sheet where the student feels comfortable and confident, and where practice will have a positive impact on helping the student begin to strengthen the skill.

Once you have selected the skill to be practiced, the next step is to ask yourself how the student will be asked to demonstrate knowledge. To answer this question, teachers will need to take learning channels into consideration. Quite simply, learning channels offer a clear way of explaining the modality students use to receive the information (the "input channel") and how we ask the child to respond (the "output channel"). In reading tasks, most often the input channel is See (see the item) and the output channel is Say (say the answer), but not always. You might elect to have the student See-Think (see the item and think the answer as in silent reading) or in some cases See-Write (see the item and write the answer) or even Hear-Write (hear the question or item and write the answer). When using Think as the input channel, a teacher is giving an initial written or verbal direction such as "Tell me all the facts you remember from the passage you read." Then the student is using information they already know cognitively to write or say (the output channel).

The following matrix will help you determine the learning channel to use with your student(s).

INPUT (Item)	OUTPUT (Answer)
See	Write
See	Say
See	Mark
Hear	Write
Hear	Say
Think	Write
Think	Say

Selecting the learning channel may in part depend upon prerequisite skills that the student has demonstrated in the past. In other words, if the reading skill has typically been presented in a See-Say format, and the student has a sense of comfort and confidence, it follows that subsequent Fluency Sheets might well be presented in similar fashion. Teachers should also view the use of learning channels as an opportunity to reinforce a skill by practicing using a different combination (e.g., Hear-Write rather than See-Say). A further explanation will be provided when we talk about practice opportunities. In the beginning select the learning channel that is the most common way students will be responding to the problems.

Setting the Fluency Goal

There should be clear expectations defining the level of performance the student must exhibit in order to be considered fluent. After selecting a starting point, it is important to set a goal indicating how accurately and quickly the student must demonstrate the skill before moving on. Remember, a fluent student is one who can perform the skill accurately with little or no hesitation. Accuracy plus speed results in automaticity.

When clear and high expectations are set and are reasonable, students are more likely to engage and attempt to reach the goal. In some cases, however, it might be necessary to establish short-term aim rather than expect the student to immediately reach a final fluency standard. In this way, teachers can help students celebrate reaching short-term aims, which is reinforcing and demonstrates that skill acquisition is progressing.

With One-Minute Fluency Builders we use "aims" to represent intermediate or short-term goals. We use "fluency standards" to represent a level of performance that ensures retention over time, ease in transferring the skill to more complex learning tasks, and generalization.

Fluency standards help guide students to a level where the skill becomes automatic, thus instantly available. The following are suggested fluency standards for reading. It is assumed the student may need to engage in repeated timings on the same skill or Fluency Sheet over a period of days in order to reach these standards.

Task	Fluency Standard
Think to Say Alphabet	400 letters/minute
See to Say Letter Names	80–100 letters/minute
See to Say Sounds	40–60 sounds/minute
See to Say Phonetic Words	40–60 words/minute
See to Say Sight Words	80–100 words/minute
Oral Reading of Passages	200 words/minute
Silent Reading of Passages	400 words/minute
Think to Say Facts (about a passage)	15–30 facts/minute

If setting aims based on fluency standards seems unrealistic, intermediate goals or aims can be set. An easy way to set initial oral reading aims for young students is to merely double their first day score. For example, if the student reads a passage at 45 words per minute on the first attempt, the aim will be set at 90 words per minute. A caution: Be careful not to set an aim so low that the student moves on to a new skill without being competent in the previous skill.

Two procedures commonly used to set aims or standards are (1) to use the performance of students who are considered fluent in the class, or (2) another is to use an adult's fluency in the skill and adjust to the skill level and grade level of the students.

Peer performance is often a fair and effective method for determining aims, particularly if there are no established fluency standards, or little is known about the specific tasks. It is helpful to have three or four peers who are considered fluent take at least three timed practices and average these students' scores for the individual or classwide fluency standard.

Rather than use peer data, the teacher might instead use his or her performance as a beginning standard and, dependent upon the age and grade level of the student, adjust accordingly. Fluency is the smooth, effortless performance of a skill at the student's achievement level. By fifth and sixth grade the students, if fluent readers, should be able to perform the task, when proficient, at close to the same rate as the teacher.

You may want to set fluency ranges, e.g., 80–100, rather than a single specific number. Remember that aims are not set in stone; aims are just short-term goals. For every aim that you set, you will have students who will not only achieve the aim, but will exceed it. As the teacher you need to ensure that students have realistic aims, and also realize that aims can change as students become more fluent in both the tool skills and the basic skills. Set clear and high expectations for your students.

Step II. Providing Practice Opportunities

Once the skill has been taught, a closely related Fluency Sheet has been selected, and an aim or fluency standard has been established, it is time to start conducting daily practice sessions with the students. Fluency building is guided by timed practice. Pioneers in the movement found that one-minute timed practice provides a sufficient time frame in which students can maximize their performance and that teachers can fit into their busy daily schedules while collecting data on student growth each day.

Managing the Practice Time

Each student has his or her own Fluency Sheet to use, with a second copy of the same sheet for the listener to use in the monitoring and correction process. To manage the materials, students use a manila folder with a sheet of clear acetate taped inside upon which to write their responses or on which student errors can be noted. Acetate is a heavier grade material than a typical sheet of transparency and increases the life span of the folder.

NOTE: Student materials such as the acetate and marking pens are sold separately and are available through Sopris West Educational Services.

If the student is performing an oral reading task, he or she uses one copy of the Fluency Sheet; the second copy of the Fluency Sheet is placed under the acetate and with a dry erase or water-soluble pen, the listener marks, underlines, or circles any incorrect responses on the acetate cover sheet. A skipped word is not counted as either a correct or incorrect response; self-corrected errors are counted as correct responses. When the one-minute time sample is complete, the listener and/or the reader count the number of correct and incorrect responses. It is important to let your students know that they are not expected to complete the entire sheet in one minute, but the expectation is that with each timed practice they will increase the number of responses.

At the end of each row, you will see a number in parentheses; this number is the number of correct answers for that row.

Timings can be conducted in several different ways.

1. The teacher, paraprofessional, or other adult can individually listen to each student read for one minute using a stopwatch or the second hand of a clock or watch as a timer.
2. Students can work with a cross-age tutor. All students can complete their one-minute timing simultaneously. The teacher will start and stop all students at the same time.
3. Students can work with a classmate as a partner. One student reads while the other student times and records errors. They then switch roles.
4. An audio tape with music that includes a tone at one-minute intervals can be used. It should have 10–15 minutes of timed music where individual students or student pairs can start or stop on their own and don't have to wait for others to be ready. Students should manage their own timed practice, starting/stopping, counting corrects and errors, and self-recording their scores daily.
   NOTE: Fluency Building: Practicing the Skills has a video that demonstrates the management of the practice session.

Many teachers find that starting each reading class with the timed practice session sets the tone for the remainder of the class period. Students are ready to work and have practiced a basic skill before moving into the lesson to be taught that day. Another option is to set up the timed practice to occur right after a recess or a break. In this method, materials can be set out before the break; as students file back into the classroom, the music tape begins and students start as they are ready. This also helps to set the stage for the next class and to bring students into the classroom quietly with a purpose.

Practice Options

Use a Different Channel to Make the Skill Easier:

The See-Write or paper pencil activity is the easiest channel to manage in a classroom because all of the students can be working at the same time (as a group activity), possibly on different Fluency Sheets. Many reading activities involve the See-Say channel, and most teachers elect to use the Fluency Sheets in this manner. However, they can also be used as a Hear-Say or echo or paired reading activity if independent decoding is a problem for a student. For both of these options the student needs a partner, (a peer, a cross-age tutor, volunteer, or teacher) who can listen as the student says the answers and mark the errors when they occur.

Use Paired Timings:

A teacher might also elect to practice a tool skill sheet before doing the See-Say Fluency Sheet. This strategy is called Paired Timings. A tool skill is a prerequisite skill or building block for the basic skill. For a third grader working on third grade passage reading, the tool skill might be automatically recognizing and reading all the Dolch words; this skill of reading high frequency sight words needs to be at a fluent level, allowing the student to use this information to fluently read prose or words in context. What is a basic skill at one level becomes a tool skill at a more advanced grade level. Identifying letter sounds is a basic skill for kindergarten or first grade students. However, recognizing and saying isolated letter sounds is more likely to be considered a tool skill for upper elementary or middle school students. If the older reader is not fluent in this prerequisite tool skill, the teacher may want to pair a timing on saying sounds prior to the basic skill timing on passage reading.

Change the Learning Channel to Make the Skill More Challenging:

Learning channels might also be used during the practice session as a way to reinforce a basic skill that has been practiced to fluency using another channel. An example would be to use any Fluency Sheet for passage reading, first as an oral reading or See-Say activity until the students are fluent and then, using the same Fluency Sheet, change the learning channel to a silent reading or See-Think activity. Another example would be to have students initially practice comprehension of read material by performing an oral Think-Say facts about the chapter or story, but then transition to having them perform the same type of task as a written or Think-Write activity to strengthen this skill.

Teachers should always start with the largest slice of the curriculum possible to help students move through the curriculum quickly and efficiently. If all students started working for fluency on only two or three new sight words, and then progressed to another two or three words and so on, students would fall quickly behind in the curriculum. For most students working on fluency building, it is best to start large and then "slice back" when you see that you have taken too large a slice. One way to determine where to start is to analyze the more complex Fluency Sheets to see where the breakdown is and what skills are giving a student trouble, then use this as either a starting point or provide more teaching or practice in that slice of the skill. Another way to start is to tie the Fluency Sheet to the actual skill being taught in the curriculum that day or week so that practice is *directly* related to instruction.

Step III. Monitoring and Charting Progress The most compelling argument for monitoring student performance is in the use of data to make more informed instructional and curricular decisions. By keeping track of performance, you—and more importantly, the students—can see where they have been, where they are now, and where they might be in the future. This continuous monitoring allows us to analyze the past, examine the present, and predict the future. As a by-product, the students have the benefit of immediate feedback and a continual visual display of their progress.

Several options exist for tracking students' daily scores. The first is a simple score sheet where the date is posted, the Fluency Sheet is listed, and the correct and error counts are recorded. This procedure allows a student to directly view their progress from day to day.

Score Sheet

Date	**Fluency Sheet**	**Correct**	**Error**
10/15	Third Grade Sight Words	65	5
10/16	Third Grade Sight Words	70	2
10/17	Third Grade Sight Words	75	1
10/18	Third Grade Sight Words	63	2
10/19	Third Grade Sight Words	68	1
10/22	Third Grade Sight Words	72	0

Another option is to provide a graphic picture of the scores by using a graph common in most classrooms, which shows both corrects and errors as well as the day. For example, the data recorded in the score sheet would look like this on an Equal Interval Graph:

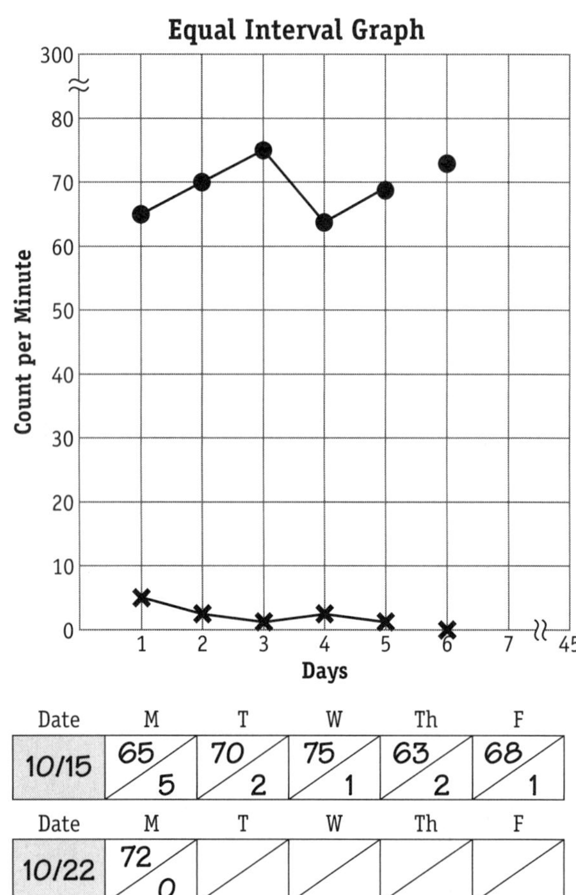

This option allows a student to see his or her progress visually as the lines on the graph show the improvement over time. Students mark the corrects (expressed by a dot •) and errors (expressed by an X) on their graphs as soon as the timed practice is completed. At the end of the week, students connect their dots with a line and connect their Xs with a line. They do not connect the lines between weeks. Growth can be tracked visually so that student and teacher can view past performance and present level of fluency.

A third and more accurate tracking option is using a chart that allows student and teacher to see growth proportionally. While this chart, the Academic Chart, may seem somewhat overwhelming at first glance, with practice and use it will become a tool that not only tracks progress, but also allows the teacher to be more precise when making instructional and curricular decisions. Data charted on this chart can be analyzed and interpreted using proportional growth statements. Because the data is displayed proportionally (the way the learning actually occurs), by extending the learning line, a teacher or student can predict when an aim will be met. On this chart you will see that the day lines have been conveniently divided into separate weeks. This allows the student to connect the number of corrects (expressed as dots •) and errors (expressed as Xs) within the week, but not across the weeks, allowing for more definition to the data.

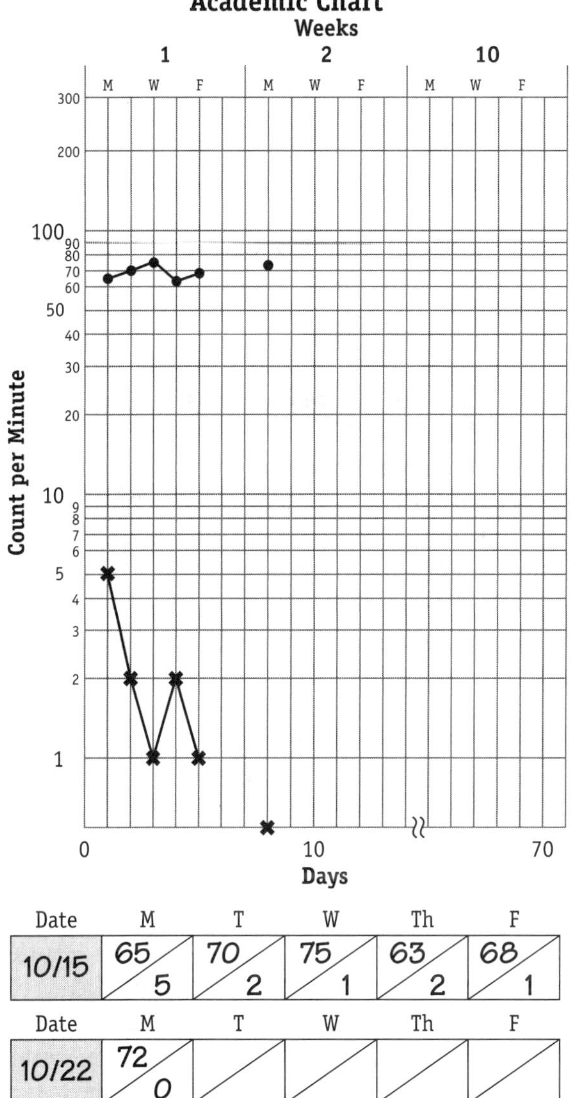

Date	M	T	W	Th	F
10/15	65 / 5	70 / 2	75 / 1	63 / 2	68 / 1

Date	M	T	W	Th	F
10/22	72 / 0				

At first and second grade levels the students can record the number of corrects and errors on the score sheet. By third grade, recording of the data on either of the charts/graphs suggested should be a student-managed activity. The recording of data is completed as soon as the timed practice is finished and students have checked for the number of correct responses and the number of errors. Both scores should be recorded; fluency building involves both accuracy and speed. You should be looking for the number of errors to decrease (accuracy) as the number of correct responses increases (speed). A fluent reader is one who can respond both quickly and accurately.

Step IV. Making Data-Based Decisions

To maximize academic achievement, students cannot waste time practicing skills they find too easy, or skills with which they have already become fluent. Nor can they afford the wasted time and frustration that occurs when they "spin their wheels" practicing a skill in a manner that does not result in increased performance or learning. To determine when it is time to move on or time to intervene, the recorded data should be frequently and regularly reviewed, at least once a week. The decision to change is based on three basic rules:

1. **IF At Aim or at Fluency Standard for Two Days, THEN Move to a More Difficult Fluency Sheet**

   If a student's scores are at or above the previously set aim or fluency standard, it is time for a change. To ensure that scores are valid, students are typically expected to demonstrate performance for more than one timed practice.

   When students reach their aim or fluency standard on the first day, teachers may want to check their performance on the second day to ensure that the aim or fluency standard has truly been reached. A teacher might want to have students who are "going for aim" do their second timed practice with the listener recording errors using pencil and paper rather than the acetate so that the teacher has a hard copy on the final day to review. Another method is to have a separate table set up for those students "going for aim" so that the teacher can monitor their timed practice to ensure that the aim is reached.

2. **IF Three Days of Little or No Growth, THEN Change**

   It is possible that students might stop making progress before reaching the set aim or fluency standard. When the data "flattens out" as displayed on the graph or chart, it suggests that the learning has stalled. Once students have three consecutive days of these "flat data," it is unlikely that further increases in performance will occur without some kind of instructional intervention to reactivate learning. Interventions will be discussed in the next section.

3. **IF Less Than 25% Growth Per Week, THEN Change**

Learning may be occurring, but at such a minimal level that we cannot expect students to reach their aims in any reasonable number of days. Experience and research suggest that we should see at least 25% growth from one week to the next.

Mathematically a teacher can divide the median (middle score) of the first week into the median score of the second week. For example, if the median score in week one was 30 correct and in week two 35 correct, begin by dividing 35 by 30, carry the decimal two places and you should have computed 1.16% growth. This is interpreted as a 16% growth from week one to week two. In this case there was not the minimum of 25% growth.

Another method is to draw a line through the data points for the two weeks that best represents the slope of the data set, and determine if there is at least 25% growth. A template is provided below that can be used in determining whether there is at least a 25% growth pattern.

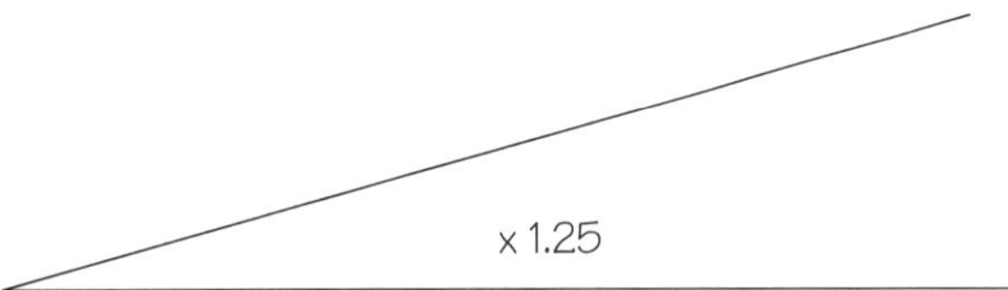

Perhaps the simplest method to determine growth is to draw a line (free hand) through the data, then place a pencil over the line and judge whether the slope is acceptable. Following is an example:

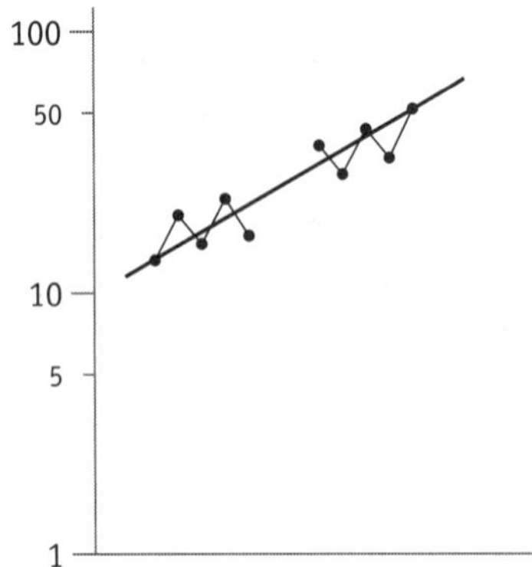

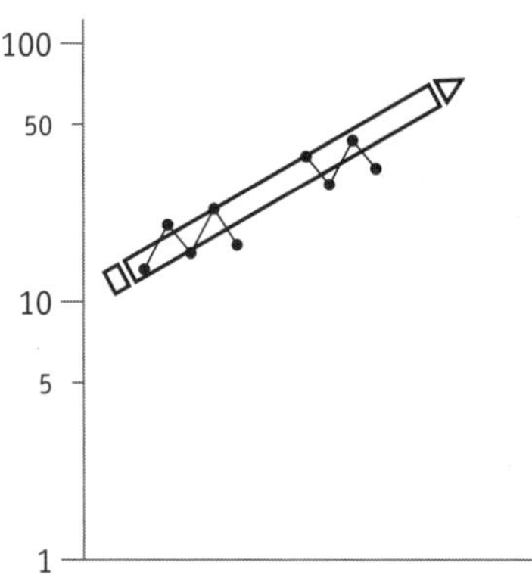

Once a decision has been made that a change is necessary, the next step is: What Change? What Next?

Step V. Refining, Reviewing, Selecting the Next Skill to Practice

You have reviewed the data; you have looked at the decision rules and see that a change is warranted. How do you decide the next step? This decision will depend on several factors including the level of skill development at which the student is operating with respect to the skill being practiced. When learning a new skill students typically move through a series of specific skill development levels or stages.

In the **acquisition stage** students are acquiring a new skill. Their scores are usually below 25 answers per minute on sheets with isolated items such as See-Say Letter Naming or below 40 correct responses per minute on tasks such as passage reading. In the acquisition stage, students are learning how to correctly respond to the targeted skill. Timed practice with Fluency Sheets should not replace teacher instruction, but can be used to monitor the effectiveness of a teaching strategy. If a change is needed and students are performing at the acquisition level, consider:

- Providing more direct instruction on the skill.
- Working on tool skills along with or instead of the current skill, a paired timing.
- Using paired timings with a related easier skill as a warm-up activity before the regular skill.
- Slicing the skill to a subset of the skill (e.g., reading four Dolch words instead of the entire primer list).
- Stepping back to an easier skill or level to build fluency and confidence.
- Changing the learning channel to one that is easier for the student.

- Providing more frequent feedback, possibly even reinforcing each response.

In the **fluency building** or **practice stage** students are not yet at their aim but can respond at a rate of more than 25–40 correct responses per minute. They are refining a skill they have previously acquired. They are becoming more accurate, as well as increasing their frequency. It is at this level that students are working toward mastery of the skill as well as fluency. If a change is necessary when the student is performing at this level, consider:

- Providing instruction specifically addressing the errors made.
- Providing many short, repeated practice opportunities of 15 seconds, 30 seconds, or one minute in length.
- Practicing identified errors:
  - Use flash cards to practice the words missed on previous timings.
  - Leave "yesterday's" errors circled on the acetate and practice them before doing "today's" timing.
- Using paired timings to increase fluency (don't record the score of the warm-up timing):
  - Warm up with a slice of the total skill by having the student read and reread the first two or three sentences of a passage before the regular passage timing.
  - Warm up with a tool skill practice (e.g., practicing an isolated sounds sheet before doing the regular timing on reading "CVC" words).
  - Warm-up timings using different learning channels (e.g., Hear-Point answers on a sheet related to reading letter names).
- Using guided reading as a one-minute warm-up: read with the student, but read a little bit faster than the student does.
- Using "echo reading": listener reads a sentence and then has the student read it back.
- Doing multiple timings: do the timing twice and record and chart the best score.
- Keeping the learning channel consistent from day to day, unless a learning channel change is necessary to facilitate growth.

In the **fluency stage** students are strengthening their command of the skill. A fluent learner can demonstrate both accuracy and speed. For example, fluent performance is the difference between knowing how to type accurately but slowly, and being a competent typist. The skill has become automatic and can now be generalized and applied to other, more complex situations. Change is necessary at this level to continue to challenge the student. Consider:

- Continuing the skill past the aim or fluency standard until the chart flattens and there is no growth.
- Raising the aim.
- Having the child establish his or her own aim.
- Changing the task to a more difficult, related one (e.g., moving from a fourth grade level passage to a fifth grade passage).
- Changing the task to another set of skills (e.g., from oral reading of a story passage to saying facts about a passage read silently).
- Changing the learning channel (e.g., switching from See-Say oral to See-Think silent reading of a passage).
- Doing maintenance timings on the skill periodically to ensure retention.

Whatever the new task, it should add enough curriculum weight that the student's initial scores drop back down to the acquisition or fluency building stage, allowing for continued learning or growth.

Material Management

Before implementing the use of Fluency Sheets, gather and organize all the necessary materials needed for each student, including:

- A stopwatch, timer, or watch/clock with a second-hand, or an audio timing tape.
- Two copies of the Fluency Sheet.
- A manila folder with an acetate sheet taped inside to be used by the listener to mark errors and a score sheet or chart for recording student progress.
- A water-soluble marking or dry-erase pen to use on the acetate.
- A paper towel or sponge to use to erase the acetate.
- A pencil to use in charting.

Because reading is typically a see to say activity, each student needs to read one-on-one with someone. If more than one student at a time is being timed, consider using:

- peer tutors
- cross-age tutors
- paraprofessionals
- parent or community volunteers

One of the keys to successful implementation of One-Minute Fluency Builders is establishing a routine for daily practice sessions. Years of practical experience has demonstrated that students must be skilled in participating in timed practice, scoring and then recording their individual performances. Much like practicing a new academic skill, students should also practice the steps in conducting and scoring one-minute timed practices. The following is a typical day:

1. Request that students retrieve their individual folders. Skill folders have been previously constructed by taping a clear piece of acetate to the inside of the folder and an Academic Chart or Equal Interval Graph on the outside of the folder. The folder and the chart are labeled with the student's name. The curriculum area, "Reading," is written in the lower right corner of the chart. One copy of the Fluency Sheet is placed under the acetate and is used by the listener. A second copy of the Fluency Sheet is used by the reader. The folders can be kept at the individual student's desk, or at a central location in the classroom.
2. Once the folders are available and opened, the students should check to confirm that they have the appropriate Fluency Sheet and one copy is properly placed under the clear acetate.
3. Students are reminded to read as many sounds, letters or words as possible during the one-minute timed practice.
4. Several options exist for conducting the one-minute timed practice. The teacher can time the entire class using a stopwatch, wall clock, or other timing device. The teacher instructs the students to "Please begin," and then in 60 seconds says "Thank you, stop."

   A second possibility is for each pair of students (the reader and the listener) to work independently. The listener uses the clock, stopwatch, etc., to prompt the reader to begin the timing task.

   A third choice involves a music or tone audiotape. In this instance, start a tape player and allow the music to run for 60-second intervals, which are marked by a distinct tone or beep. You can also use a tape with no music, just a tone every 60 seconds. Students score and record the number of corrects and errors from their first trial and prepare for a second try. Give students a second try with the same Fluency Sheet.
5. Scoring is relatively simple. As the student reads the letters, sounds, words, etc., aloud, the listener marks any errors on the acetate covering one copy of the Fluency Sheet. All letters, sounds, or words mispronounced or provided by the listener, are counted as errors. Skipped responses are counted neither as correct nor incorrect. To facilitate quickly counting the number of correct responses, there is a number in parentheses at the end

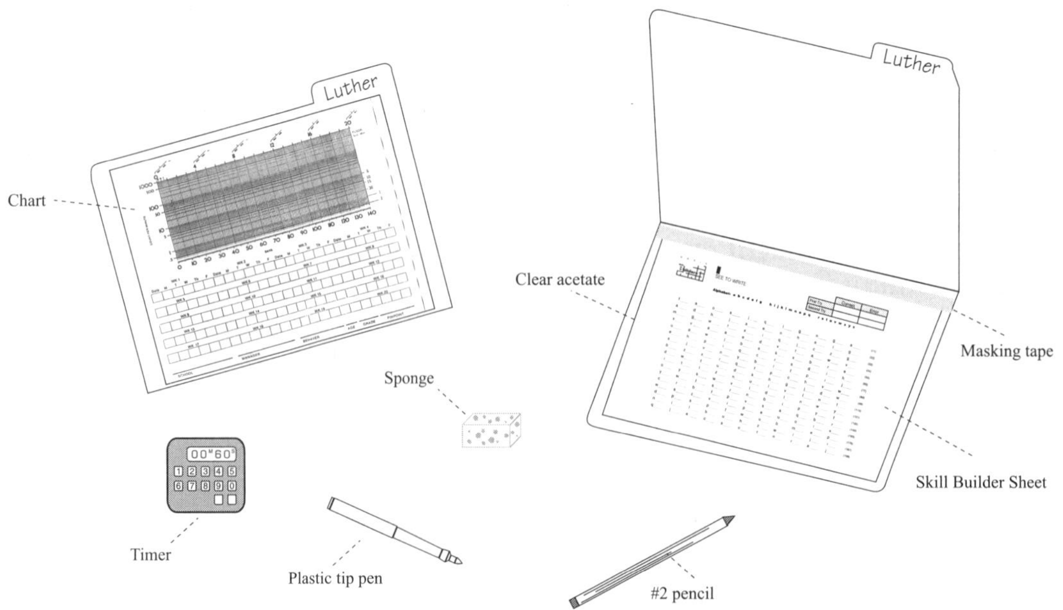

of each row on the Fluency Sheet. This number represents the cumulative number of items on the sheet up that point.

If more than one try is encouraged, students clean the acetate using a small sponge or paper towel. The listener or student records the better of the two trials.

NOTE: Keep sponges collected in a jar with a teaspoon of vinegar and rinse out regularly so that they retain a fresh smell.

6. The next step is putting the data on the chart/graph. If using the Academic Chart, instruct students how to take the raw scores (corrects and errors) and write them in the appropriate day of the week box on the lower half of the chart. Next, instruct students to plot the corrects and errors on the appropriate day line and frequency line intersection on the chart itself. From third grade on, students should be able to do their own charting. Be sure to use a pencil when charting, because it is difficult if not impossible to erase marks made with an ink or marking pen. If using the graph form, students should still chart both corrects and errors.
7. At this point, depending on the overall plan, students can either move on to completing additional timed practices on other Fluency Sheets in other curriculum areas, meet with the teacher for further feedback, or store their folders until they use them again. In any case, teachers should review students' performances at least once a week, and more often if students are at aim or seem to be struggling with the task.

Working with students with special needs or in a remedial placement requires essentially the same materials and procedures as working with regular classroom students. For example, the difference between managing a group of 25 to 30 general classroom students and 15 special needs or at-risk students is that the latter require more individual planning. Teaching at-risk students often means more curriculum slices, tool skill exercises, opportunities to practice, and more time spent in decision making. Additional procedural differences are:

- In these classes there are typically fewer students, but they may have highly complex tasks. The challenge is to individualize, while at the same time managing the timed practice without constant attention. It may be helpful to establish an area or station where students can take their timed practices.
- Establishing a Fluency Sheets "bank" similar to the one found in regular classrooms, allows for the storage of reproducible masters, as well as a place for students to store their individual folders.
- Once students are familiar with the location of their individual folders and the timing procedure, they will become their own best managers.

The following management procedures can be used for several different applications of the Reading Fluency Sheets process.

OPTION I: ORAL PASSAGE READING

Time Required: Approximately 5–10 minutes

First Day of Timed Readings

1. Put your copy of the Fluency Sheet under the acetate sheet that has been taped to the inside cover of the manila file folder.
2. Give the student the other copy of the Fluency Sheet.
3. Prior to starting the timing, explain that the student will read for one minute.
   - Suggest that the student read as quickly as possible during the one minute.
   - Suggest that the student skip any words he or she is unable to read quickly using decoding skills.
   - Explain that if the student reaches the bottom of the page before the timing ends, he or she should start over at the top.
4. Have the student read for one minute using the following verbal cues:
   - "Ready." (Pause **2–3** seconds.)
   - "Please begin."
   - (One minute later.) "Thank you, please stop."

5. If the student is unable to decode a word, immediately tell him or her the word and record it as an error.
6. Mark all errors (words mispronounced or provided) by circling the words on the acetate covering your copy of the Fluency Sheet.
7. At the end of the timing, count all words read correctly and words missed, ignoring that part of the Fluency Sheet or passage the student didn't get to attempt.
8. Using a pencil, record or have the student record the number of corrects and errors on the score sheet or chart. Make sure the date of the timing is marked correctly.
9. Using a damp sponge or cloth, erase the acetate.
10. Place the two copies of the Fluency Sheet and the recording sheet in the student's folder and put away all materials.
NOTE: If an aim hasn't yet been set, double the score from the first day and set that as the aim.

Following Days
1. Use exactly the same Fluency Sheet.
2. Do a one-minute timing starting with Step 4 listed for Day 1.
3. After charting the day's score, help the student compare "today's" performance with the performance for the past few days.

Each Friday or Once a Week
1. Look at each individual student's scores.
2. Decide to continue or change:
   - If the student is making good progress but has not reached the aim, continue doing daily timings as you have been.
   - If the student reached the set aim for at least two days, go to a new, more challenging Fluency Sheet.
   - If the student has shown little or no progress during the past week and if the student's daily rate is *very* low (e.g., less than 15–20 correct responses per minute), it may be necessary to select an easier or lower-level Fluency Sheet.
   - If the student is showing little progress but the number of correct responses is above 15–20 per minute, continue to use the same Fluency Sheet but try some sort of intervention before each day's timing. For example:
     - □ Use flash cards to practice the words missed on yesterday's timing.
     - □ Do a 30-second warm-up timing on the first two or three sentences or rows before doing the regular timing.
     - □ Use guided reading as a warm-up for one minute. Read with the student a little bit faster than he or she does.
     - □ Use parroting. Read a response (sound, letter, word, phrase, or sentence), then have the student read it back to you.

Classwide Timed Readings

Use the process described above, but instead of listening to each student read (which could take 30–45 minutes out of the instructional day), pair students to read:

- With each other. One student reads while the other listens and records errors, then they switch roles.
- With parent or other classroom volunteers.
- With older cross-age tutor.

OPTION II: ORAL READING OF A PASSAGE OR STORY WITH ERROR FLASH CARD PRACTICE

Time Required: Approximately 10 minutes

Day 1 of Story
1. Put one copy of the story under the acetate in the student's folder.
2. Hand the student a second copy of the story. Have him or her read for one minute. If he or she reaches the bottom of the sheet before the end of one minute, have the student start over at the top and keep reading.
3. If the student is unable to decode a word immediately, say the word and record it as an error.
4. Record all errors (words mispronounced or provided by you, the listener) by circling the word on the acetate. Do not erase until the next day.
5. Make flash cards of all missed words.
6. Count all the words read correctly and all the words missed in the one-minute timing, ignoring that part of the story the student didn't get to read.
7. Have the student record corrects and errors on the score sheet.
8. Chart or help the student chart corrects and errors on the appropriate day line.

Following Days (Reread exactly the same story passage.)

1. Before doing the story timing:
   a. Practice words using flash cards: Do a one-minute warm-up timing using flash cards spread out in rows on a table. Have the student read them for one minute.
   b. Read words circled on acetate once or twice. Do not record this score.
   c. Erase the acetate.
2. Take timing following all steps listed for Day 1.
3. After charting the score, compare today's performance with performances of the past few days.

Each Friday you should:

1. Look at the student's scores.
2. Decide to continue or change. A change is necessary if:
   a. The student has been achieving his or her aim for two days; go on to the next story or passage.
   b. The student's chart has been "flat" for three days or is showing very little growth; you may need to continue to work on the same skill again in a new way.

OPTION III: PRACTICING MORE THAN ONE READING SKILL AT A TIME

Time Required: Approximately 30 minutes
If time allows, students will benefit greatly from working on several different but related components of reading during each session.

Daily Schedule

1. Flash Cards — 3 minutes
2. Fluency Sheet—Isolated Sounds
   a. Sound Dictation — 3 minutes
   b. Reading Sounds — 3 minutes
   c. Timing — 1 minute
   d. Recording and Charting — 1 minute
3. Fluency Sheet—Isolated Decodable Real Words
   a. Word Dictation — 3 minutes
   b. Blending/Reading Words — 3 minutes
   c. Timing — 1 minute
   d. Recording and Charting — 1 minute
4. Fluency Sheet—High Frequency Sight Words: Isolated Words
   a. Reading Words — 3 minutes
   b. Timing — 1 minute
   c. Recording and Charting — 1 minute
5. Fluency Sheet—Grade Level Passages
   a. Reading — 3 minutes
   b. Timing — 1 minute
   c. Recording and Charting — 1 minute

TOTAL 29 minutes

Schedule Expansion

1. Flash Cards—Flash cards can fall into four different categories:
   a. Consonant and/or vowel sounds
   b. Phonetic words
   c. Sight words
   d. Words missed during passage reading
2. Fluency Sheet—Isolated Sounds and Isolated Decodable Real Words
   a. Dictation—After the teacher or tutor says the sound or word, the student writes it either on paper, an acetate sheet, a chalkboard, or dry erase board. Corrections are made immediately. "No, not 'eat.' Write 'can'."
   b. Reading—The student begins reading the Fluency Sheet. Errors are corrected immediately. "This says, 'was.' What does it say?"
   c. One-Minute Timing—The student starts reading at the beginning of the sheet. If he or she reaches the bottom of the sheet before the end of the timing, the student should start over at the top. Errors are noted and subtracted from the total responses made. Corrections are made after the completion of the timing.
   d. Recording—Tutor and student record the number of correct and incorrect answers on the student's score sheet or chart.
3. Fluency Sheet—-High Frequency Sight Words: Isolated Words
   Follow the same steps as above, but consider skipping the dictation step.
4. Fluency Sheet—Grade Level Passages
   Reading a story or passage proficiently is the final goal.
   a. Reading—The student reads the entire passage. Corrections are made immediately.
   b. Timing—The student reads the passage starting at the beginning of the skill sheet. If the student finishes, he or she starts over at the top and continues reading. Corrections are noted and subtracted from the total words read.

c. Recording—Tutor and student record words read correctly and errors made on student's score sheet or chart.

5. Materials are returned to student's folder and placed in a desk or file.
6. Recorded or charted data is reviewed weekly and appropriate changes are made.

NOTE: Instead of using a Fluency Sheet passage, the teacher may use a basal reading or library book written at the appropriate level of difficulty. In this instance, use the following steps for the passage reading phase of the session.

a. Reading—Student reads for three minutes beginning where he or she left off the day before. Errors are corrected immediately.

b. Timing—Student chooses one page he or she has just read and rereads it while being timed for one minute. Errors are not corrected until the timing ends.

c. Recording—Teacher and student record words read correctly and errors made.

When using a book, the teacher should divide the pages into three to five sections. The student does not need to reach his or her aim on every page, but should reach his or her aim in the first part of the book before moving on to the next section.

OPTION IV: BUILDING COMPREHENSION

Eighty percent of students experience reading difficulty because of their inability to decode and read words in print easily. Once they can decode the print they see, their ability to comprehend the material read reaches a satisfactory level. However, it is possible to use One-Minute Fluency Builder techniques to practice and monitor the development of comprehension skills before students reach that level of proficiency.

Tool Skill Practice

The teacher may first want to focus on comprehension tool skills such as those listed below. Note that these skills are not dependent upon the student's decoding skill level.

Tool Skill

Think to Say Things I See in the Room
Think to Say Things I See in a Picture
Think to Say Ideas about a Topic, e.g. Mammals
See to Say or Think to Say Describe an Object
Think to Say People I Know
Think to Say Things I Like to Do

Reading Comprehension Practice

Time Required: Approximately 10 minutes
A student may also practice comprehension of material read.

1. Pair students as partners.
2. Both students read silently from copies of the same book or passage for three minutes.
3. The first student is timed for one minute by the second student as he or she lists facts about the material read (Think to Say Facts). The number of facts is recorded.
4. Both students read for another three minutes.
5. The second student is timed for one minute as he or she completes the Think to Say Facts activity. The number of facts is recorded on his or her score sheet or chart.
6. The teacher reviews the recorded data at least once a week and makes appropriate changes.

NOTE: Once students are able to fluently Think to Say Facts, the teacher may want to focus on a different skill:

Think to Say Details in Sequence
Think to Say Main Idea and Details
Think to Say Inferences
Think to Say Questions About the Passage

Practicing Basic Skills in Reading is a program developed to build basic skills and remediate skill deficits. This program is for educators who believe that in order to be successful in academic settings or the world of work, students need to be fluent in the core skills. The Fluency Sheets and related materials enable teachers to implement a practice program that will improve the students' ability to:

- Learn new skills.
- Maintain newly acquired skills.
- Transfer skills to more complex tasks.
- Apply these skills across the curriculum and to everyday life.

For teachers, One-Minute Fluency Builders provides immediate and positive change in student performance; for students, it provides clear objectives, meaningful feedback, and most importantly, a dynamic tool for learning critical skills.

Suggested materials include acetate, manila folders, and marking pens.
Student materials are available through Sopris West Educational Services.
(800) 547-6747
www.sopriswest.com

REFERENCES

Beck, R. (1979a). *Report for the Office of Education joint dissemination review panel.* Great Falls, MT: Precision Teaching Project.

Beck, R. (1979b). *Remediation of learning deficits through precision teaching: A follow-up study.* Unpublished doctoral dissertation. University of Montana, Missoula.

Beck, R., & Clement, R. (1991). The Great Falls precision teaching project: An historical review. *Journal of Precision Teaching, 8*(2), 8–12.

Binder, C. (1996). Behavioral fluency: Evolution of a new paradigm. *The Behavior Analyst, 19*(2), 163–197.

Binder, C. (2003). *Doesn't everybody need fluency? Performance Improvement—Special Master's Series Issue. 42*(3), 14–20.

Good, R. H. III, & Kaminski, R. (2003). *DIBELS: Dynamic indicators of basic early literacy skills.* Longmont, CO: Sopris West Educational Services.

Johnson, K. R., & Layng, T. V. J. (1992). Breaking the structuralist barrier: Literacy and numeracy with fluency. *American Psychologist. 47,* 1,475–1,490.

Kubina, R. M. Jr., & Morrison, R. S. (2000). Fluency in education. *Behavior and Social Issues,* (10), 83–99.

National Reading Panel. (2000). *Report of the National Reading Panel: Teaching children to read.* Retrieved from http://www.nichd.nih.gov/publications/hrppubskey.cfm.

Sprick, M., Howard., L., Fidanque, A., & Jones, S. (2006). *Read well 1.* Longmont, CO: Sopris West Educational Services.

Sprick, M., & Jones, S. (2006). *Read well plus.* Longmont, CO: Sopris West Educational Services.

Sprick, M., Jones, S., Dunn, R., & Gunn, B. (2008). *Read well K.* Longmont, CO: Sopris West Educational Services.

Sprick, M., Watanabe, A., Akiyama-Paik, K., & Jones, S. (2009). *Read well 2.* Longmont, CO: Sopris West Educational Services.

Torgesen, J. K., Rashotte, C. A., & Alexander, A. W. (2001). Principles of fluency instruction in reading: Relationships with established empirical outcomes. In M. Wolf (Ed.), *Dyslexia, fluency and the brain.* Timonium, MD: York Press.

Williams, J. P. (Ed.) (2001). [Special issue]. *Scientific Studies of Reading, 5*(3), 203–288.

Scoring Guide

Scoring is relatively simple. Each Fluency Sheet has an answer sheet printed on the reverse side. Each student compares his or her answers to those on the answer sheet and determines how many **correct and incorrect** letters, words, phrases, or notations he or she has completed at the end of each timing. As described earlier, with each successive timing a student should be able to increase the number of correct answers (correct letters, words, phrases, or notations).

How to Determine Corrects and Errors

After the students have completed each timing, they determine how many errors (letters, words, phrases, or notations) they completed in the timing. This number is recorded at the top of the page under "Error." They then determine the total number of possible letters, words, phrases, or notations that could have been part of the answer and subtract any errors from the total possible. This is the total and is recorded at the top of the page under "Correct." You may choose to have students graph both their number of errors and corrects or only the number of corrects.

To make it easier to determine the number of possible letters, words, phrases, or notations, the number at the end of each line or column is the total number of letters, words, phrases, or notations (e.g., underlines, arrows, etc.) in that line or column.

Determining Number of Letters, Words, Phrases, or Notations

Count all letters, words, phrases, or notations that are part of the answer. For instance, a phoneme segmentation item may ask the student to say the sounds of a word pronounced by the teacher. If the word is comprised of three phonemes, one point is given for the correct production of each individual phoneme. Thus, there are 3 points possible.

Additional Points and Examples

- Some Fluency Sheets do not have answer sheets; for those the cumulative scores appear on the student sheet.
- An important element in scoring is to remain consistent and score each timing using the same criteria.

Prereading Skills

Grades K–2

	Correct	Error
First Try		
Second Try		

PREREADING SKILLS
Personal Information

Directions to Teacher: Start the timing device and ask the following questions. Work through all questions and stop the watch or give as many of the questions as possible in one minute.

1–3. What is your name? (Count as three responses. Prompt for all three names—first, middle, last.) (3)

4. How old are you? (4)

5. What is your telephone number? (5)

6. Where do you live? (address) (6)

7. When is your birthday? (7)

8. What is your friend's name? (8)

9. How many people are in your family? (9)

10. How many brothers? (10)

11. How many sisters? (11)

12. What color are your eyes? (12)

13. What color is your hair? (13)

14. How many fingers do you have? (14)

15. What day is it? (15)

16. What is it like outside? (warm, cool, etc.) (16)

SEE TO SAY

	Correct	Error
First Try		
Second Try		

PREREADING SKILLS

Big

Directions: Mark or touch the **big** “X” in each circle and say, *big*.

(5)

(10)

(15)

(20)

ONE MINUTE FLUENCY
SOPRIS WEST SKILL BUILDERS SERIES

SEE TO SAY

	Correct	Error
First Try		
Second Try		

PREREADING SKILLS

Little

Directions: Mark or touch the **little** "x" in each circle and say, *little*.

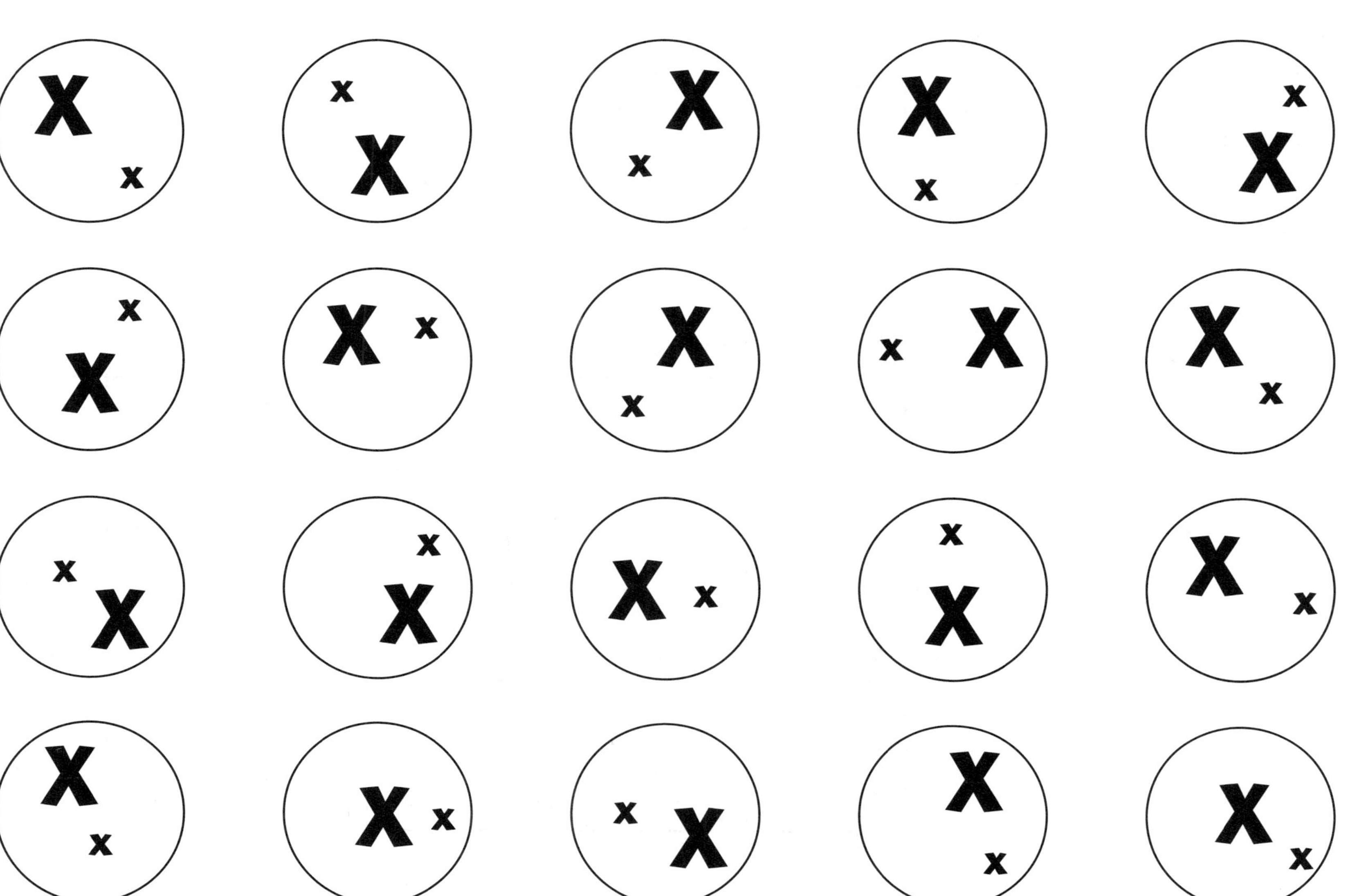

(5)

(10)

(15)

(20)

ONE MINUTE FLUENCY
SOPRIS WEST SKILL BUILDERS SERIES

SEE TO MARK

PREREADING SKILLS
Big
Directions: Mark the **big** circle in each square.

	Correct	Error
First Try		
Second Try		

(9)

(18)

(27)

(36)

(45)

(54)

SEE TO MARK

	Correct	Error
First Try		
Second Try		

PREREADING SKILLS
Little

Directions: Mark the **little** circle in each square.

(9)

(18)

(27)

(36)

(45)

(54)

ONE-MINUTE FLUENCY
SOPRIS WEST SKILL BUILDERS SERIES

SEE TO SAY

	Correct	Error
First Try		
Second Try		

PREREADING SKILLS
In

Directions: Mark or touch each circle with the dot **in** the square and say, *in*.

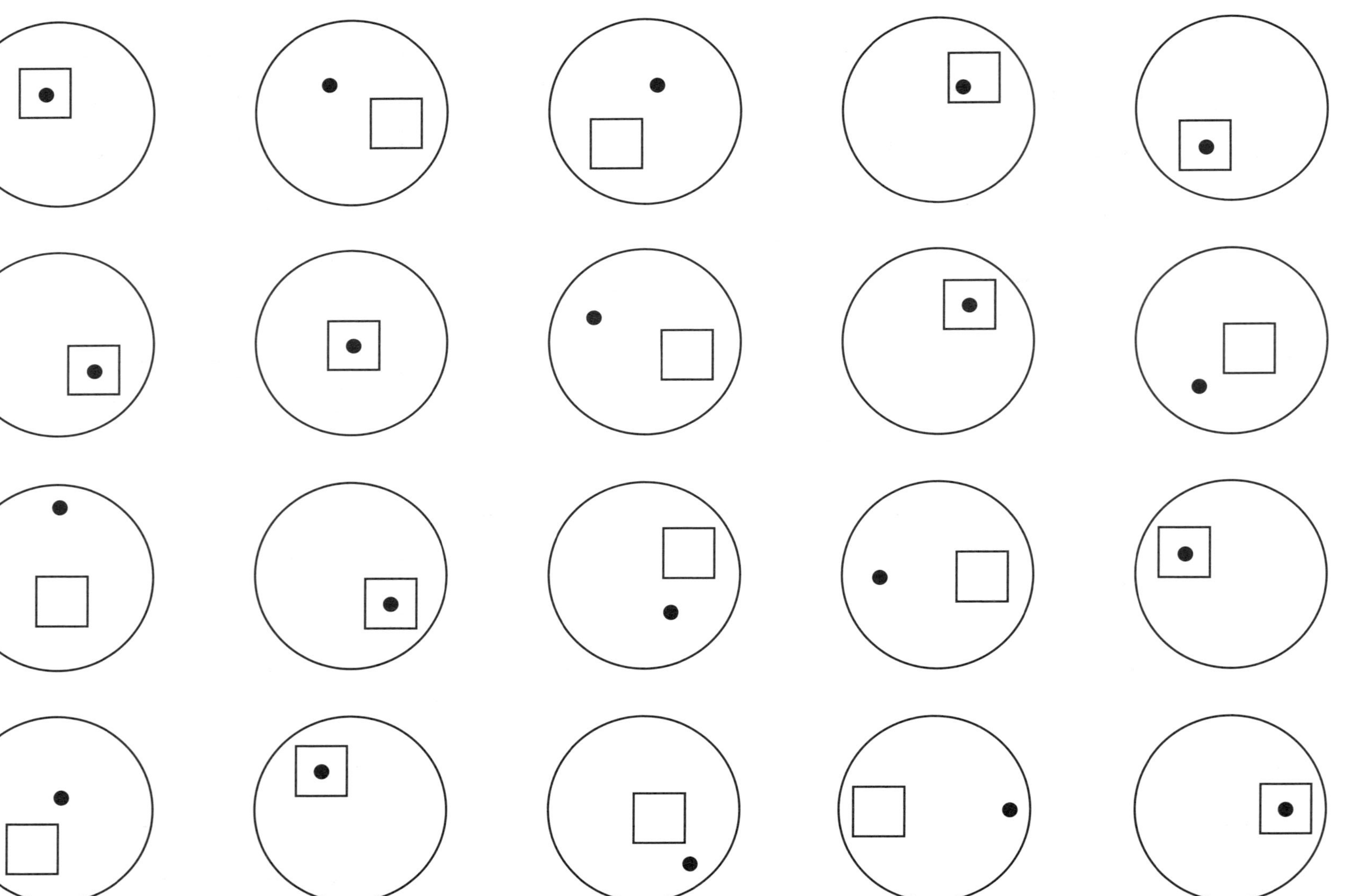

(5)

(10)

(15)

(20)

	Correct	Error
First Try		
Second Try		

PREREADING SKILLS
Out

Directions: Mark or touch each circle with the dot **out** of the square and say, *out*.

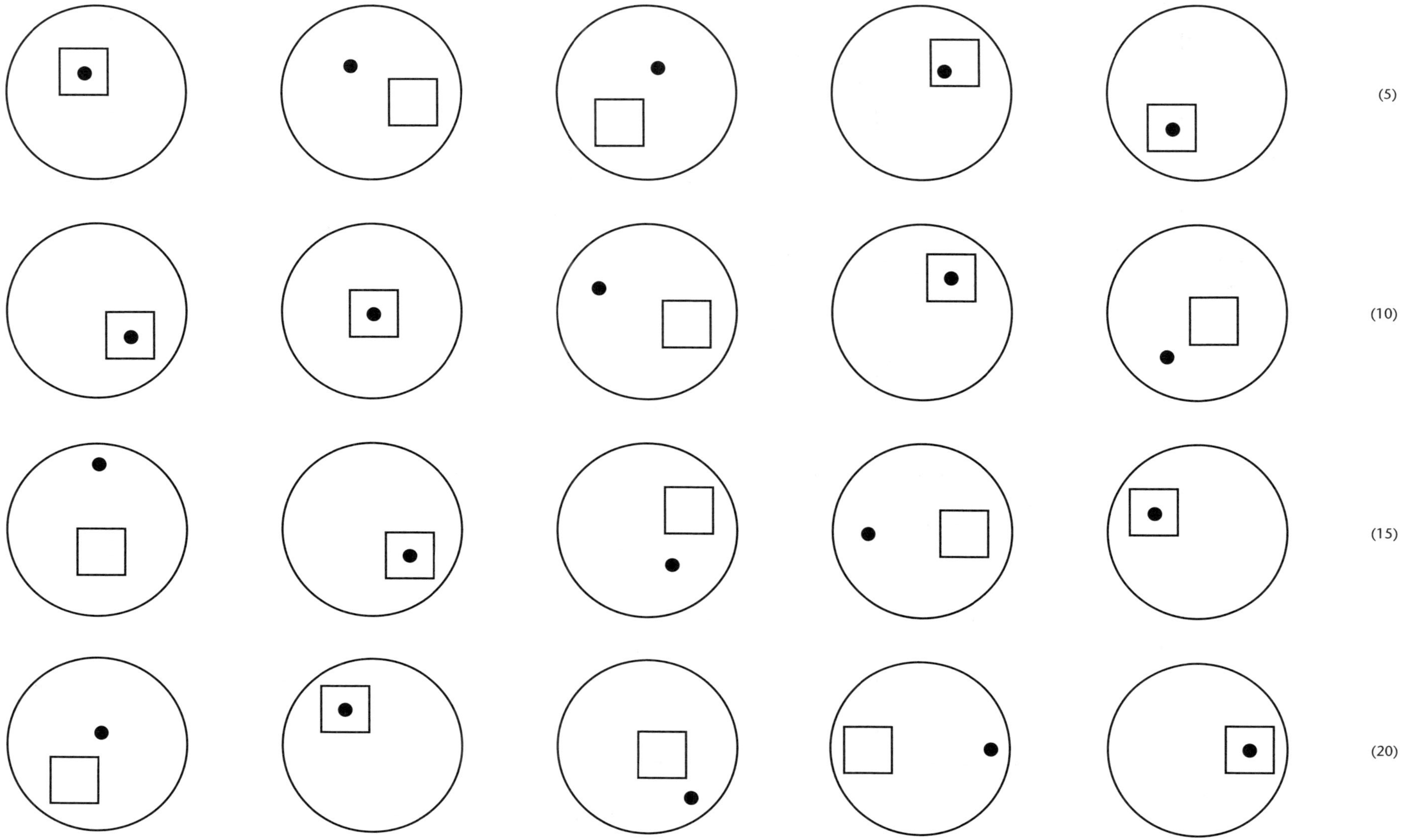

(5)

(10)

(15)

(20)

ONE MINUTE FLUENCY
SOPRIS WEST SKILL BUILDERS SERIES

SEE TO MARK

	Correct	Error
First Try		
Second Try		

PREREADING SKILLS
In

Directions: Mark each square with the dot **in** the circle.

(9)

(18)

(27)

(36)

(45)

(54)

PREREADING SKILLS
Out

Directions: Mark each square with the dot **out** of the circle.

	Correct	Error
First Try		
Second Try		

(9)

(18)

(27)

(36)

(45)

(54)

SEE TO SAY

PREREADING SKILLS

On

Directions: Mark or touch each circle with the square **on** the line and say, *on*.

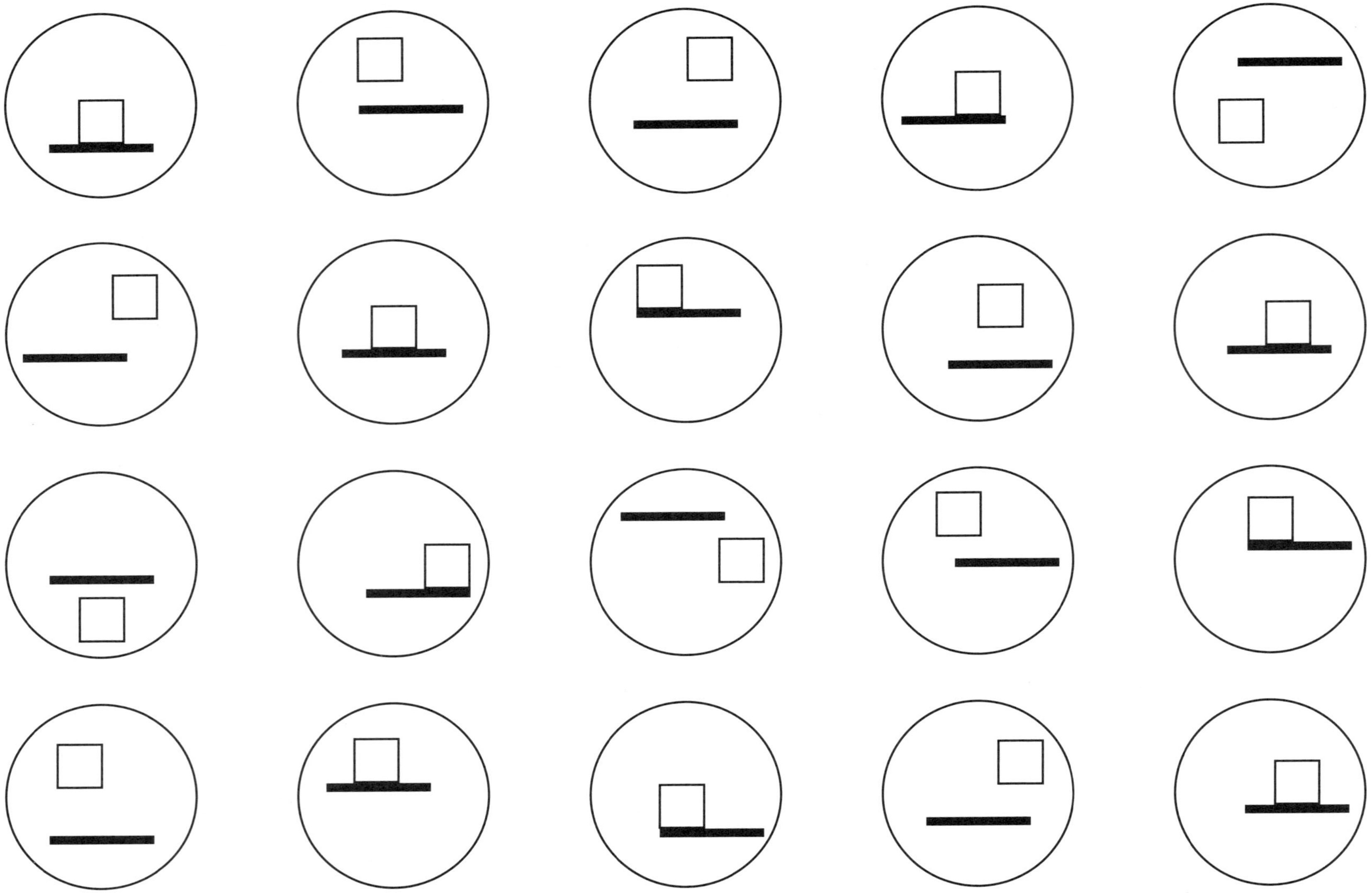

	Correct	Error
First Try		
Second Try		

(5)

(10)

(15)

(20)

ONE-MINUTE FLUENCY
SOPRIS WEST SKILL BUILDERS SERIES

	Correct	Error
First Try		
Second Try		

PREREADING SKILLS
Off

Directions: Mark or touch each circle with the square **off** the line and say, *off*.

(5)

(10)

(15)

(20)

SEE TO MARK

PREREADING SKILLS

On

Directions: Mark each square with the circle **on** the line.

	Correct	Error
First Try		
Second Try		

(9)

(18)

(27)

(36)

(45)

(54)

One Minute Fluency — Sopris West Skill Builders Series

SEE TO MARK

	Correct	Error
First Try		
Second Try		

PREREADING SKILLS
Off

Directions: Mark each square with the circle **off** the line.

(9)

(18)

(27)

(36)

(45)

(54)

ONE-MINUTE FLUENCY
SOPRIS WEST SKILL BUILDERS SERIES

SEE TO SAY

	Correct	Error
First Try		
Second Try		

PREREADING SKILLS
Up/Down

Directions: *See* the arrows and *Say* the direction the arrow is pointing.

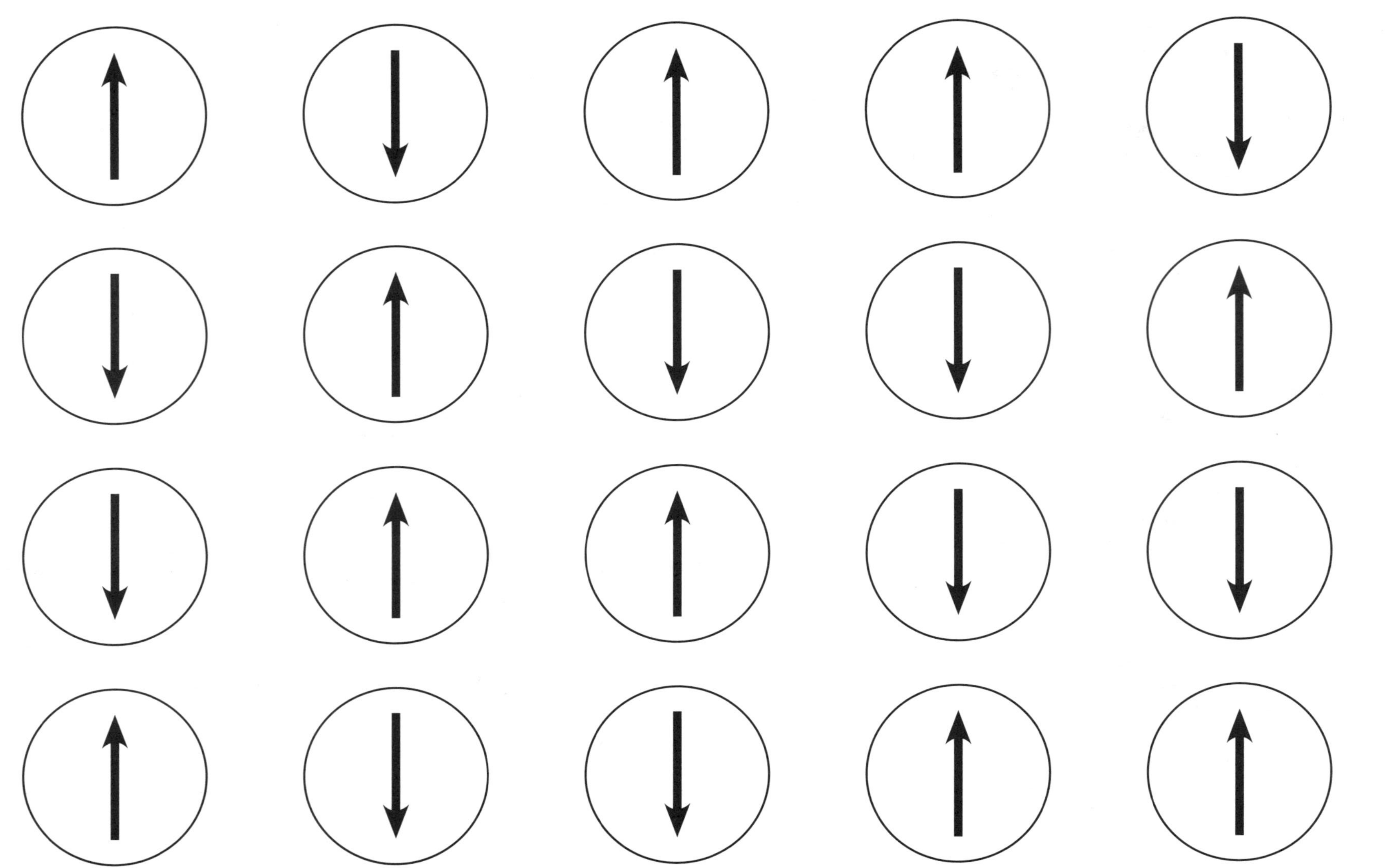

(5)

(10)

(15)

(20)

ONE-MINUTE FLUENCY
SOPRIS WEST SKILL BUILDERS SERIES

SEE TO SAY

PREREADING SKILLS
Left/Right

Directions: *See* the arrows and *Say* the direction the arrow is pointing.

	Correct	Error
First Try		
Second Try		

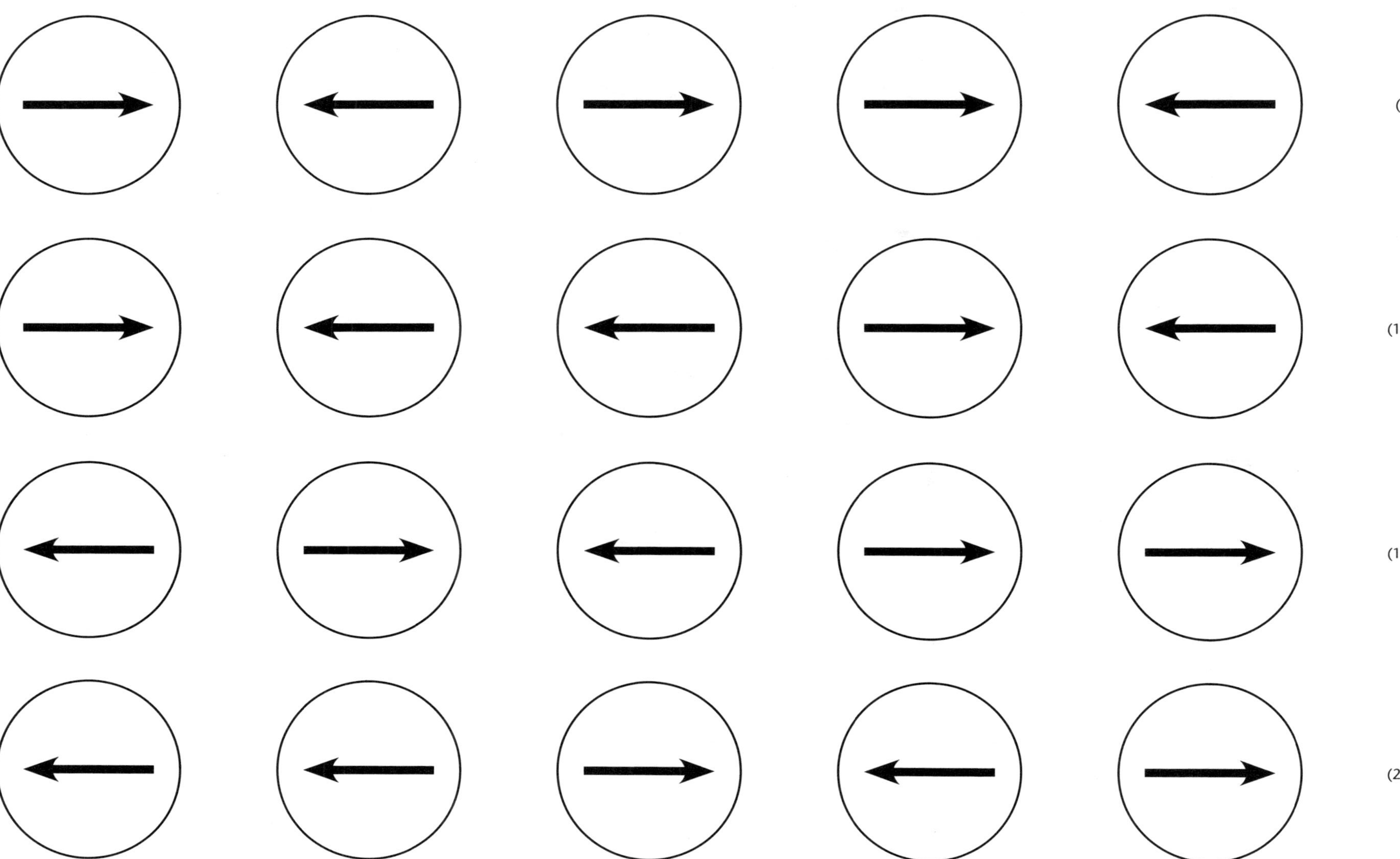

ONE-MINUTE FLUENCY
SOPRIS WEST SKILL BUILDERS SERIES

SEE TO SAY

PREREADING SKILLS
Up/Down, Left/Right

Directions: *See* the arrows and *Say* the direction the arrow is pointing.

	Correct	Error
First Try		
Second Try		

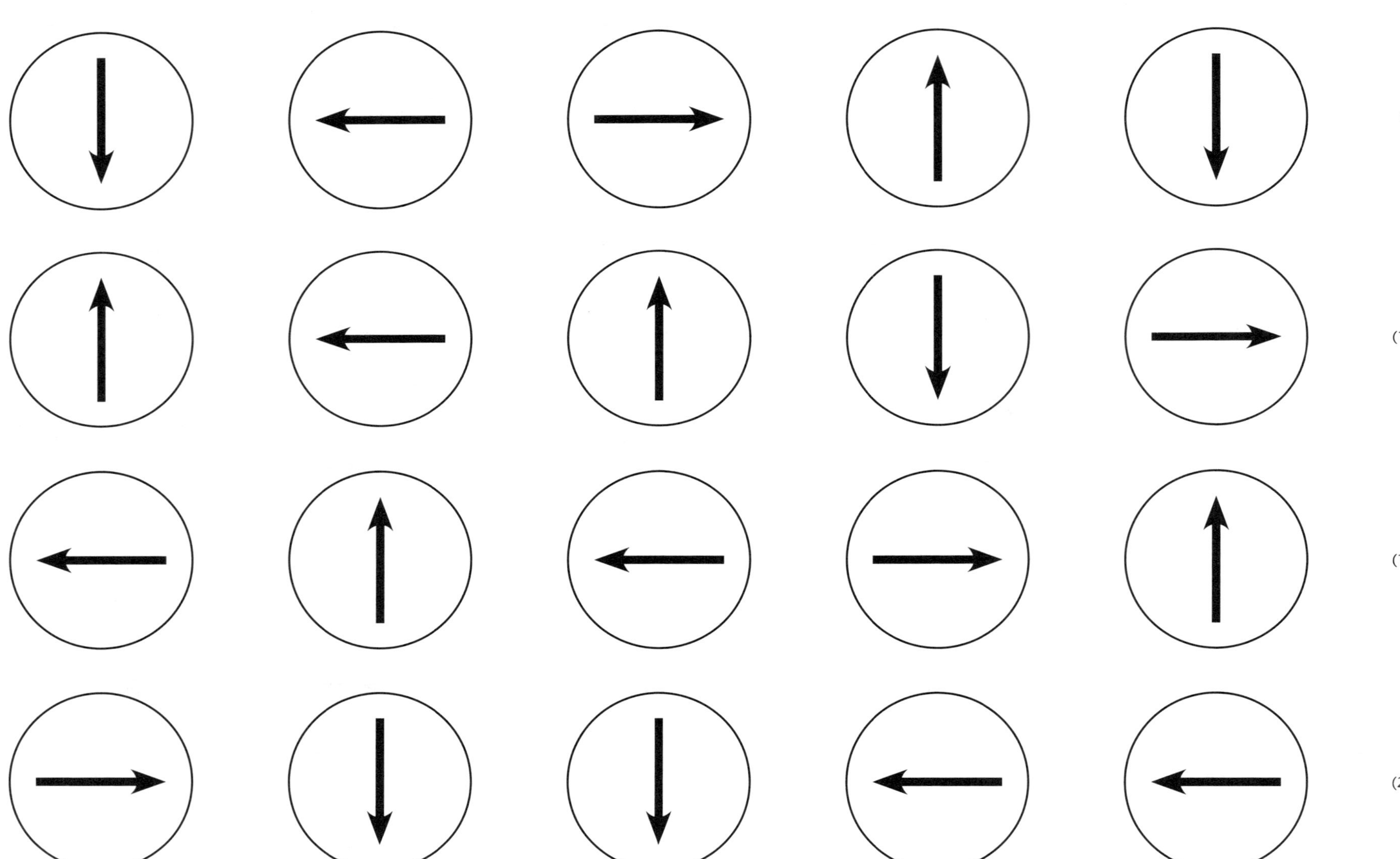

(5)

(10)

(15)

(20)

	Correct	Error
First Try		
Second Try		

PREREADING SKILLS
Up/Down, Left/Right

Directions: *See* the arrows and *Say* the direction the arrow is pointing.

↓	→	↓	↓	←	↑	↓	→	↓	(9)
→	←	→	↑	↑	←	→	↓	→	(18)
→	→	↑	→	↓	←	←	→	↓	(27)
↓	←	←	↑	↓	→	↓	→	↓	(36)
←	←	→	↑	←	↓	→	↓	→	(45)
↑	↓	←	→	↑	←	↑	→	↓	(54)

	Correct	Error
First Try		
Second Try		

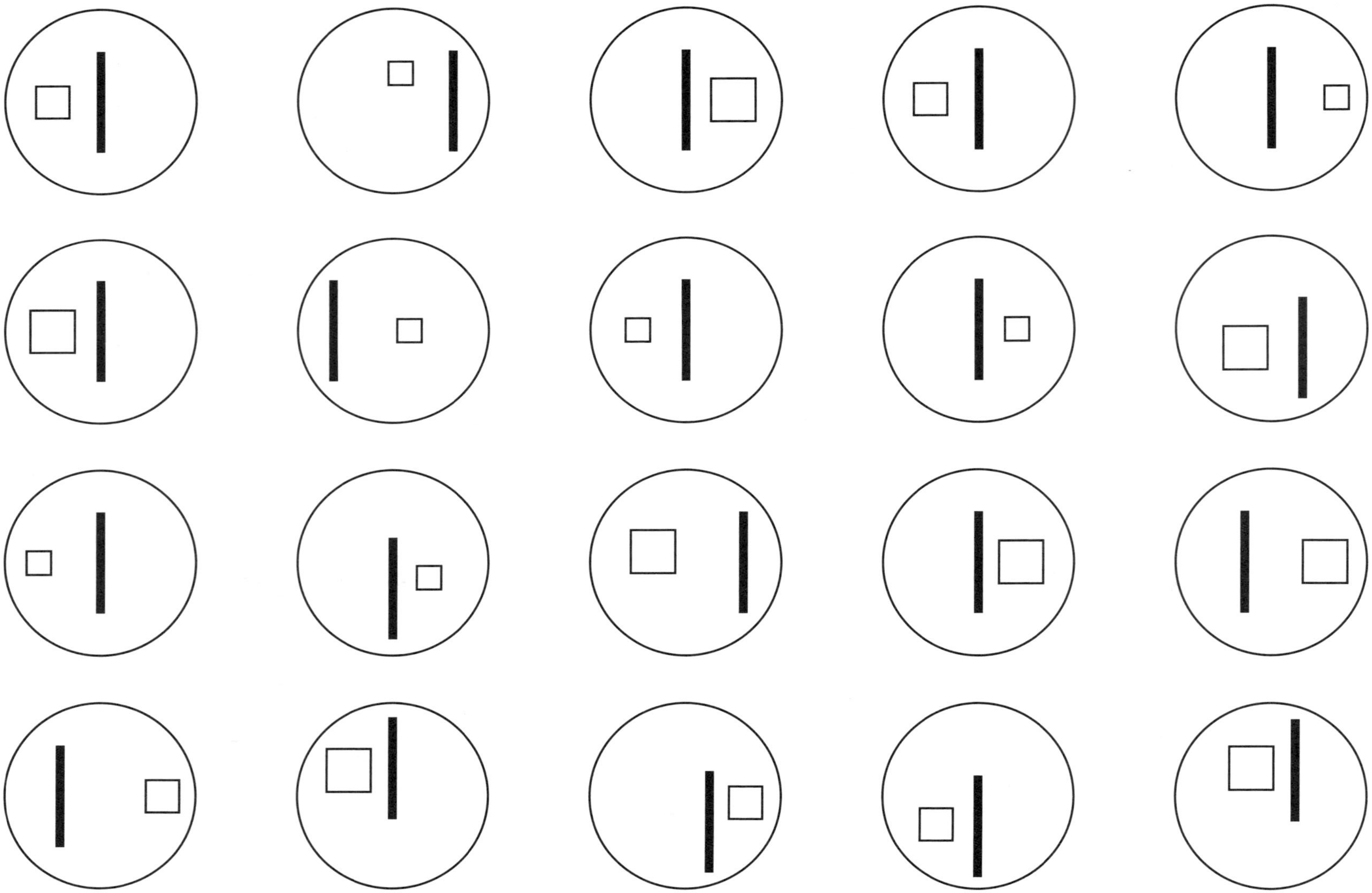

PREREADING SKILLS

Before

Directions: Mark or touch each circle with the square **before** the line and say, *before*.

(5)

(10)

(15)

(20)

ONE MINUTE FLUENCY
SOPRIS WEST SKILL BUILDERS SERIES

SEE TO SAY

PREREADING SKILLS
After

Directions: Mark or touch each circle with the square **after** the line and say, *after*.

	Correct	Error
First Try		
Second Try		

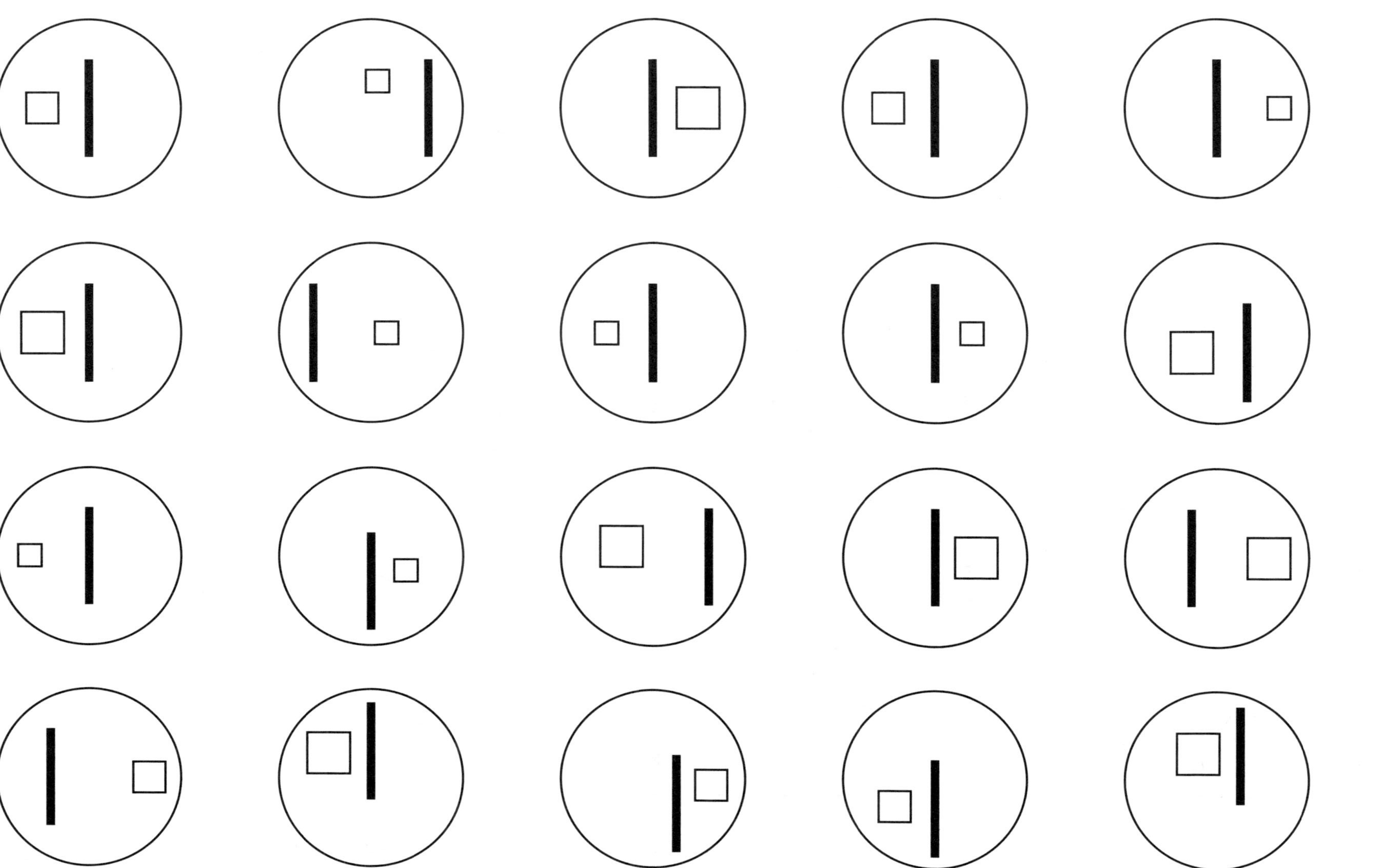

(5)
(10)
(15)
(20)

ONE MINUTE FLUENCY
SOPRIS WEST SKILL BUILDERS SERIES

SEE TO MARK

PREREADING SKILLS
Before—Left

Directions: Mark each square with the circle **before** the line or to the **left** of the line.

	Correct	Error
First Try		
Second Try		

(9)

(18)

(27)

(36)

(45)

(54)

ONE MINUTE FLUENCY
SOPRIS WEST SKILL BUILDERS SERIES

SEE TO MARK

	Correct	Error
First Try		
Second Try		

PREREADING SKILLS
After—Right

Directions: Mark each square with the circle **after** the line or to the **right** of the line.

(9)

(18)

(27)

(36)

(45)

(54)

HEAR/SEE TO MARK

	Correct	Error
First Try		
Second Try		

PREREADING SKILLS
Colors

Directions: Hear the color name and mark it.

red	purple	yellow	green	orange	(5)
black	brown	blue	purple	red	(10)
orange	yellow	blue	green	brown	(15)
black	red	green	blue	yellow	(20)

	Correct	Error
First Try		
Second Try		

PREREADING SKILLS
Colors

Directions: Say each color.

red	blue	yellow	green	brown	(5)
purple	black	orange	red	green	(10)
blue	brown	black	yellow	orange	(15)
purple	blue	green	red	brown	(20)

ONE MINUTE FLUENCY
SOPRIS WEST SKILL BUILDERS SERIES

SEE TO SAY

PREREADING SKILLS
Color Words

Directions: Say each word.

	Correct	Error
First Try		
Second Try		

red	green	black	blue	purple	yellow	orange	brown	(8)
green	blue	red	black	yellow	purple	brown	orange	(16)
black	orange	green	blue	red	yellow	orange	brown	(24)
yellow	purple	brown	red	blue	green	black	orange	(32)
purple	orange	yellow	green	black	blue	red	brown	(40)
brown	green	red	black	purple	orange	blue	yellow	(48)
green	orange	brown	yellow	red	blue	black	purple	(56)
blue	red	green	black	orange	brown	purple	black	(64)
orange	green	blue	brown	black	red	purple	yellow	(72)
red	purple	yellow	orange	green	blue	black	brown	(80)
purple	blue	brown	black	yellow	red	orange	green	(88)

Letter Naming

Grades K–2; Intervention Grade 3 and Above

THINK TO SAY

	Correct	Error
First Try		
Second Try		

LETTER NAMING
Alphabet in Sequence

Directions to Teacher: Ask the student to say the alphabet (saying or singing is acceptable) and start the timing device. Have the student repeat the alphabet as many times as possible in the one minute. This task may also be measured in a 30-second timing.

Helpful Hint:

a	b	c	d	e	f	g	h	i	j	k	l	m	n	o	p	q	r	s	t	u	v	w	x	y	z
1	2	3	4	5	6	7	8	9	10	11	12	13	14	15	16	17	18	19	20	21	22	23	24	25	26

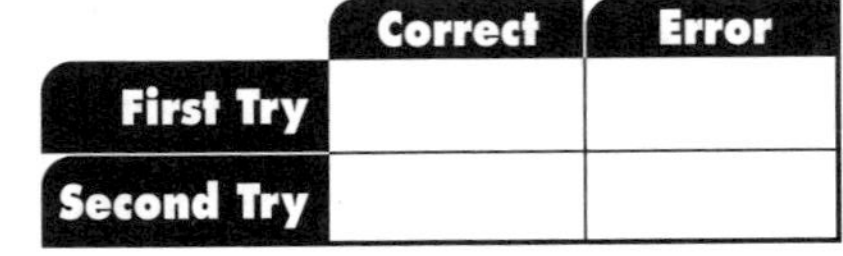

SEE TO SAY

LETTER NAMING

Uppercase Letters—Random, Large Print

Directions: Say each letter.

	Correct	Error
First Try		
Second Try		

B	I	M	F	W	S	Z	D	N	(9)
P	J	X	Q	A	U	H	V	O	(18)
K	T	C	G	Y	R	L	E	M	(27)
C	U	R	F	X	D	Z	N	T	(36)
V	G	E	S	O	L	Y	I	A	(45)
P	W	K	Q	B	J	H	E	C	(54)

SEE TO SAY

LETTER NAMING

Lowercase Letters—Random, Large Print

Directions: Say each letter.

	Correct	Error
First Try		
Second Try		

b	g	a	j	p	c	u	x	q	(9)
n	k	v	z	d	s	y	i	r	(18)
f	t	o	h	m	e	w	l	m	(27)
k	e	r	y	f	w	q	x	a	(36)
o	b	j	v	d	p	s	h	t	(45)
n	g	z	l	i	u	c	a	k	(54)

ONE-MINUTE FLUENCY
SOPRIS WEST SKILL BUILDERS SERIES

SEE TO SAY

LETTER NAMING

Upper and Lowercase Letters—Random, Large Print

Directions: Say each letter.

	Correct	Error
First Try		
Second Try		

F	o	S	a	E	H	B	J	I	(9)
p	D	G	L	m	K	r	T	z	(18)
A	U	X	y	c	O	W	n	Q	(27)
r	b	a	V	x	f	s	P	g	(36)
u	Y	h	e	M	C	q	d	I	(45)
l	R	k	Z	j	N	b	t	v	(54)

ONE MINUTE FLUENCY
SOPRIS WEST SKILL BUILDERS SERIES

SEE TO SAY

LETTER NAMING

Uppercase Letters—Random, Small Print

Directions: Say each letter.

	Correct	Error
First Try		
Second Try		

G L Y W O Q A H M Z C F H O L B X E T P A B D U Y (25)

N Z I U W Q N B X T P W L A E R U F K V N X W A D (50)

S Z L P E T H L K J U N B V C X O Y Z A S D F N K (75)

P T U R W P B H D L J Z A T Y U F L J E A M N O R (100)

F O Y J S P E W M J C S P D V B O E L P J C F R T (125)

A M G T P O W R S E K G L D B M R Q T U Z W R L I (150)

K B R U F P W S B H U I M F V P T Y U I C E O X F (175)

E W J W L R G E R Y N H L D Y U A K O R T I F U Z (200)

SEE TO SAY

	Correct	Error
First Try		
Second Try		

LETTER NAMING
Lowercase Letters—Random, Small Print
Directions: Say each letter.

g l y w o q a h m z c f h o l b x e t p a b d u y (25)

n z i u w q n b x t p w l a e r u f k v n x w a d (50)

s z l p e t h l k j u n b v c x o y z a s d f n k (75)

p t u r w q b h d l j z a t y u f l j e a m n o r (100)

f o y j s p e w m j c s p d v b o e l p j c f r t (125)

a m g t p o w r s e k g l d b m r q t u z w r l i (150)

k b r u f p w s b h u i m f v p t y u i c e o x f (175)

e w j w l r g e r y n h l d y u a k o r t i f u z (200)

ONE-MINUTE FLUENCY
SOPRIS WEST SKILL BUILDERS SERIES

SEE TO SAY

LETTER NAMING

Upper and Lowercase Letters—Random, Small Print

Directions: Say each letter.

	Correct	Error
First Try		
Second Try		

g L y w o q A H m z C f h o l B X e T p a b D u Y (25)

N Z i U W Q n b x t P w L a E R u F k v n x W a d (50)

S z G p e T H l K j u N B V c X O y z A s D f n k (75)

P t u R w Q b h d l j Z a t y u f l J E a M n O r (100)

F o y J s p e W M j c S p D V b O e l p j c f r T (125)

A m g t P o w R s E k G L d B M r Q t U Z w r l i (150)

K b R u f p w S b h u I m F v p t Y u i C e o X f (175)

E w j W l r G e r y N H l D y U a K o R T I f u z (200)

Phonemic Awareness—Phoneme Isolation

Grades K–2; Intervention Grade 3 and Above

Initial Sounds

Skill Sheets 1–6 include increasingly more challenging words. A short description is provided of each of these skill sheets.

Skill Sheets 7–16 contain single and multisyllabic words related to specific topic.

Final Sounds

Skill Sheets 1–6 include increasingly more challenging words. A short description is provided of each of these skill sheets.

Combination of Initial and Final Sounds

Timing Note:
The directions to the teacher are to:
(1) Point to the picture.
(2) Say, "This is (say name of picture). What sound does (picture) begin/end with?"

After providing this initial direction to the student, the teacher may choose to prompt each individual response by merely pointing to the picture and saying the name of the picture. The student says the beginning or ending sound and the teacher immediately points to and names the next picture. The student is timed for one minute, then the number of correct and incorrect responses is recorded.

Scoring Note:
Answer sheets indicate the correct isolated initial or final phoneme for each picture name. Depending on the reading series being used with the student, the teacher may choose to modify the scoring process to count as correct letter blends or even initial or final clusters of sounds.

Word	Initial Phoneme	Initial Blend	Sound Cluster
train	/t/	/t/ /r/	/t/ /r/ /ai/

If some modified response is accepted as correct, all sounds must be produced accurately and in the correct sequence.

Pronunciation Guide
Answer sheets indicate the correct isolated phoneme using the following conventions:

Phoneme	Phoneme Example
/ai/	rain, day
/ea/	bead, see
/ie/	tie, fine
/oa/	coat, doe
/oo/	moon
/a/	dad
/e/	bed, head
/i/	did
/o/	log, law
/u/	cup and "a" in about
/uu/	book
/ow/	how
/oi/	noise, boy
/ar/	(1 phoneme) car
/ir/	(1 phoneme) girl, fur
/or/	(1 phoneme) for, more, four
/ai/ /r/	(2 phonemes) fair
/ea/ /r/	(2 phonemes) dear
/oo/ /r/	(2 phonemes) tour
/ĕr/	winter, sister
/b/	bad
/k/	cat, kite, back
/d/	dad
/f/	fat
/g/	go, big
/h/	hat
/j/	jet, edge
/l/	let
/m/	man, ham
/n/	no, knob, can
/p/	pat, cap
/kw/	queen
/r/	rat, frog
/s/	sat, cats
/t/	top, pot
/v/	van
/w/	wet
/ks/	box
/z/	zoo
/sh/	show
/SH/	measure, beige
/th/	thin
/TH/	the
/ch/	chick
/hw/	whale
/ng/	sing

PHONEMIC AWARENESS—PHONEME ISOLATION
Beginning Sound—Skill Sheet 1

	Correct	Error
First Try		
Second Try		

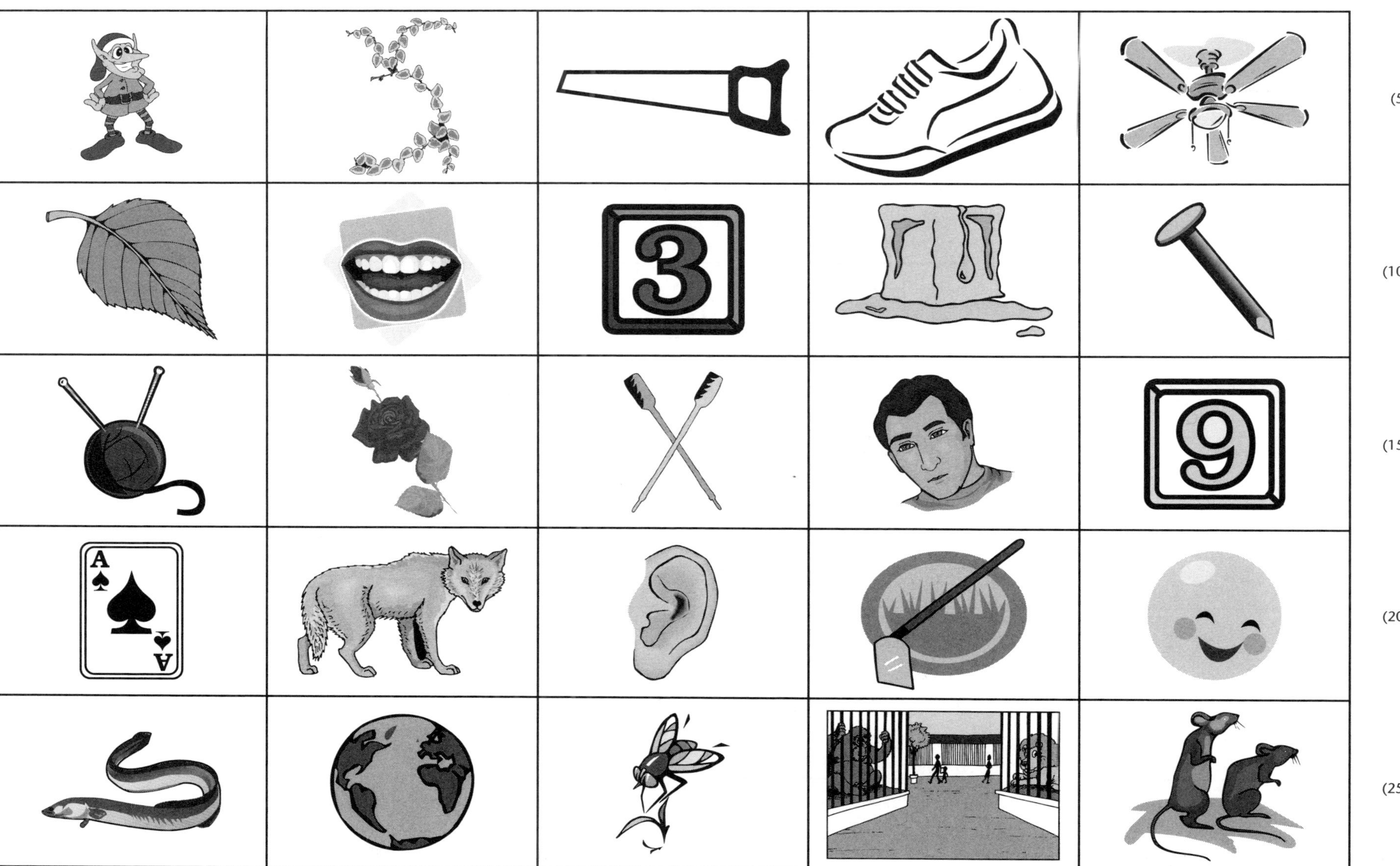

	Correct	Error
First Try		
Second Try		

PHONEMIC AWARENESS—PHONEME ISOLATION
Beginning Sound—Skill Sheet 1

Directions to Teacher: Point to the picture. Say, "This is (say name of picture). What sound does (picture) begin with?"

elf /e/	vine /v/	saw /s/	shoe /sh/	fan /f/	(5)
leaf /l/	mouth /m/	three /th/	ice /ie/	nail /n/	(10)
yarn /y/	rose /r/	oars /or/	face /f/	nine /n/	(15)
ace /ai/	wolf /w/	ear /ea/	hoe /h/	smile /s/	(20)
eel /ea/	earth /er/	fly /f/	zoo /z/	mice /m/	(25)

ONE-MINUTE FLUENCY
SOPRIS WEST SKILL BUILDERS SERIES

HEAR/SEE TO SAY

PHONEMIC AWARENESS—PHONEME ISOLATION
Beginning Sound—Skill Sheet 2

	Correct	Error
First Try		
Second Try		

(5)

(10)

(15)

(20)

(25)

HEAR/SEE TO SAY

PHONEMIC AWARENESS—PHONEME ISOLATION
Beginning Sound—Skill Sheet 2

Directions to Teacher: Point to the picture. Say, "This is (say name of picture). What sound does (picture) begin with?"

	Correct	Error
First Try		
Second Try		

ape /ai/	elk /e/	fist /f/	lock /l/	wood /w/	(5)
match /m/	net /n/	ox /o/	rope /r/	ant /a/	(10)
six /s/	ship /sh/	ax /ă/	foot /f/	wig /w/	(15)
log /l/	knot /n/	hill /h/	sack /s/	lip /l/	(20)
robe /r/	eight /ai/	shrub /sh/	leg /l/	string /s/	(25)

ONE MINUTE FLUENCY
SOPRIS WEST SKILL BUILDERS SERIES

HEAR/SEE TO SAY

PHONEMIC AWARENESS—PHONEME ISOLATION
Beginning Sound—Skill Sheet 3

	Correct	Error
First Try		
Second Try		

(5)

(10)

(15)

(20)

(25)

	Correct	Error
First Try		
Second Try		

PHONEMIC AWARENESS—PHONEME ISOLATION
Beginning Sound—Skill Sheet 3

Directions to Teacher: Point to the picture. Say, "This is (say name of picture). What sound does (picture) begin with?"

award /u/	hatchet /h/	ladder /l/	motorcycle /m/	alarm /u/	(5)
slippers /s/	airplane /ai/	ladybug /l/	igloo /i/	suitcases /s/	(10)
xylophone /z/	newspaper /n/	rocket /r/	mittens /m/	lightbulb /l/	(15)
cellphone /s/	emus /ea/	shovel /sh/	violin /v/	snowman /s/	(20)
elephant /e/	rabbit /r/	zebra /z/	thumbtack /th/	wheelbarrow /hw/	(25)

ONE-MINUTE FLUENCY
SOPRIS WEST SKILL BUILDERS SERIES

HEAR/SEE TO SAY

PHONEMIC AWARENESS—PHONEME ISOLATION
Beginning Sound—Skill Sheet 4

	Correct	Error
First Try		
Second Try		

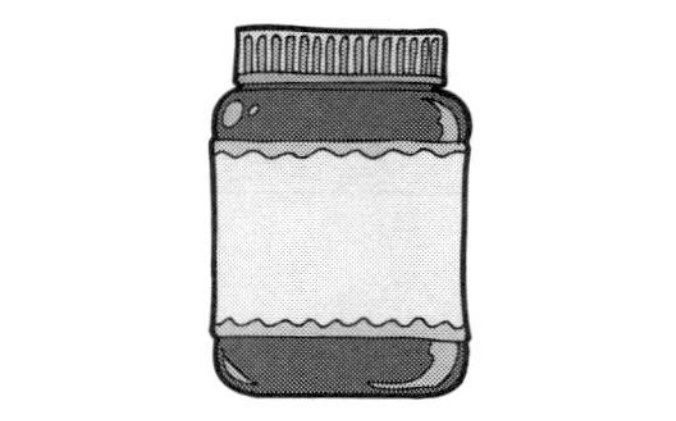

(5)

(10)

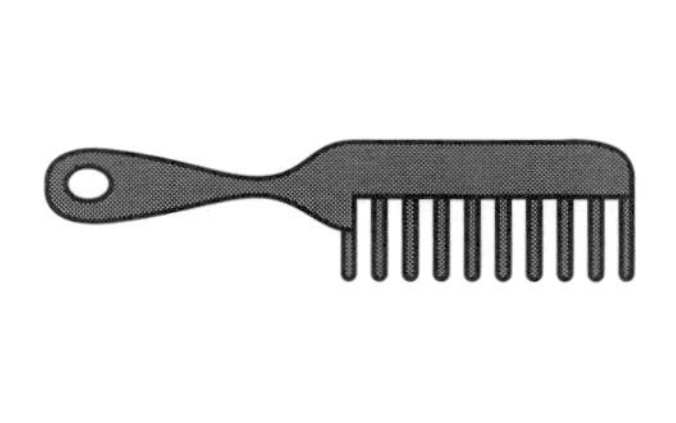

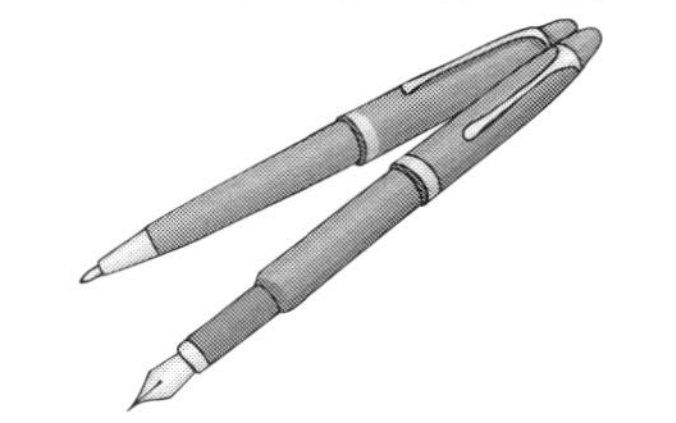

(15)

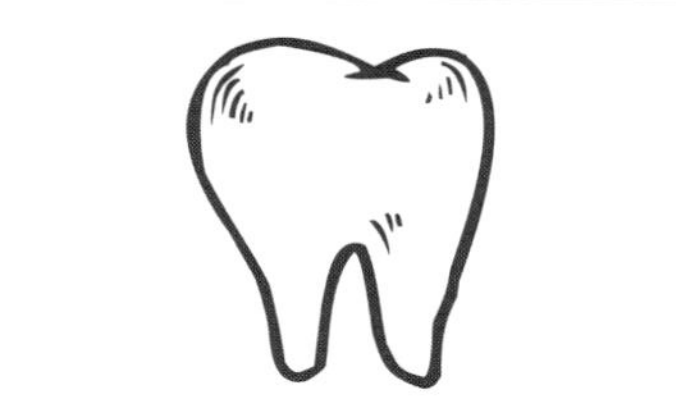

(20)

(25)

HEAR/SEE TO SAY

	Correct	Error
First Try		
Second Try		

PHONEMIC AWARENESS—PHONEME ISOLATION
Beginning Sound—Skill Sheet 4

Directions to Teacher: Point to the picture. Say, "This is (say name of picture). What sound does (picture) begin with?"

boy /b/	can /k/	dove /d/	girl /g/	jar /j/	(5)
car /k/	pail /p/	queen /kw/	ten /t/	bow /b/	(10)
comb /k/	door /d/	gloves /g/	jam /j/	pens /p/	(15)
quail /kw/	tire /t/	wall /w/	bill /b/	tooth /t/	(20)
dice /d/	keys /k/	bee /b/	cows /k/	drum /d/	(25)

PHONEMIC AWARENESS—PHONEME ISOLATION
Beginning Sound—Skill Sheet 5

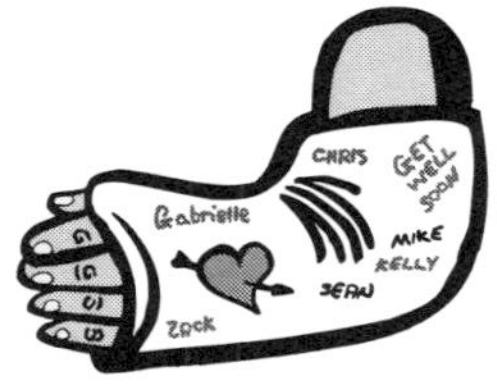

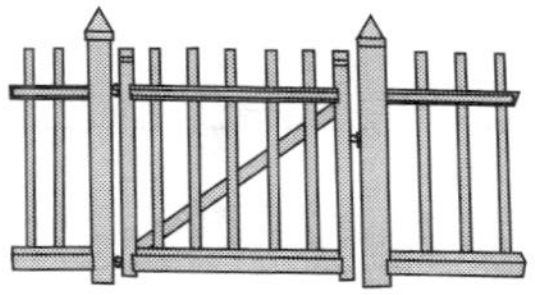

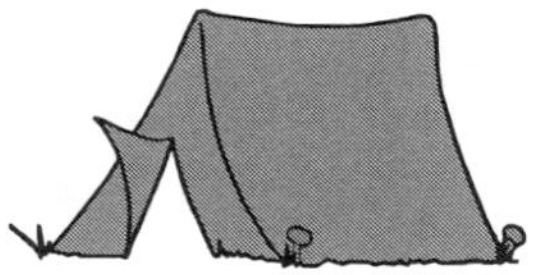

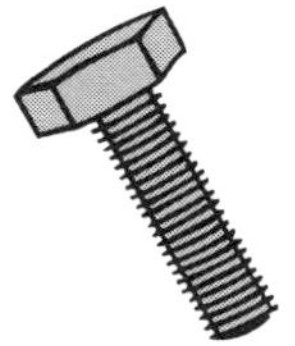

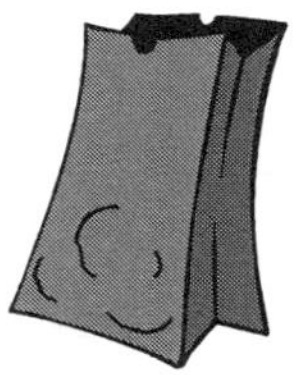

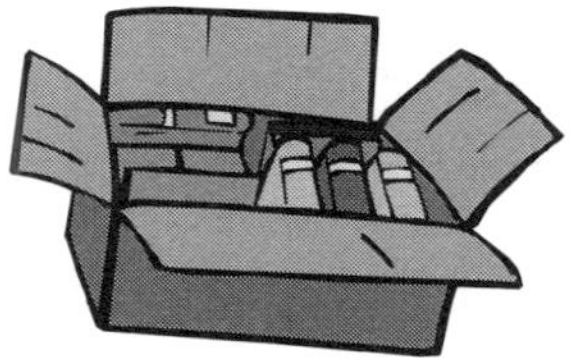

	Correct	Error
First Try		
Second Try		

(5)

(10)

(15)

(20)

(25)

	Correct	Error
First Try		
Second Try		

PHONEMIC AWARENESS—PHONEME ISOLATION
Beginning Sound—Skill Sheet 5

Directions to Teacher: Point to the picture. Say, "This is (say name of picture). What sound does (picture) begin with?"

bank /b/	cast /k/	gate /g/	cloud /k/	jeep /j/	(5)
pot /p/	king /k/	quilt /kw/	tent /t/	wand /w/	(10)
bolt /b/	chick /ch/	jet /j/	duck /d/	watch /w/	(15)
cart /k/	web /w/	church /ch/	bird /b/	dart /d/	(20)
bag /b/	harp /h/	box /b/	chimp /ch/	bridge /b/	(25)

HEAR/SEE TO SAY

PHONEMIC AWARENESS—PHONEME ISOLATION
Beginning Sound—Skill Sheet 6

	Correct	Error
First Try		
Second Try		

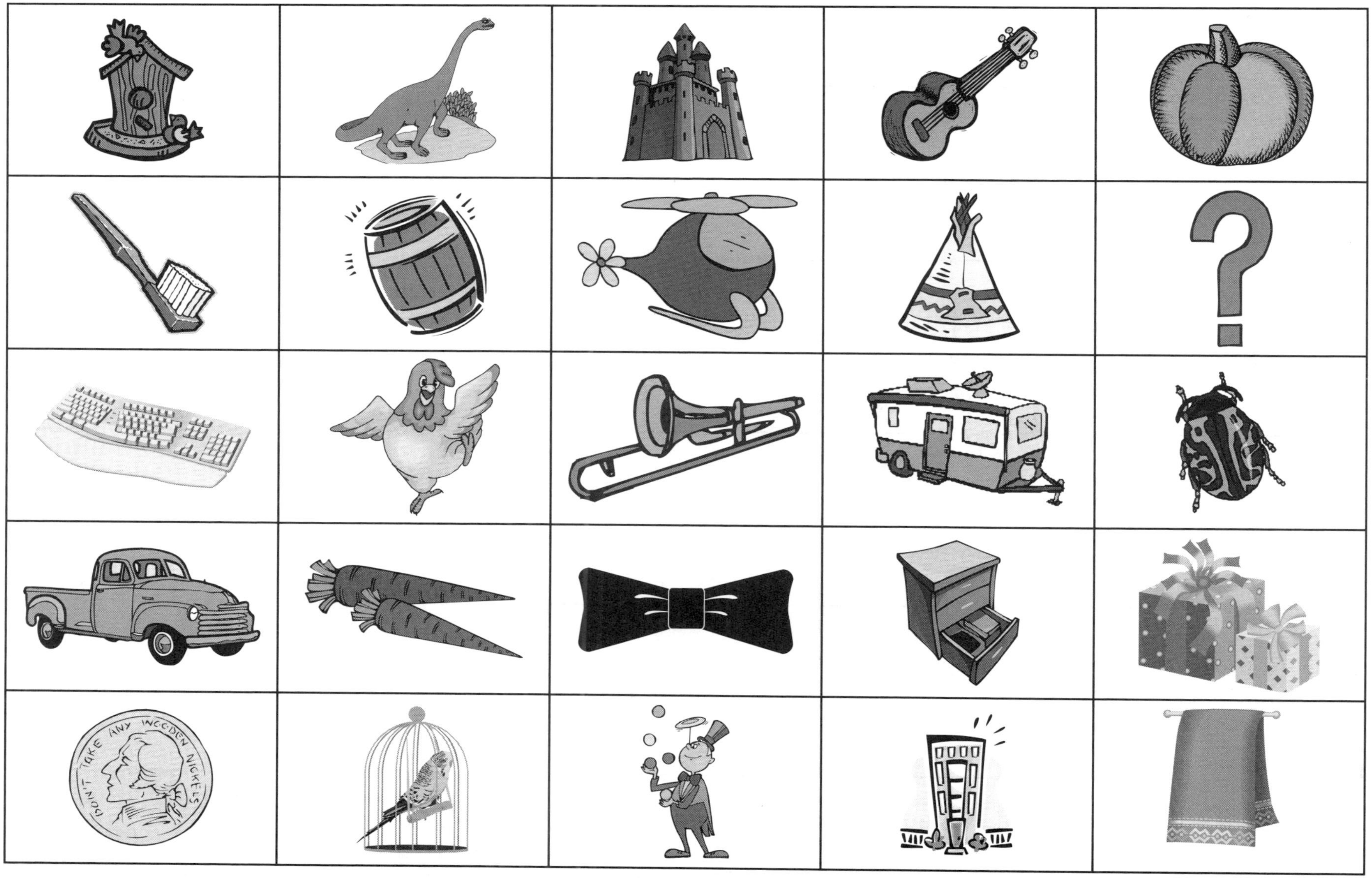

(5)
(10)
(15)
(20)
(25)

PHONEMIC AWARENESS—PHONEME ISOLATION
Beginning Sound—Skill Sheet 6

Directions to Teacher: Point to the picture. Say, "This is (say name of picture). What sound does (picture) begin with?"

	Correct	Error
First Try		
Second Try		

birdhouse /b/	dinosaur /d/	castle /k/	guitar /g/	pumpkin /p/	(5)
toothbrush /t/	barrel /b/	helicopter /h/	teepee /t/	question /kw/	(10)
keyboard /k/	chicken /ch/	trombone /t/	camper /k/	beetle /b/	(15)
pickup /p/	carrots /k/	bowtie /b/	drawer /d/	presents /p/	(20)
nickel /n/	birdcage /b/	juggler /j/	building /b/	towel /t/	(25)

PHONEMIC AWARENESS—PHONEME ISOLATION
Beginning Sound—Skill Sheet 7, Household

	Correct	Error
First Try		
Second Try		

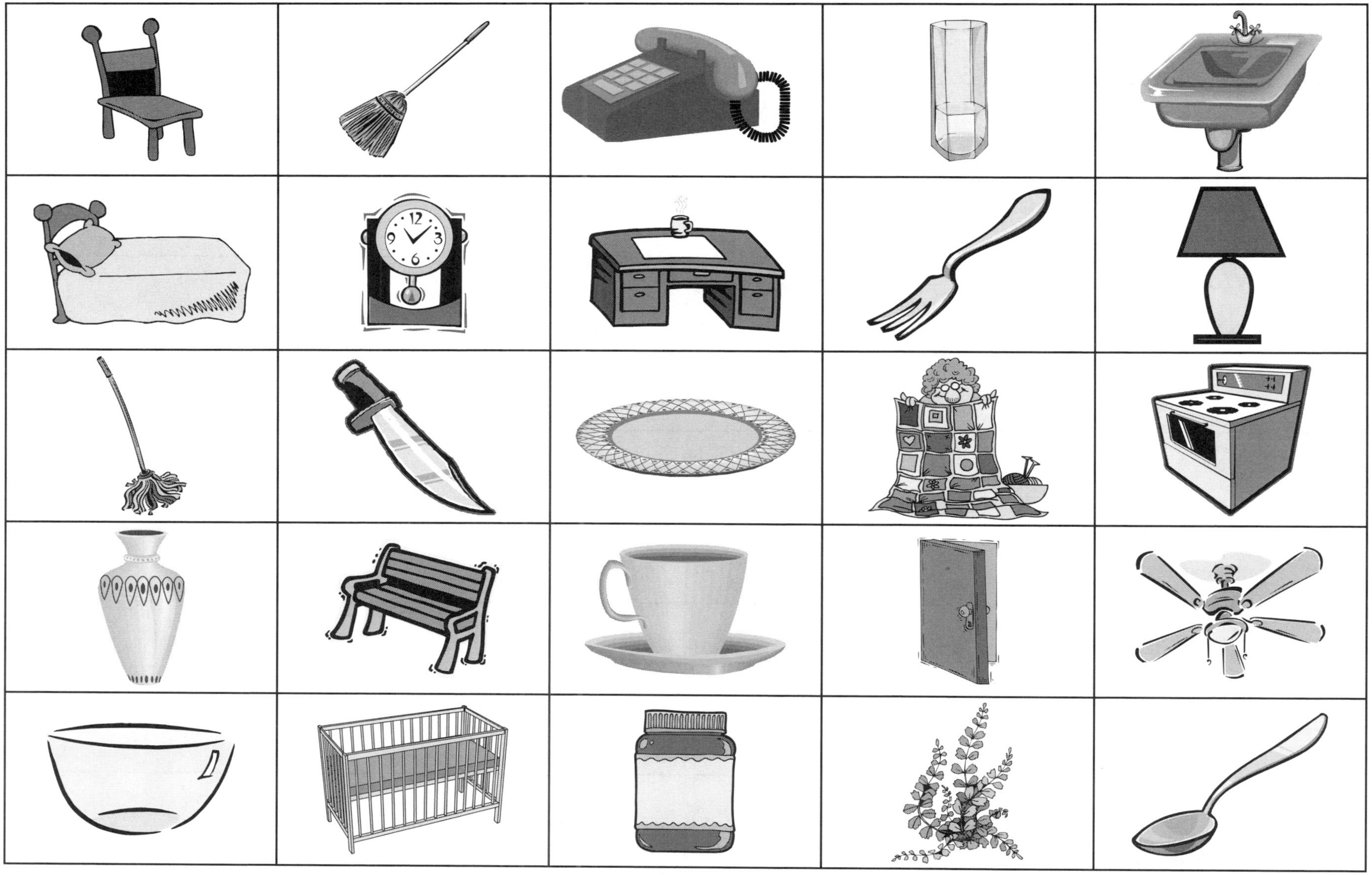

(5)

(10)

(15)

(20)

(25)

	Correct	Error
First Try		
Second Try		

PHONEMIC AWARENESS—PHONEME ISOLATION
Beginning Sound—Skill Sheet 7, Household

Directions to Teacher: Point to the picture. Say, "This is (say name of picture). What sound does (picture) begin with?"

chair /ch/	broom /b/	phone /f/	glass /g/	sink /s/	(5)
bed /b/	clock /k/	desk /d/	fork /f/	lamp /l/	(10)
mop /m/	knife /n/	plate /p/	quilt /kw/	stove /s/	(15)
vase /v/	bench /b/	cup /k/	door /d/	fan /f/	(20)
bowl /b/	crib /k/	jar /j/	plant /p/	spoon /s/	(25)

ONE MINUTE FLUENCY
SOPRIS WEST SKILL BUILDERS SERIES

HEAR/SEE TO SAY

PHONEMIC AWARENESS—PHONEME ISOLATION
Beginning Sound—Skill Sheet 8, Household

	Correct	Error
First Try		
Second Try		

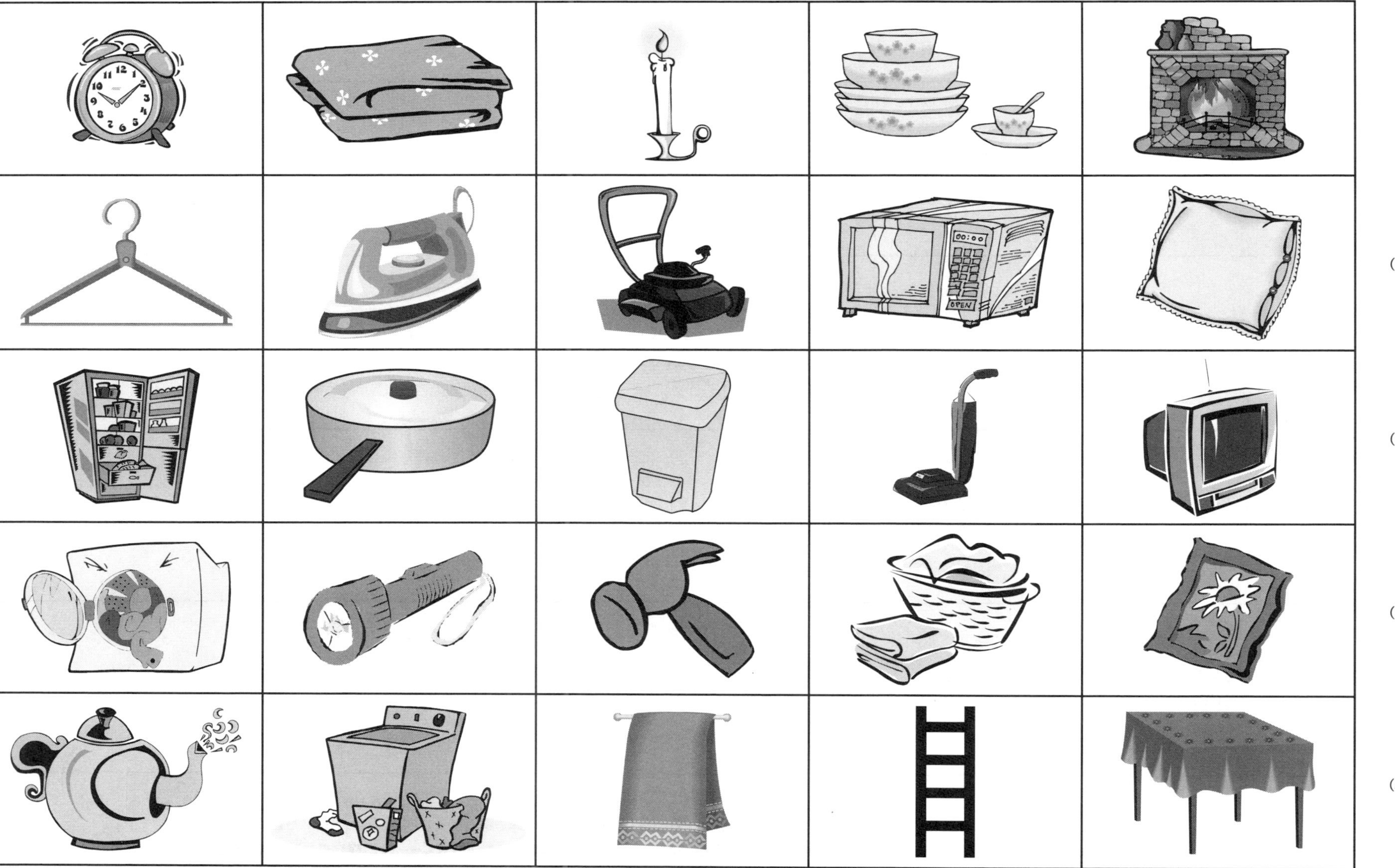

(5)
(10)
(15)
(20)
(25)

ONE-MINUTE FLUENCY
SOPRIS WEST SKILL BUILDERS SERIES

HEAR/SEE TO SAY

	Correct	Error
First Try		
Second Try		

PHONEMIC AWARENESS—PHONEME ISOLATION
Beginning Sound—Skill Sheet 8, Household

Directions to Teacher: Point to the picture. Say, "This is (say name of picture). What sound does (picture) begin with?"

alarm /u/	blanket /b/	candle /k/	dishes /d/	fireplace /f/	(5)
hanger /h/	iron /ie/	lawnmower /l/	microwave /m/	pillow /p/	(10)
refrigerator /r/	skillet /s/	wastebasket /w/	vacuum /v/	television /t/	(15)
dryer /d/	flashlight /f/	hammer /h/	laundry /l/	picture /p/	(20)
teapot /t/	washer /w/	towel /t/	ladder /l/	table /t/	(25)

ONE-MINUTE FLUENCY
SOPRIS WEST SKILL BUILDERS SERIES

HEAR/SEE TO SAY

PHONEMIC AWARENESS—PHONEME ISOLATION
Beginning Sound—Skill Sheet 9, Clothes

	Correct	Error
First Try		
Second Try		

					(5)
					(10)
					(15)
					(20)
					(25)

HEAR/SEE TO SAY

	Correct	Error
First Try		
Second Try		

PHONEMIC AWARENESS—PHONEME ISOLATION
Beginning Sound—Skill Sheet 9, Clothes

Directions to Teacher: Point to the picture. Say, "This is (say name of picture). What sound does (picture) begin with?"

gown /g/	jeans /j/	shorts /sh/	pajamas /p/	necktie /n/	(5)
apron /ai/	blouse /b/	nightgown /n/	raincoat /r/	skirt /s/	(10)
vest /v/	umbrella /u/	watch /w/	coat /k/	ring /r/	(15)
t-shirt /t/	glasses /g/	sweatshirt /s/	dress /d/	earrings /ea/	(20)
hat /h/	mittens /m/	necklace /n/	shirt /sh/	purse /p/	(25)

ONE-MINUTE FLUENCY
SOPRIS WEST SKILL BUILDERS SERIES

HEAR/SEE TO SAY

PHONEMIC AWARENESS—PHONEME ISOLATION
Beginning Sound—Skill Sheet 10, School

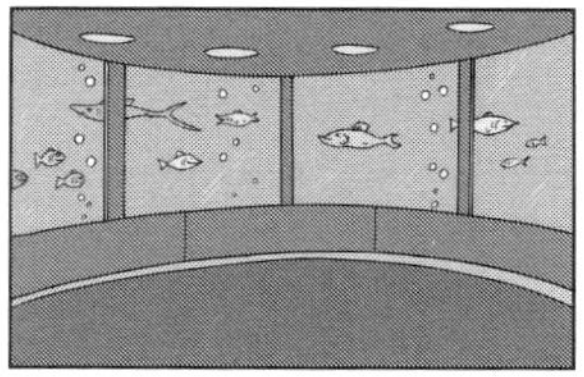

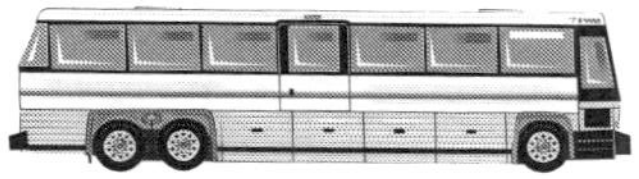

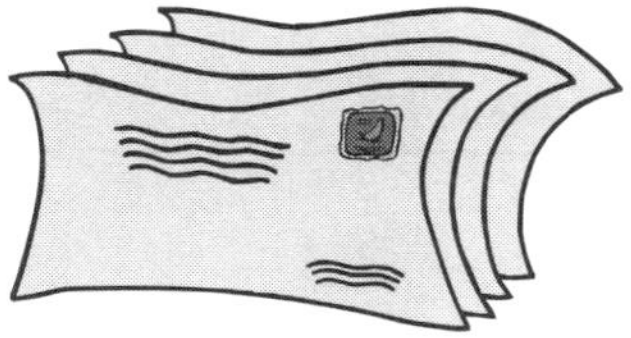

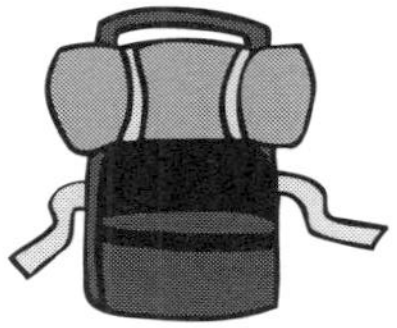

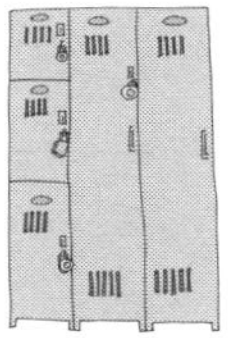

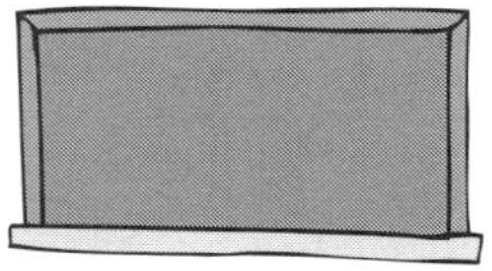

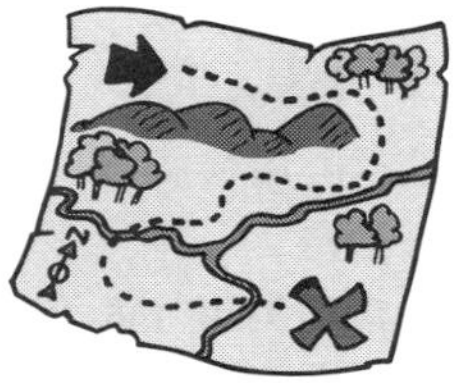

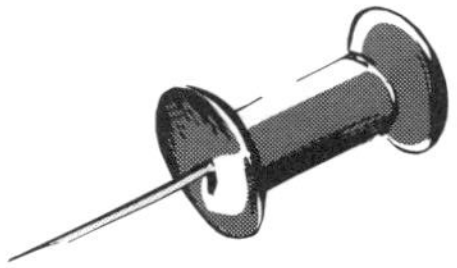

	Correct	Error
First Try		
Second Try		

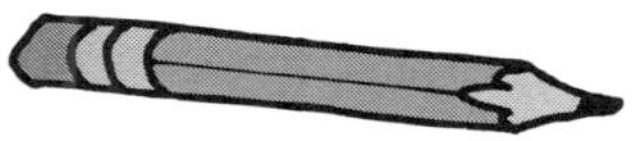

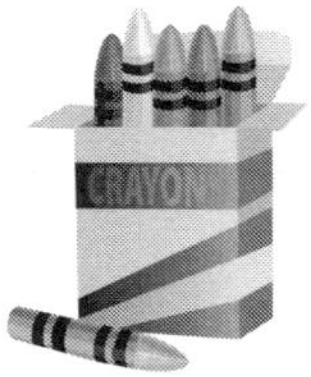

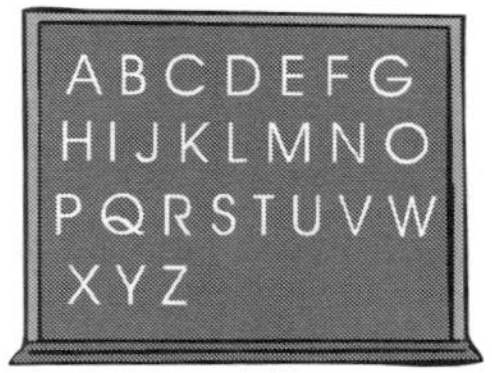

ABCDEFG
HIJKLMNO
PQRSTUVW
XYZ

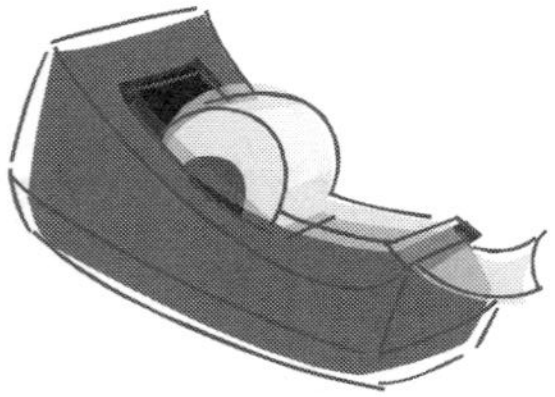

(5)

(10)

(15)

(20)

(25)

HEAR/SEE TO SAY

	Correct	Error
First Try		
Second Try		

PHONEMIC AWARENESS—PHONEME ISOLATION
Beginning Sound—Skill Sheet 10, School

Directions to Teacher: Point to the picture. Say, "This is (say name of picture). What sound does (picture) begin with?"

desk /d/	notebook /n/	pencil /p/	scissors /s/	crayons /k/	(5)
aquarium /u/	bus /b/	flag /f/	books /b/	letters /l/	(10)
globe /g/	earphones /ea/	alphabet /a/	tape /t/	sharpener /sh/	(15)
chair /ch/	backpack /b/	lockers /l/	marker /m/	paints /p/	(20)
chalkboard /ch/	numbers /n/	ruler /r/	map /m/	thumbtack /th/	(25)

ONE-MINUTE FLUENCY
SOPRIS WEST SKILL BUILDERS SERIES

HEAR/SEE TO SAY

PHONEMIC AWARENESS—PHONEME ISOLATION
Beginning Sound—Skill Sheet 11, Play

	Correct	Error
First Try		
Second Try		

(5)

(10)

(15)

(20)

(25)

	Correct	Error
First Try		
Second Try		

PHONEMIC AWARENESS—PHONEME ISOLATION
Beginning Sound—Skill Sheet 11, Play

Directions to Teacher: Point to the picture. Say, "This is (say name of picture). What sound does (picture) begin with?"

airplane /ai/	balloon /b/	cards /k/	doll /d/	football /f/	(5)
golf /g/	horse /h/	kite /k/	marbles /m/	puzzle /p/	(10)
swing /s/	tricycle /t/	yo-yo /y/	whistle /hw/	checkers /ch/	(15)
basketball /b/	car /k/	dominoes /d/	horn /h/	mitt /m/	(20)
sled /s/	teeter-totter /t/	blocks /b/	crayons /k/	train /t/	(25)

ONE MINUTE FLUENCY
SOPRIS WEST SKILL BUILDERS SERIES

HEAR/SEE TO SAY

PHONEMIC AWARENESS—PHONEME ISOLATION
Beginning Sound—Skill Sheet 12, Farm

	Correct	Error
First Try		
Second Try		

(5)

(10)

(15)

(20)

(25)

HEAR/SEE TO SAY

PHONEMIC AWARENESS—PHONEME ISOLATION
Beginning Sound—Skill Sheet 12, Farm

Directions to Teacher: Point to the picture. Say, "This is (say name of picture). What sound does (picture) begin with?"

	Correct	Error
First Try		
Second Try		

barn /b/	colt /k/	ducklings /d/	eggs /e/	hen /h/	(5)
lamb /l/	cow /k/	pig /p/	rooster /r/	scarecrow /s/	(10)
tractor /t/	weathervane /w/	sheep /sh/	chick /ch/	wheelbarrow /hw/	(15)
calf /k/	duck /d/	hay /h/	goose /g/	ox /o/	(20)
pickup /p/	turkey /t/	goat /g/	truck /t/	farmer /f/	(25)

ONE-MINUTE FLUENCY
SOPRIS WEST SKILL BUILDERS SERIES

HEAR/SEE TO SAY

PHONEMIC AWARENESS—PHONEME ISOLATION
Beginning Sound—Skill Sheet 13, Food (Fruits and Vegetables)

	Correct	Error
First Try		
Second Try		

(5)

(10)

(15)

(20)

(25)

	Correct	Error
First Try		
Second Try		

PHONEMIC AWARENESS—PHONEME ISOLATION
Beginning Sound—Skill Sheet 13, Food (Fruits and Vegetables)

Directions to Teacher: Point to the picture. Say, "This is (say name of picture). What sound does (picture) begin with?"

apple /a/	banana /b/	carrot /k/	grapes /g/	onion /u/	(5)
celery /s/	radishes /r/	peach /p/	tomato /t/	watermelon /w/	(10)
cherries /ch/	beans /b/	corn /k/	fruit /f/	lemon /l/	(15)
pineapple /p/	strawberry /s/	grapefruit /g/	cucumber /k/	lettuce /l/	(20)
vegetables /v/	mushrooms /m/	potatoes /p/	pear /p/	spinach /s/	(25)

HEAR/SEE TO SAY

PHONEMIC AWARENESS—PHONEME ISOLATION
Beginning Sound—Skill Sheet 14, Food (General)

	Correct	Error
First Try		
Second Try		

(5)

(10)

(15)

(20)

(25)

	Correct	Error
First Try		
Second Try		

PHONEMIC AWARENESS—PHONEME ISOLATION
Beginning Sound—Skill Sheet 14, Food (General)

Directions to Teacher: Point to the picture. Say, "This is (say name of picture). What sound does (picture) begin with?"

bread /b/	cupcake /k/	donut /d/	egg /e/	hotdog /h/	(5)
gelatin /j/	turkey /t/	salad /s/	yogurt /y/	nuts /n/	(10)
sandwich /s/	meat /m/	cheese /ch/	pie /p/	hamburger /h/	(15)
pumpkin /p/	drumstick /d/	cookie /k/	milk /m/	fries /f/	(20)
jam /j/	chocolate /ch/	walnut /w/	pizza /p/	tea /t/	(25)

ONE-MINUTE FLUENCY
SOPRIS WEST SKILL BUILDERS SERIES

HEAR/SEE TO SAY

PHONEMIC AWARENESS—PHONEME ISOLATION
Beginning Sound—Skill Sheet 15, Animals

	Correct	Error
First Try		
Second Try		

(5)

(10)

(15)

(20)

(25)

HEAR/SEE TO SAY

PHONEMIC AWARENESS—PHONEME ISOLATION
Beginning Sound—Skill Sheet 15, Animals

Directions to Teacher: Point to the picture. Say, "This is (say name of picture). What sound does (picture) begin with?"

	Correct	Error
First Try		
Second Try		

alligator /a/	butterfly /b/	camel /k/	eagle /ea/	Dachshund /d/	(5)
frog /f/	goldfish /g/	giraffe /j/	kangaroo /k/	lion /l/	(10)
hippopotamus /h/	monkey /m/	ostrich /o/	parrot /p/	raccoon /r/	(15)
squirrel /s/	woodpecker /w/	zebra /z/	owl /ow/	chipmunk /ch/	(20)
elephant /e/	gorilla /g/	flamingo /f/	penguin /p/	tiger /t/	(25)

HEAR/SEE TO SAY

PHONEMIC AWARENESS—PHONEME ISOLATION
Beginning Sound—Skill Sheet 16, Ocean

	Correct	Error
First Try		
Second Try		

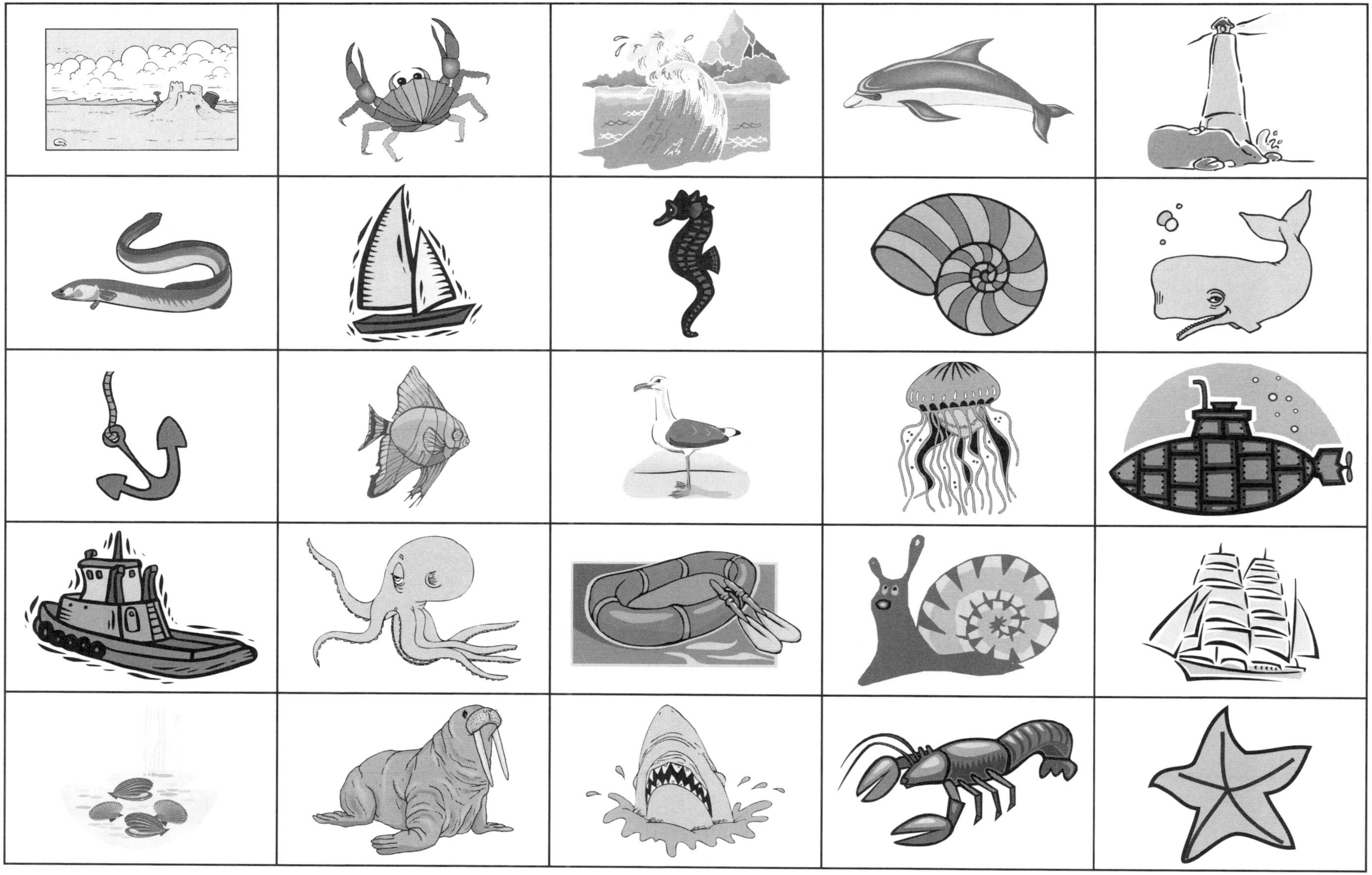

(5)

(10)

(15)

(20)

(25)

HEAR/SEE TO SAY

	Correct	Error
First Try		
Second Try		

PHONEMIC AWARENESS—PHONEME ISOLATION
Beginning Sound—Skill Sheet 16, Ocean

Directions to Teacher: Point to the picture. Say, "This is (say name of picture). What sound does (picture) begin with?"

beach /b/	crab /k/	waves /w/	dolphin /d/	lighthouse /l/	(5)
eel /ea/	sailboat /s/	seahorse /s/	shell /sh/	whale /hw/	(10)
anchor /a/	fish /f/	gull /g/	jellyfish /j/	submarine /s/	(15)
tugboat /t/	octopus /o/	raft /r/	snail /s/	ship /sh/	(20)
clams /k/	walrus /w/	shark /sh/	lobster /l/	starfish /s/	(25)

HEAR/SEE TO SAY

PHONEMIC AWARENESS—PHONEME ISOLATION
Ending Sound—Skill Sheet 1

	Correct	Error
First Try		
Second Try		

					(5)
		3			(10)
				5	(15)
A A					(20)
					(25)

	Correct	Error
First Try		
Second Try		

PHONEMIC AWARENESS—PHONEME ISOLATION

Ending Sound—Skill Sheet 1

Directions to Teacher: Point to the picture. Say, "This is (say name of picture). What sound does (picture) end with?"

elf /f/	vine /n/	saw /o/	shoe /oo/	fan /n/	(5)
leaf /f/	mouth /th/	three /ea/	ice /s/	nail /l/	(10)
yarn /n/	rose /z/	ear /r/	face /s/	five /v/	(15)
ace /s/	arm /m/	oars /z/	hoe /oa/	smile /l/	(20)
owl /l/	Earth /th/	fly /ie/	zoo /oo/	mice /s/	(25)

ONE-MINUTE FLUENCY
SOPRIS WEST SKILL BUILDERS SERIES

HEAR/SEE TO SAY

PHONEMIC AWARENESS—PHONEME ISOLATION
Ending Sound—Skill Sheet 2

	Correct	Error
First Try		
Second Try		

					(5)
					(10)
					(15)
					(20)
					(25)

HEAR/SEE TO SAY

	Correct	Error
First Try		
Second Try		

PHONEMIC AWARENESS—PHONEME ISOLATION
Ending Sound—Skill Sheet 2

Directions to Teacher: Point to the picture. Say, "This is (say name of picture). What sound does (picture) end with?"

pail /l/	bee /ea/	bear /r/	cash /sh/	bow /oa/	(5)
bone /n/	dove /v/	pan /n/	calf /f/	girl /l/	(10)
can /n/	tooth /th/	bell /l/	screw /oo/	hay /ai/	(15)
bus /s/	jar /ar/	key /ea/	trash /sh/	two /oo/	(20)
chips /s/	door /r/	fire /r/	drum /m/	comb /m/	(25)

ONE-MINUTE FLUENCY
SOPRIS WEST SKILL BUILDERS SERIES

PHONEMIC AWARENESS—PHONEME ISOLATION
Ending Sound—Skill Sheet 3

	Correct	Error
First Try		
Second Try		

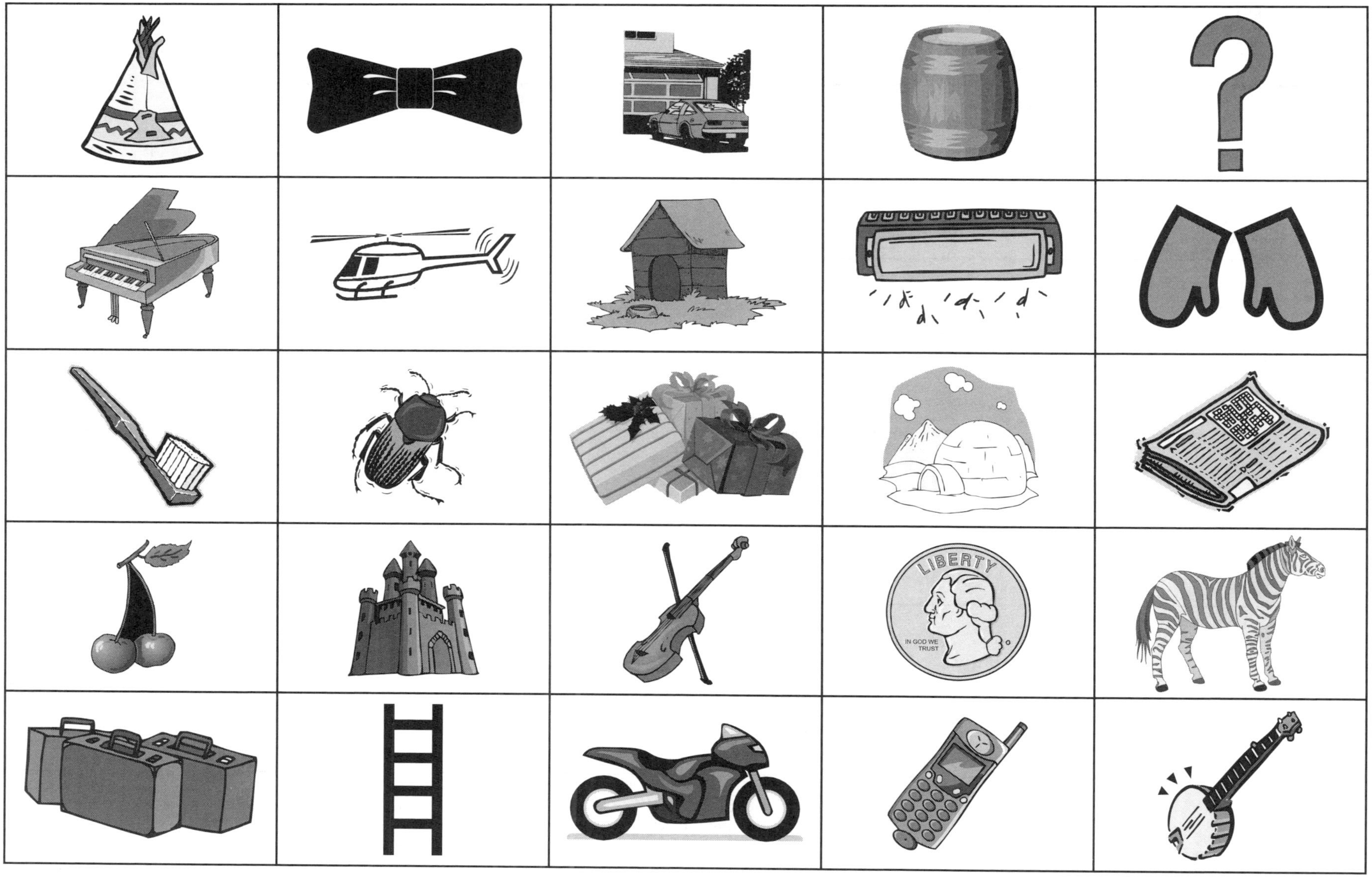

(5)
(10)
(15)
(20)
(25)

HEAR/SEE TO SAY

	Correct	Error
First Try		
Second Try		

PHONEMIC AWARENESS—PHONEME ISOLATION
Ending Sound—Skill Sheet 3

Directions to Teacher: Point to the picture. Say, "This is (say name of picture). What sound does (picture) end with?"

teepee /ea/	bowtie /ie/	garage /SH/	barrel /l/	question /n/	(5)
piano /oa/	helicopter /r/	doghouse /s/	harmonica /u/	mittens /z/	(10)
toothbrush /sh/	beetle /l/	presents /s/	igloo /oo/	newspaper /ĕr/	(15)
cherry /ea/	castle /l/	violin /n/	quarter /ĕr/	zebra /u/	(20)
suitcases /s/	ladder /ĕr/	motorcycle /l/	cellphone /n/	banjo /oa/	(25)

ONE MINUTE FLUENCY
SOPRIS WEST SKILL BUILDERS SERIES

HEAR/SEE TO SAY

PHONEMIC AWARENESS—PHONEME ISOLATION
Ending Sound—Skill Sheet 4

	Correct	Error
First Try		
Second Try		

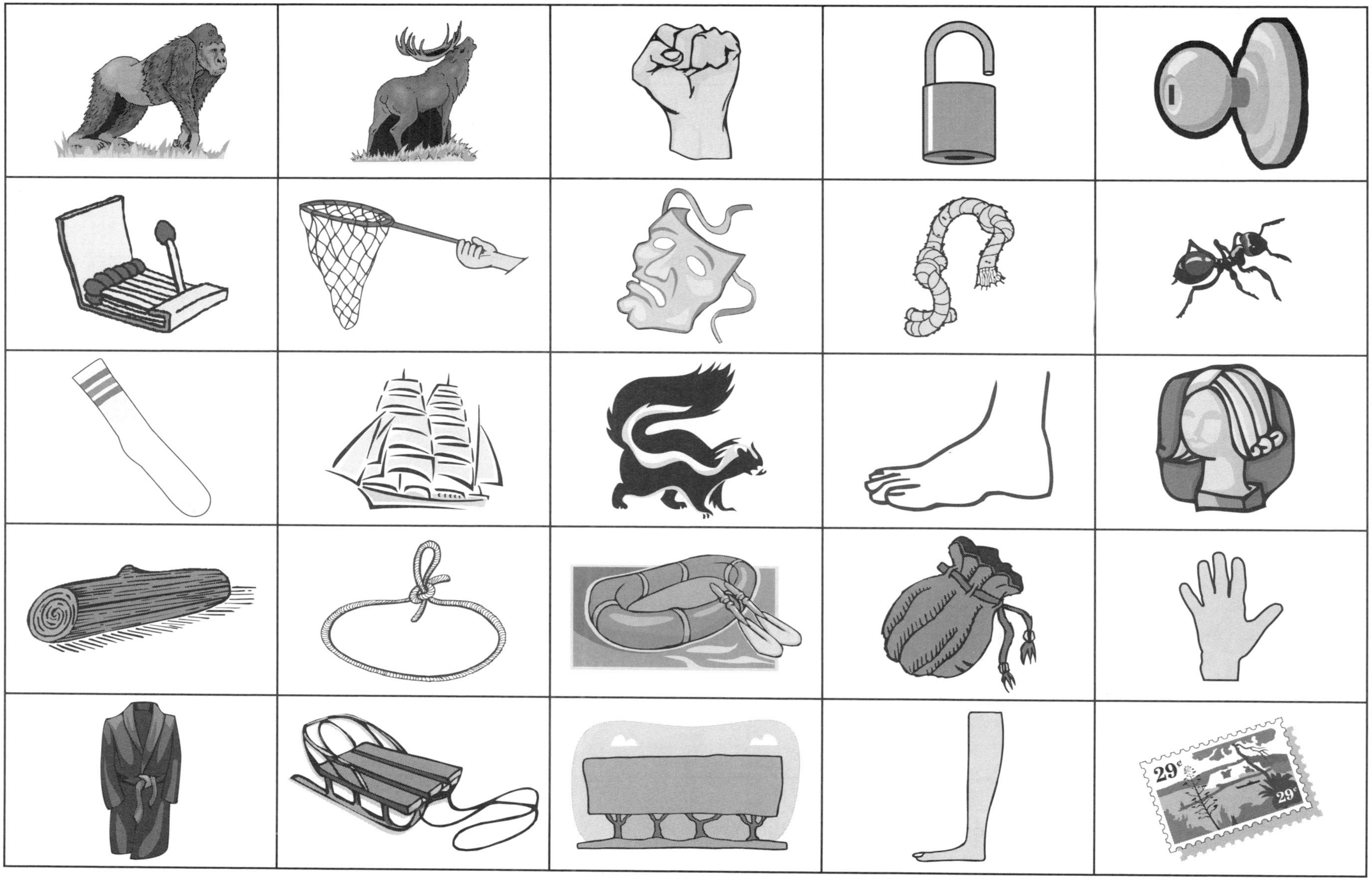

(5)
(10)
(15)
(20)
(25)

HEAR/SEE TO SAY

	Correct	Error
First Try		
Second Try		

PHONEMIC AWARENESS—PHONEME ISOLATION
Ending Sound—Skill Sheet 4

Directions to Teacher: Point to the picture. Say, "This is (say name of picture). What sound does (picture) end with?"

ape /p/	elk /k/	fist /t/	lock /k/	knob /b/	(5)
match /ch/	net /t/	mask /k/	rope /p/	ant /t/	(10)
sock /k/	ship /p/	skunk /k/	foot /t/	wig /g/	(15)
log /g/	knot /t/	raft /t/	sack /k/	hand /d/	(20)
robe /b/	sled /d/	shrub /b/	leg /g/	stamp /p/	(25)

PHONEMIC AWARENESS—PHONEME ISOLATION
Ending Sound—Skill Sheet 5

	Correct	Error
First Try		
Second Try		

(5)

(10)

(15)

(20)

(25)

HEAR/SEE TO SAY

	Correct	Error
First Try		
Second Try		

PHONEMIC AWARENESS—PHONEME ISOLATION
Ending Sound—Skill Sheet 5

Directions to Teacher: Point to the picture. Say, "This is (say name of picture). What sound does (picture) end with?"

cab /b/	bank /k/	bag /g/	bird /d/	bridge /j/	(5)
chimp /p/	cast /t/	jeep /p/	gate /t/	church /ch/	(10)
chick /k/	jet /t/	pot /t/	card /d/	bolt /t/	(15)
cart /t/	cage /j/	crab /b/	gold /d/	tack /k/	(20)
bug /g/	bat /t/	chest /t/	toast /t/	plant /t/	(25)

HEAR/SEE TO SAY

ONE MINUTE FLUENCY
SOPRIS WEST SKILL BUILDERS SERIES

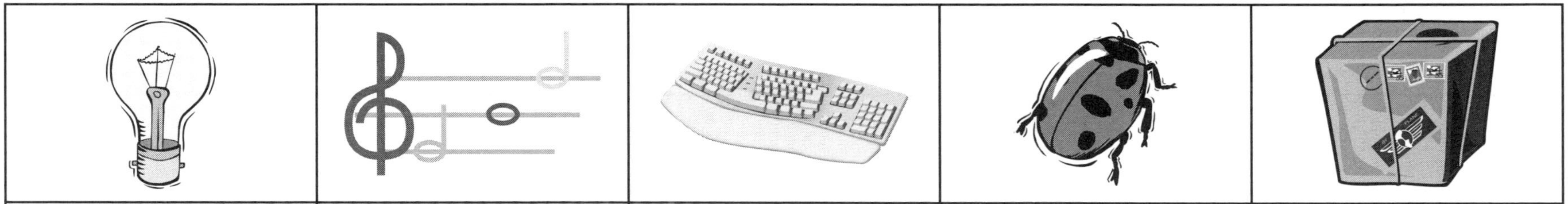

PHONEMIC AWARENESS—PHONEME ISOLATION
Ending Sound—Skill Sheet 6

	Correct	Error
First Try		
Second Try		

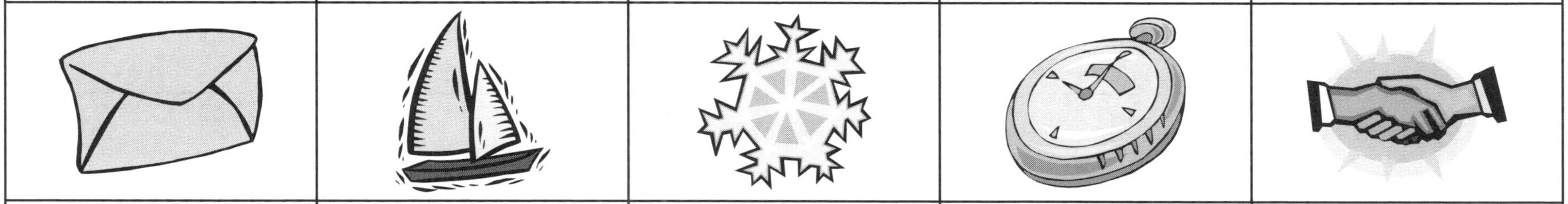

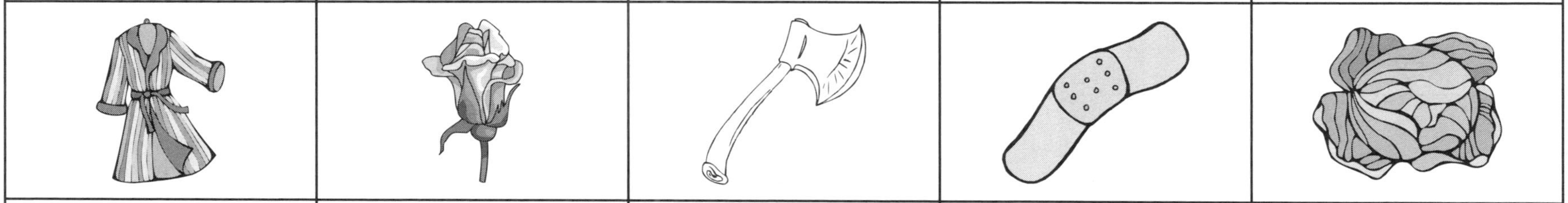

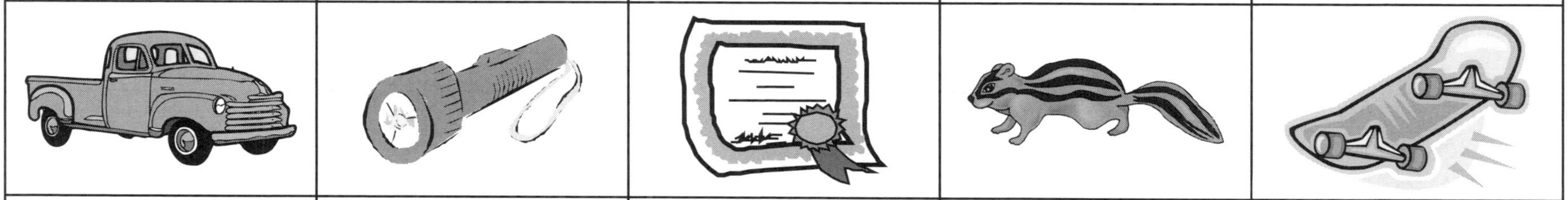

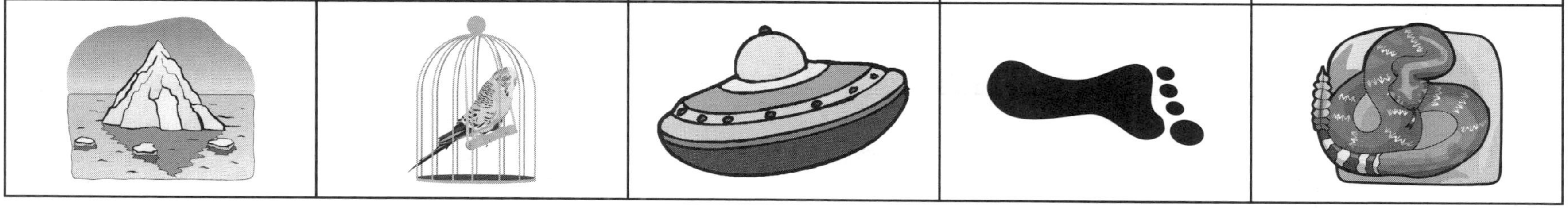

(5)

(10)

(15)

(20)

(25)

HEAR/SEE TO SAY

	Correct	Error
First Try		
Second Try		

PHONEMIC AWARENESS—PHONEME ISOLATION
Ending Sound—Skill Sheet 6

Directions to Teacher: Point to the picture. Say, "This is (say name of picture). What sound does (picture) end with?"

lightbulb /b/	music /k/	keyboard /d/	ladybug /g/	package /j/	(5)
envelope /p/	sailboat /t/	snowflake /k/	stopwatch /ch/	handshake /k/	(10)
bathrobe /b/	rosebud /d/	hatchet /t/	bandage /j/	cabbage /j/	(15)
pickup /p/	flashlight /t/	award /d/	chipmunk /k/	skateboard /d/	(20)
iceberg /g/	birdcage /j/	spaceship /p/	footprint /t/	rattlesnake /k/	(25)

SEE TO WRITE

PHONEMIC AWARENESS—PHONEME ISOLATION
Beginning and Ending Sounds—Skill Sheet 1

	Correct	Error
First Try		
Second Try		

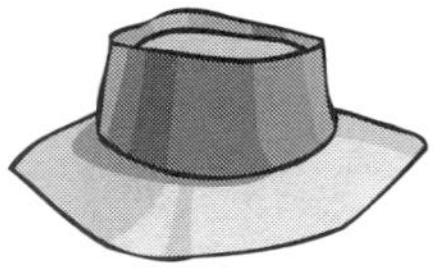

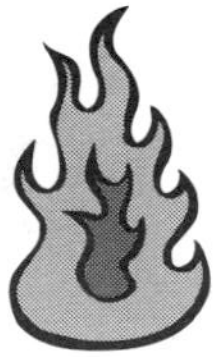

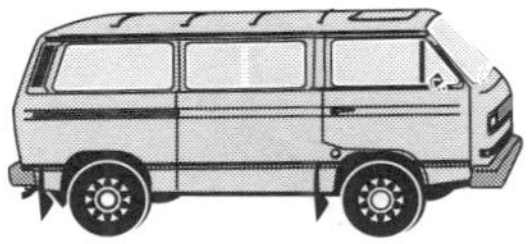

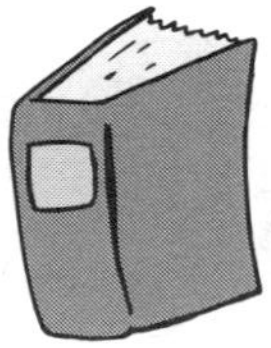

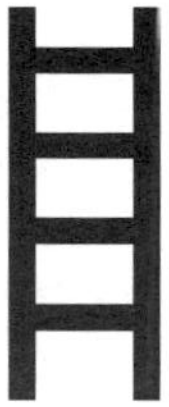

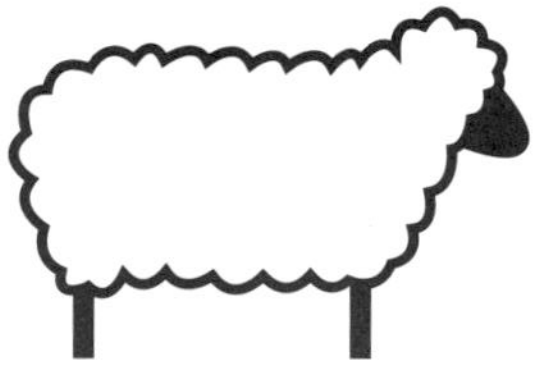

(12)

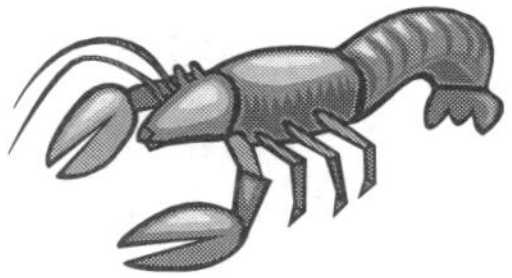

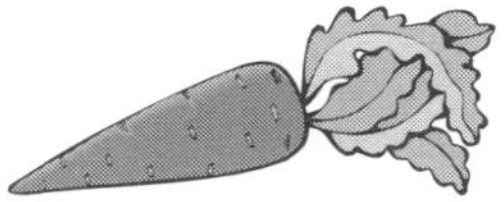

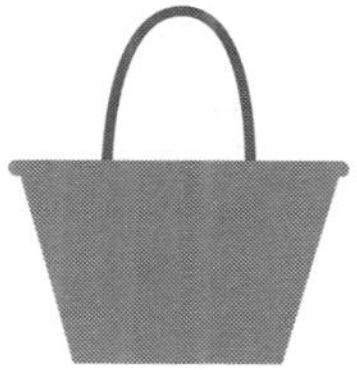

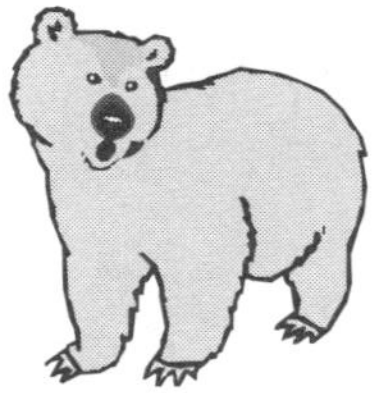

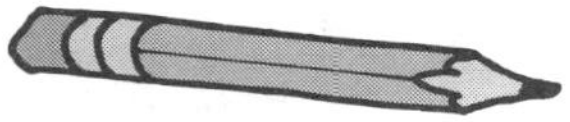

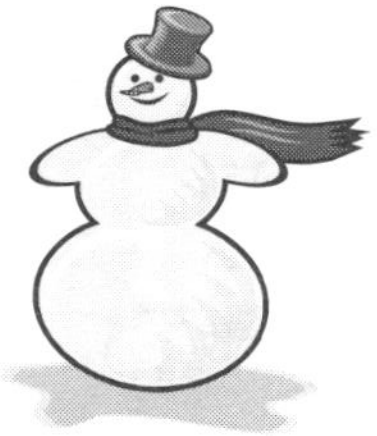

(24)

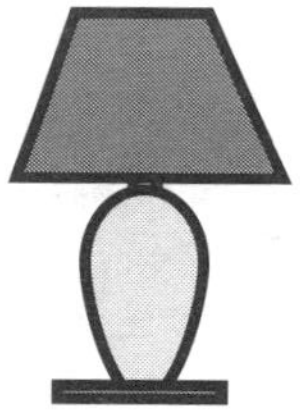

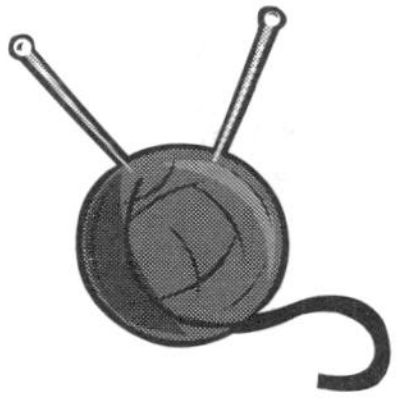

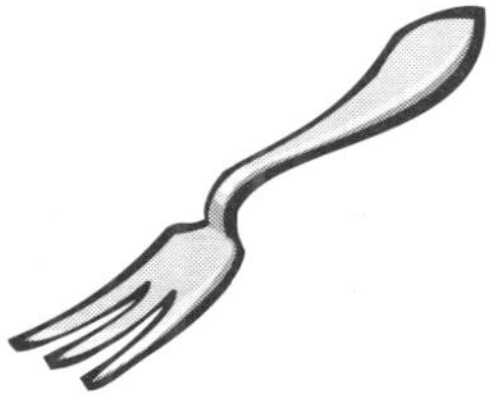

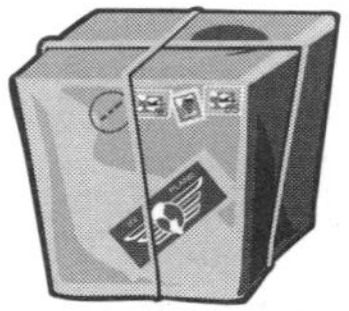

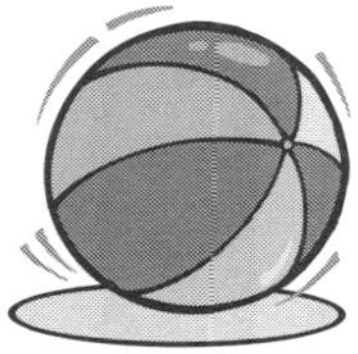

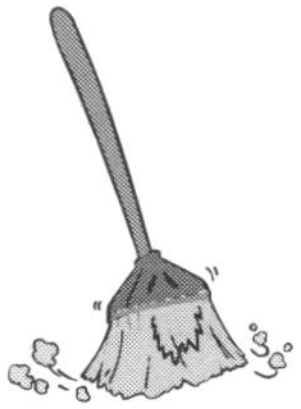

(36)

ONE-MINUTE FLUENCY
SOPRIS WEST SKILL BUILDERS SERIES

SEE TO WRITE

	Correct	Error
First Try		
Second Try		

PHONEMIC AWARENESS—PHONEME ISOLATION
Beginning and Ending Sounds—Skill Sheet 1

Directions to Teacher: Say the beginning and ending sound for the picture.

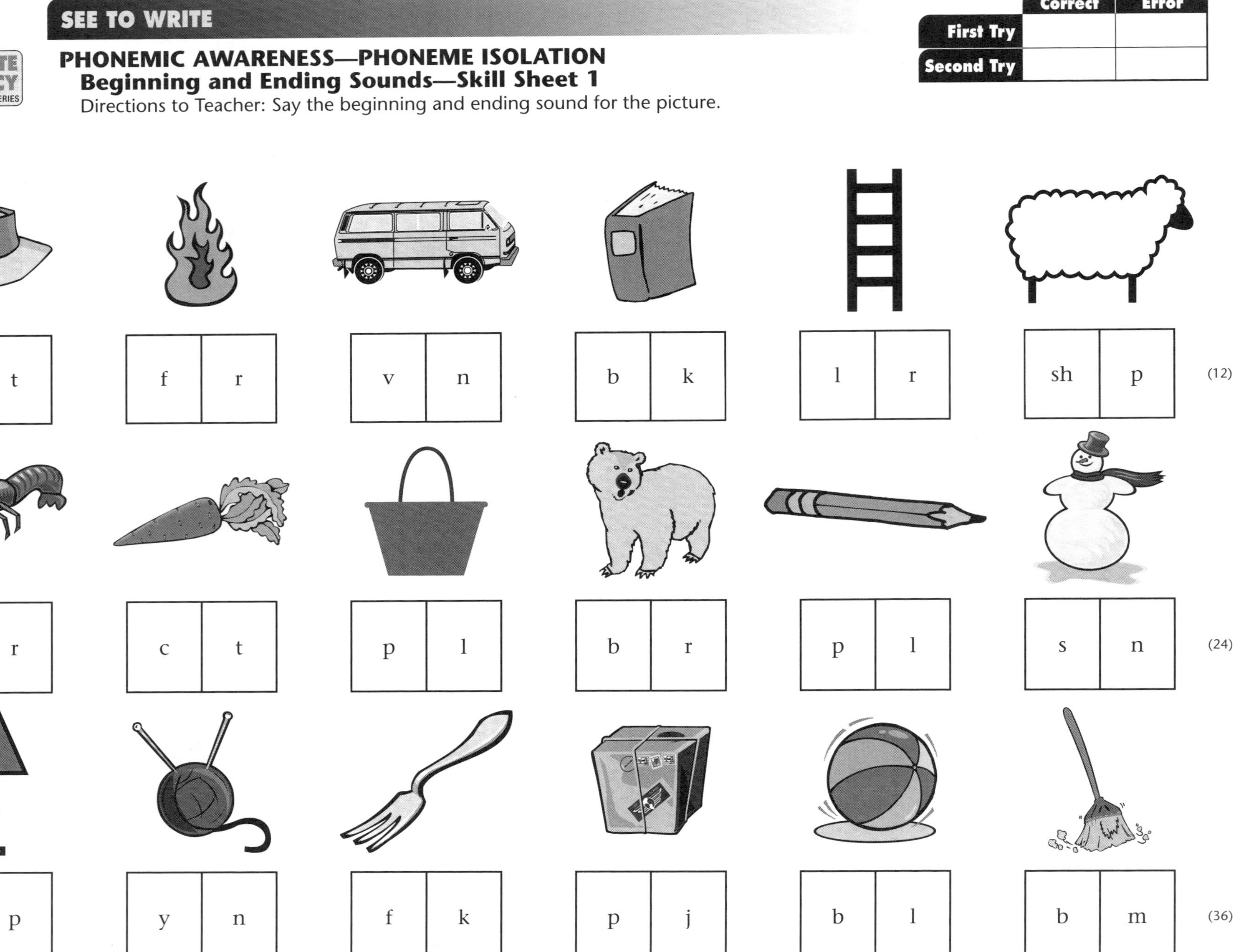

h t	f r	v n	b k	l r	sh p	(12)
l r	c t	p l	b r	p l	s n	(24)
l p	y n	f k	p j	b l	b m	(36)

ONE-MINUTE FLUENCY
SOPRIS WEST SKILL BUILDERS SERIES

SEE TO WRITE

PHONEMIC AWARENESS—PHONEME ISOLATION
Beginning and Ending Sounds—Skill Sheet 2

	Correct	Error
First Try		
Second Try		

(12)

(24)

(36)

SEE TO WRITE

PHONEMIC AWARENESS—PHONEME ISOLATION
Beginning and Ending Sounds—Skill Sheet 2

Directions to Teacher: Say the beginning and ending sound for the picture.

	Correct	Error
First Try		
Second Try		

h d	 b t	 b x	 w n	 d l	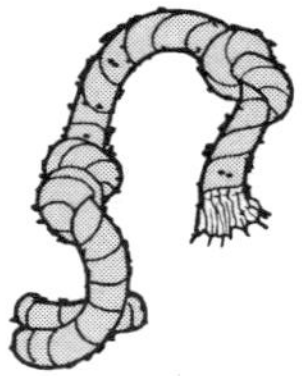 r p	(12)
g t	 k t	 c p	 m n	 n t	 v s	(24)
j p	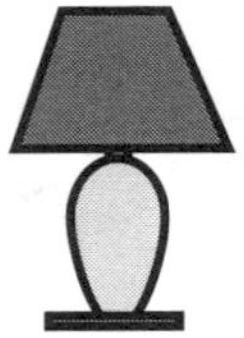 l p	 r t	 l f	 d m	 p g	(36)

Phonemic Awareness—Phoneme Segmentation

Grades K–2; Intervention Grade 3 and Above

Timing Note:
The directions to the teacher are to:

1. Point to the picture.
2. Say, "This is (say name of picture). Tell me all the sounds in (picture)."

After providing this initial direction to the student, the teacher may choose to prompt each individual response by merely pointing to the picture and saying the name of the picture. The student says the individual phonemes in the word/picture and the teacher immediately points to and names the next picture. The student is timed for one minute, then the number of correct and incorrect responses is recorded.

Scoring Note:
Answer sheets indicate the correct phonemes in sequence for each picture name. Each separate phoneme produced correctly in sequence is counted as accurate.

Word	Phonemes	Count
train	/t/ /r/ /ai/ /n/	4

Depending on the reading series being used with the student, the teacher may choose to modify the scoring process to count as correct letter blends or even clusters of sounds.

If some modified response is accepted as correct, all sounds must be produced accurately and in the correct sequence. Each separate sound/phoneme segment is counted as one correct response.

Word	Student Said	Count
train	tr...ain	2
train	tr...ai...n	3

If the student simply repeats the word heard with no attempt to segment it into component sounds, no credit is given.

Pronunciation Guide
Answer sheets indicate the correct isolated phoneme using the following conventions:

Phoneme	Phoneme Example
/ai/	rain, day
/ea/	bead, see
/ie/	tie, fine
/oa/	coat, doe
/oo/	moon
/a/	dad
/e/	bed, head
/i/	did
/o/	log, law
/u/	cup and "a" in about
/uu/	book
/ow/	how
/oi/	noise, boy
/ar/	(1 phoneme) car
/ir/	(1 phoneme) girl, fur
/or/	(1 phoneme) for, more, four
/ai/ /r/	(2 phonemes) fair
/ea/ /r/	(2 phonemes) dear
/oo/ /r/	(2 phonemes) tour
/er/	winter, sister
/b/	bad
/k/	cat, kite, back
/d/	dad
/f/	fat
/g/	go, big
/h/	hat
/j/	jet, edge
/l/	let
/m/	man, ham
/n/	no, knob, can
/p/	pat, cap
/kw/	queen
/r/	rat, frog
/s/	sat, cats
/t/	top, pot
/v/	van
/w/	wet
/ks/	box
/z/	zoo
/sh/	show
/SH/	measure, beige
/th/	thin
/TH/	the
/ch/	chick
/hw/	whale
/ng/	sing

PHONEMIC AWARENESS—PHONEME SEGMENTATION
One- and Two-Phoneme Words—Skill Sheet 1

	Correct	Error
First Try		
Second Try		

(10)

(20)

(30)

(39)

HEAR/SEE TO SAY

	Correct	Error
First Try		
Second Try		

PHONEMIC AWARENESS—PHONEME SEGMENTATION
One- and Two-Phoneme Words—Skill Sheet 1

Directions to Teacher: Point to the picture. Say, "This is (say name of picture). Tell me all the sounds in (picture)."

bow /b/ /oa/	cow /k/ /ow/	ape /ai/ /p/	hoe /h/ /oe/	eel /ea/ /l/	(10)
saw /s/ /o/	bee /b/ /ea/	tea /t/ /ea/	boy /b/ /oi/	shoe /sh/ /oo/	(20)
tie /t/ /ie/	earth /ur/ /th/	car /k/ /ar/	ice /ie/ /s/	two /t/ /oo/	(30)
doe /d/ /oa/	four /f/ /or/	egg /e/ /g/	pie /p/ /ie/	eye /ie/	(39)

HEAR/SEE TO SAY

PHONEMIC AWARENESS—PHONEME SEGMENTATION
Three-Phoneme Words—Skill Sheet 2

	Correct	Error
First Try		
Second Try		

					(15)
					(30)
					(45)
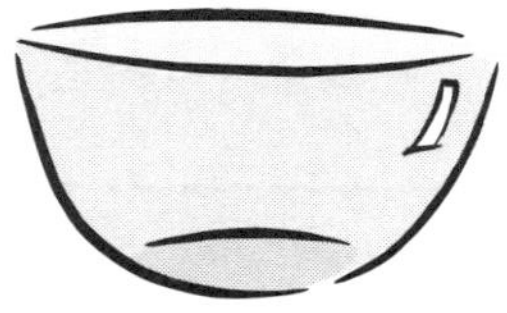					(60)

	Correct	Error
First Try		
Second Try		

PHONEMIC AWARENESS—PHONEME SEGMENTATION
Three-Phoneme Words—Skill Sheet 2

Directions to Teacher: Point to the picture. Say, "This is (say name of picture). Tell me all the sounds in (picture)."

sack /s/ /a/ /k/	elf /e/ /l/ /f/	mouse /m/ /ow/ /s/	ant /a/ /n/ /t/	deer /d/ /ea/ /r/	(15)
net /n/ /e/ /t/	tub /t/ /u/ /b/	hen /h/ /e/ /n/	comb /k/ /oa/ /m/	robe /r/ /oa/ /b/	(30)
lamb /l/ /a/ /m/	star /s/ /t/ /ar/	fly /f/ /l/ /ie/	can /k/ /a/ /n/	pear /p/ /ai/ /r/	(45)
bowl /b/ /oa/ /l/	chair /ch/ /ai/ /r/	purse /p/ /ir/ /s/	jet /j/ /e/ /t/	bed /b/ /e/ /d/	(60)

ONE MINUTE FLUENCY
SOPRIS WEST SKILL BUILDERS SERIES

HEAR/SEE TO SAY

PHONEMIC AWARENESS—PHONEME SEGMENTATION
Three-Phoneme Words—Skill Sheet 3

	Correct	Error
First Try		
Second Try		

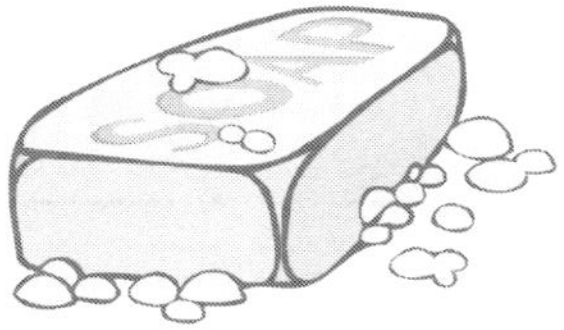

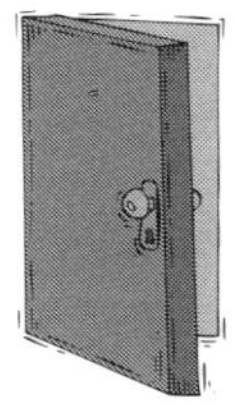

(15)

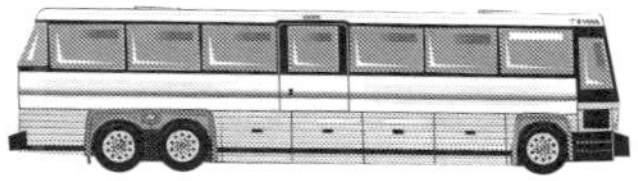

(30)

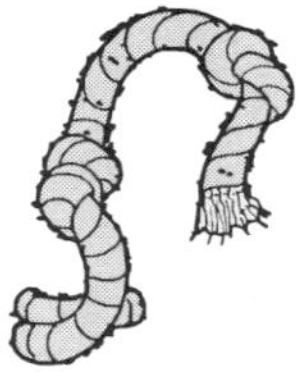

(45)

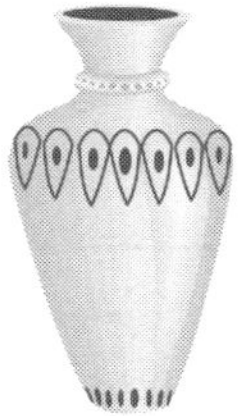

(60)

	Correct	Error
First Try		
Second Try		

PHONEMIC AWARENESS—PHONEME SEGMENTATION
Three-Phoneme Words—Skill Sheet 3

Directions to Teacher: Point to the picture. Say, "This is (say name of picture). Tell me all the sounds in (picture)."

hose /h/ /oa/ /z/	soap /s/ /oa/ /p/	fire /f/ /ie/ /r/	book /b/ /uu/ /k/	door /d/ /oa/ /r/	(15)
chick /ch/ /i/ /k/	rat /r/ /a/ /t/	bus /b/ /u/ /s/	top /t/ /o/ /p/	barn /b/ /ar/ /n/	(30)
phone /f/ /oa/ /n/	cake /k/ /ai/ /k/	ball /b/ /o/ /l/	pail /p/ /ai/ /l/	rope /r/ /oa/ /p/	(45)
bear /b/ /ai/ /r/	vase /v/ /ai/ /s/	boot /b/ /oo/ /t/	dog /d/ /o/ /g/	hat /h/ /a/ /t/	(60)

ONE-MINUTE FLUENCY
SOPRIS WEST SKILL BUILDERS SERIES

HEAR/SEE TO SAY

PHONEMIC AWARENESS—PHONEME SEGMENTATION
Three-Phoneme Words—Skill Sheet 4

	Correct	Error
First Try		
Second Try		

     (15)

     (30)

     (45)

    (60)

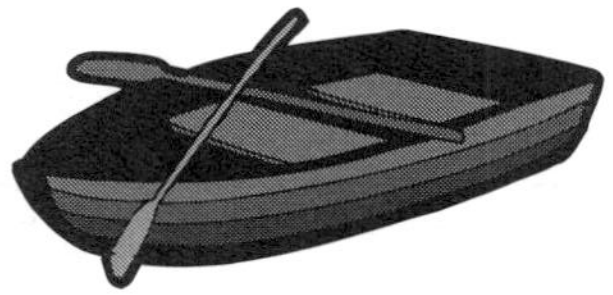

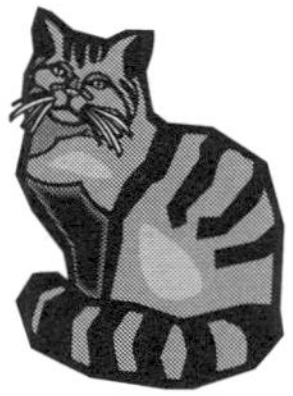

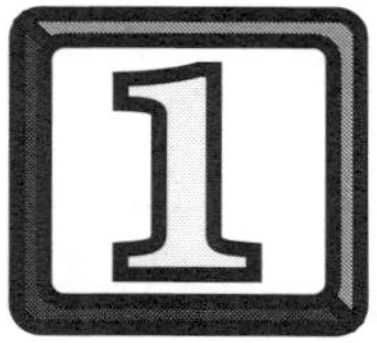

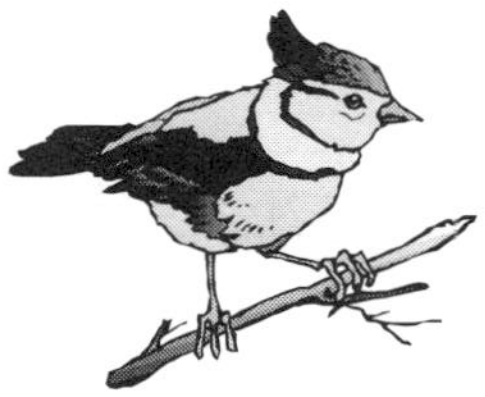

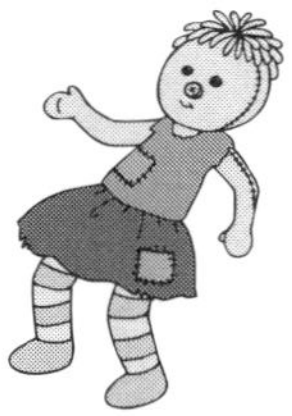

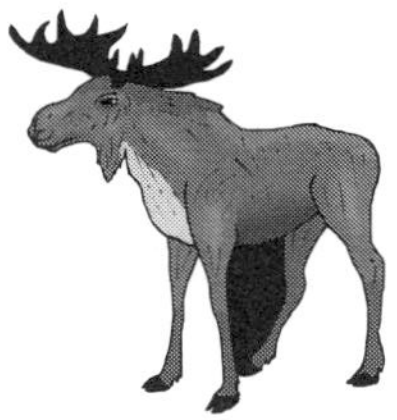

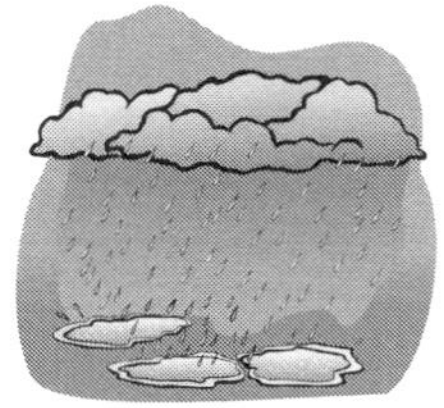

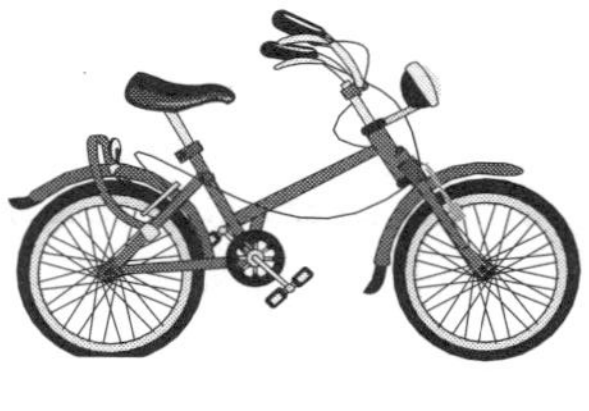

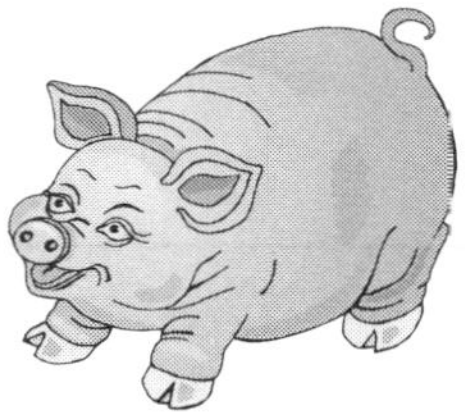

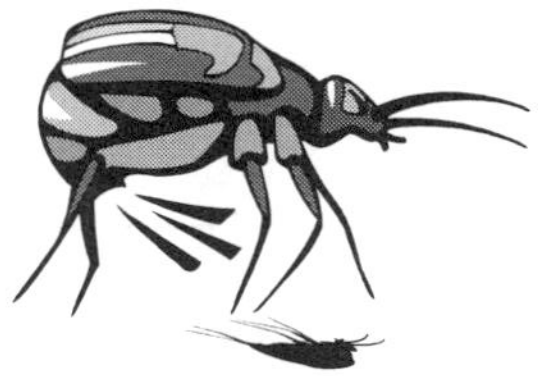

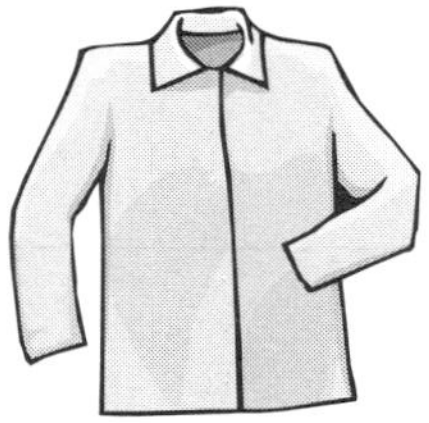

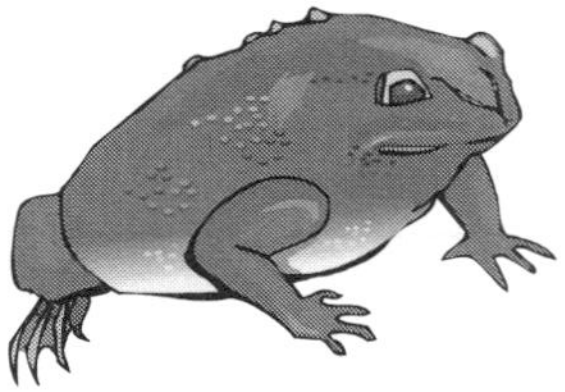

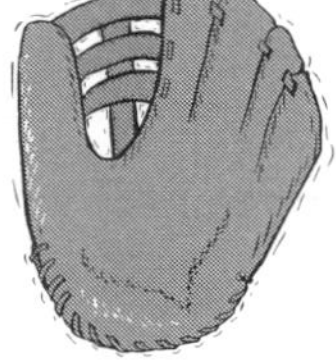

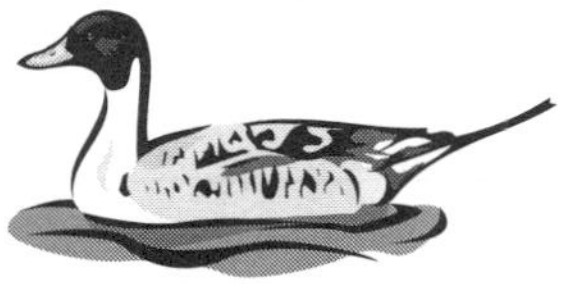

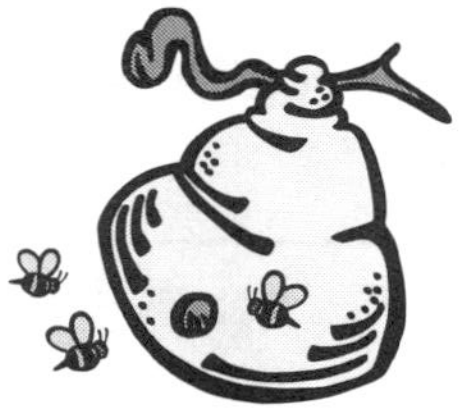

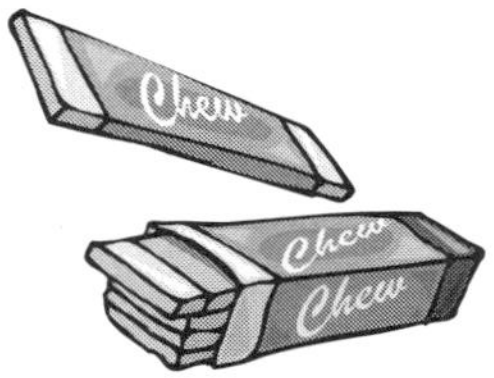

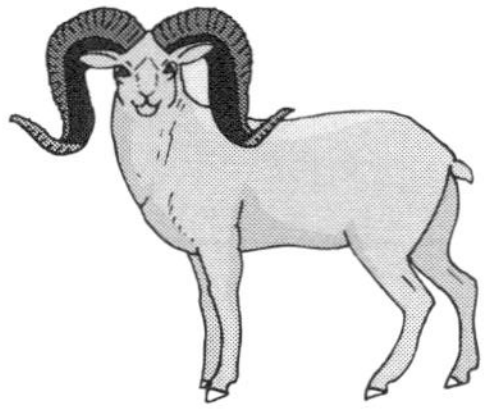

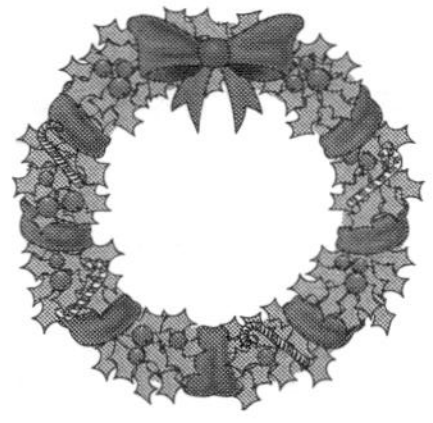

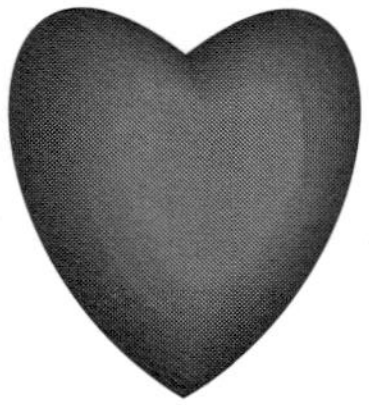

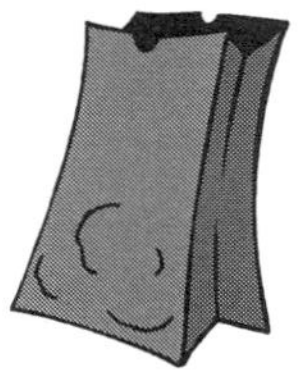

HEAR/SEE TO SAY

	Correct	Error
First Try		
Second Try		

PHONEMIC AWARENESS—PHONEME SEGMENTATION
Three-Phoneme Words—Skill Sheet 4

Directions to Teacher: Point to the picture. Say, "This is (say name of picture). Tell me all the sounds in (picture)."

boat /b/ /oa/ /t/	cat /k/ /a/ /t/	one /w/ /u/ /n/	bird /b/ /ir/ /d/	doll /d/ /o/ /l/	(15)
moose /m/ /oo/ /s/	rain /r/ /ai/ /n/	bike /b/ /ie/ /k/	hog /h/ /o/ /g/	bug /b/ /u/ /g/	(30)
shirt /sh/ /ir/ /t/	toad /t/ /oa/ /d/	mitt /m/ /i/ /t/	duck /d/ /u/ /k/	hive /h/ /ie/ /v/	(45)
gum /g/ /u/ /m/	ram /r/ /a/ /m/	wreathe /r/ /ea/ /th/	heart /h/ /ar/ /t/	bag /b/ /a/ /g/	(60)

HEAR/SEE TO SAY

PHONEMIC AWARENESS—PHONEME SEGMENTATION
Two- and Three-Phoneme Words—Skill Sheet 5

	Correct	Error
First Try		
Second Try		

					(14)
		8			(28)
				5	(42)
					(57)

	Correct	Error
First Try		
Second Try		

PHONEMIC AWARENESS—PHONEME SEGMENTATION
Two- and Three-Phoneme Words—Skill Sheet 5

Directions to Teacher: Point to the picture. Say, "This is (say name of picture). Tell me all the sounds in (picture)."

oars /or/ /z/	coat /k/ /oa/ /t/	knot /n/ /o/ /t/	mop /m/ /o/ /p/	mouth /m/ /ow/ /th/	(14)
bone /b/ /oa/ /n/	eight /ai/ /t/	leaf /l/ /ea/ /f/	rose /r/ /oa/ /z/	jeep /j/ /ea/ /p/	(28)
dove /d/ /u/ /v/	van /v/ /a/ /n/	Earth /ir/ /th/	chalk /ch/ /o/ /k/	five /f/ /ie/ /v/	(42)
kite /k/ /ie/ /t/	seal /s/ /ea/ /l/	bull /b/ /uu/ /l/	pig /p/ /i/ /g/	shark /sh/ /ar/ /k/	(57)

ONE-MINUTE FLUENCY
SOPRIS WEST SKILL BUILDERS SERIES

HEAR/SEE TO SAY

PHONEMIC AWARENESS—PHONEME SEGMENTATION
Two- and Three-Phoneme Words—Skill Sheet 6

	Correct	Error
First Try		
Second Try		

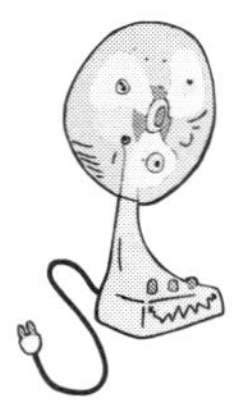

(14)

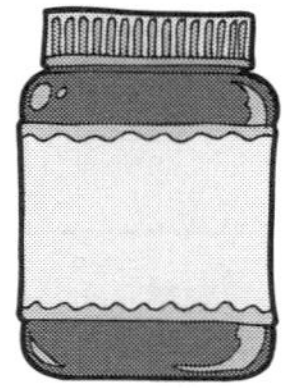

(28)

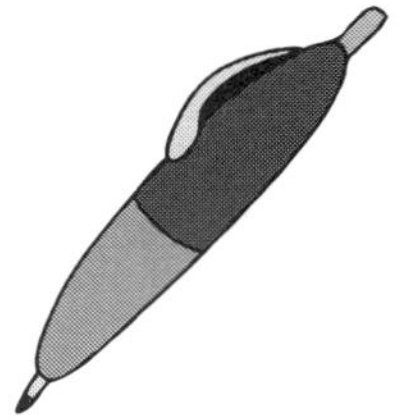

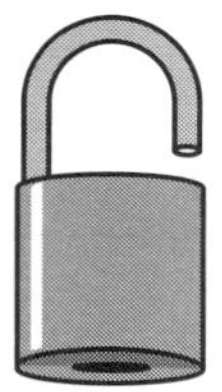

(43)

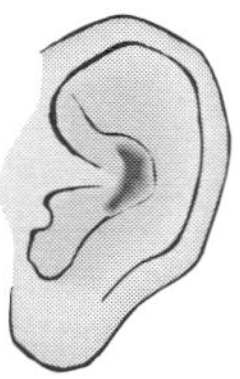

(56)

PHONEMIC AWARENESS—PHONEME SEGMENTATION
Two- and Three-Phoneme Words—Skill Sheet 6

Directions to Teacher: Point to the picture. Say, "This is (say name of picture). Tell me all the sounds in (picture)."

	Correct	Error
First Try		
Second Try		

sheep /sh/ /ea/ /p/	cap /k/ /a/ /p/	hay /h/ /ai/	sun /s/ /u/ /n/	fan /f/ /a/ /n/	(14)
jar /j/ /ar/	nail /n/ /ai/ /l/	bell /b/ /e/ /l/	goose /g/ /oo/ /s/	ten /t/ /e/ /n/	(28)
pen /p/ /e/ /n/	keys /k/ /ea/ /z/	rake /r/ /ai/ /k/	vine /v/ /ie/ /n/	lock /l/ /o/ /k/	(43)
pan /p/ /a/ /n/	moon /m/ /oo/ /n/	three /th/ /r/ /ea/	sea /s/ /ea/	ear /ea/ /r/	(56)

ONE MINUTE FLUENCY
SOPRIS WEST SKILL BUILDERS SERIES

HEAR/SEE TO SAY

PHONEMIC AWARENESS—PHONEME SEGMENTATION
Four-Phoneme Words—Skill Sheet 7

	Correct	Error
First Try		
Second Try		

(20)

(40)

(60)

(80)

	Correct	Error
First Try		
Second Try		

PHONEMIC AWARENESS—PHONEME SEGMENTATION

Four-Phoneme Words—Skill Sheet 7

Directions to Teacher: Point to the picture. Say, "This is (say name of picture). Tell me all the sounds in (picture)."

tent /t/ /e/ /n/ /t/	nest /n/ /e/ /s/ /t/	lamp /l/ /a/ /m/ /p/	colt /k/ /o/ /l/ /t/	books /b/ /uu/ /k/ /s/	(20)
mask /m/ /a/ /s/ /k/	hand /h/ /a/ /n/ /d/	desk /d/ /e/ /s/ /k/	ghost /g/ /oa/ /s/ /t/	screw /s/ /k/ /r/ /oo/	(40)
spool /s/ /p/ /oo/ /l/	flame /f/ /l/ /ai/ /m/	chest /ch/ /e/ /s/ /t/	frog /f/ /r/ /o/ /g/	raft /r/ /a/ /f/ /t/	(60)
glass /g/ /l/ /a/ /s/	trike /t/ /r/ /ie/ /k/	gift /g/ /i/ /f/ /t/	leaves /l/ /ea/ /v/ /z/	spoon /s/ /p/ /oo/ /n/	(80)

ONE-MINUTE FLUENCY
SOPRIS WEST SKILL BUILDERS SERIES

PHONEMIC AWARENESS—PHONEME SEGMENTATION
Four-Phoneme Words—Skill Sheet 8

	Correct	Error
First Try		
Second Try		

				SCHOOL	(20)
					(40)
			CHRIS GET WELL SOON Gabrielle MIKE KELLY SEAN Zack		(60)
	A B				(80)

	Correct	Error
First Try		
Second Try		

PHONEMIC AWARENESS—PHONEME SEGMENTATION
Four-Phoneme Words—Skill Sheet 8

Directions to Teacher: Point to the picture. Say, "This is (say name of picture). Tell me all the sounds in (picture)."

fist /f/ /i/ /s/ /t/	plane /p/ /l/ /ai/ /n/	stool /s/ /t/ /oo/ /l/	clam /k/ /l/ /a/ /m/	school /s/ /k/ /oo/ /l/	(20)
spade /s/ /p/ /ai/ /d/	sled /s/ /l/ /e/ /d/	blouse /b/ /l/ /ow/ /s/	plate /p/ /l/ /ai/ /t/	stove /s/ /t/ /oa/ /v/	(40)
fruit /f/ /r/ /oo/ /t/	salt /s/ /o/ /l/ /t/	crib /k/ /r/ /i/ /b/	cast /k/ /a/ /s/ /t/	spool /s/ /p/ /oo/ /l/	(60)
truck /t/ /r/ /u/ /k/	block /b/ /l/ /o/ /k/	smile /s/ /m/ /ie/ /l/	broom /b/ /r/ /oo/ /m/	shrub /sh/ /r/ /u/ /b/	(80)

ONE-MINUTE FLUENCY
SOPRIS WEST SKILL BUILDERS SERIES

HEAR/SEE TO SAY

PHONEMIC AWARENESS—PHONEME SEGMENTATION
Two-, Three-, and Four-Phoneme Words—Skill Sheet 9

	Correct	Error
First Try		
Second Try		

					(16)
					(33)
					(51)
					(66)

HEAR/SEE TO SAY

	Correct	Error
First Try		
Second Try		

PHONEMIC AWARENESS—PHONEME SEGMENTATION
Two-, Three-, and Four-Phoneme Words—Skill Sheet 9

Directions to Teacher: Point to the picture. Say, "This is (say name of picture). Tell me all the sounds in (picture)."

foot /f/ /uu/ /t/	shell /sh/ /e/ /l/	nose /n/ /oa/ /z/	girls /g/ /ir/ /l/ /z/	church /ch/ /ir/ /ch/	(16)
bat /b/ /a/ /t/	nine /n/ /ie/ /n/	bulb /b/ /u/ /l/ /b/	cup /k/ /u/ /p/	wolf /w/ /uu/ /l/ /f/	(33)
yarn /y/ /ar/ /n/	flag /f/ /l/ /a/ /g/	bread /b/ /r/ /e/ /d/	tack /t/ /a/ /k/	vest /v/ /e/ /s/ /t/	(51)
sock /s/ /o/ /k/	calf /k/ /a/ /f/	drum /d/ /r/ /u/ /m/	tire /t/ /ie/ /r/	arm /ar/ /m/	(66)

HEAR/SEE TO SAY

PHONEMIC AWARENESS—PHONEME SEGMENTATION
Three- and Four-Phoneme Words—Skill Sheet 10

	Correct	Error
First Try		
Second Try		

					(17)
					(33)
					(49)
					(67)

HEAR/SEE TO SAY

	Correct	Error
First Try		
Second Try		

PHONEMIC AWARENESS—PHONEME SEGMENTATION
Three- and Four-Phoneme Words—Skill Sheet 10

Directions to Teacher: Point to the picture. Say, "This is (say name of picture). Tell me all the sounds in (picture)."

peas /p/ /ea/ /z/	snail /s/ /n/ /ai/ /l/	feet /f/ /ea/ /t/	toast /t/ /oa/ /s/ /t/	rug /r/ /u/ /g/	(17)
tooth /t/ /oo/ /th/	tree /t/ /r/ /ea/	bench /b/ /e/ /n/ /ch/	gown /g/ /ow/ /n/	elk /e/ /l/ /k/	(33)
cash /k/ /a/ /sh/	clown /k/ /l/ /ow/ /n/	knife /n/ /ie/ /f/	cab /k/ /a/ /b/	house /h/ /ow/ /s/	(49)
trash /t/ /r/ /a/ /sh/	train /t/ /r/ /ai/ /n/	farm /f/ /ar/ /m/	plug /p/ /l/ /u/ /g/	log /l/ /o/ /g/	(67)

HEAR/SEE TO SAY

PHONEMIC AWARENESS—PHONEME SEGMENTATION
Three- and Four-Phoneme Words—Skill Sheet 11

	Correct	Error
First Try		
Second Try		

(20)

(39)

(59)

(78)

HEAR/SEE TO SAY

	Correct	Error
First Try		
Second Try		

PHONEMIC AWARENESS—PHONEME SEGMENTATION
Three- and Four-Phoneme Words—Skill Sheet 11

Directions to Teacher: Point to the picture. Say, "This is (say name of picture). Tell me all the sounds in (picture)."

wasp /w/ /o/ /s/ /p/	clock /k/ /l/ /o/ /k/	belt /b/ /e/ /l/ /t/	chimp /ch/ /i/ /m/ /p/	crab /k/ /r/ /a/ /b/	(20)
mug /m/ /u/ /g/	tools /t/ /oo/ /l/ /z/	skirt /s/ /k/ /ir/ /t/	bolt /b/ /oa/ /l/ /t/	cloud /k/ /l/ /ow/ /d/	(39)
scarf /s/ /k/ /ar/ /f/	snake /s/ /n/ /ai/ /k/	chicks /ch/ /i/ /k/ /s/	swan /s/ /w/ /o/ /n/	paint /p/ /ai/ /n/ /t/	(59)
crown /k/ /r/ /ow/ /n/	grass /g/ /r/ /a/ /s/	gate /g/ /ai/ /t/	gold /g/ /oa/ /l/ /d/	wand /w/ /o/ /n/ /d/	(78)

Reading Isolated Sounds

Grades K–2; Intervention Grade 3 and Above

ONE-MINUTE FLUENCY
SOPRIS WEST SKILL BUILDERS SERIES

SEE TO SAY

READING ISOLATED SOUNDS

Consonant Sounds—Large Print

Directions: Say each sound.

	Correct	Error
First Try		
Second Try		

m	t	d	h	n	s	f	c	r	l	w	b	(12)
g	p	v	j	k	x	qu	y	z	t	w	g	(24)
m	z	c	n	d	s	l	r	p	b	v	k	(36)
j	qu	y	m	x	w	f	h	d	t	r	l	(48)
n	b	g	v	y	x	k	p	j	c	g	f	(60)
s	h	z	m	d	h	s	f	r	w	g	p	(72)
j	qu	y	t	n	c	l	w	b	g	p	v	(84)

SEE TO SAY

	Correct	Error
First Try		
Second Try		

READING ISOLATED SOUNDS

Consonant Sounds and Digraphs
(th – the, sh – she, wh – whale, ch – chicken)—Large Print

Directions: Say each sound.

s	m	d	th	n	t	w	h	c	r	(10)
sh	k	wh	l	b	g	f	p	v	j	(20)
qu	x	z	ch	m	th	c	w	k	sh	(30)
b	f	t	v	ch	l	s	d	n	h	(40)
r	wh	g	p	j	x	qu	z	s	n	(50)

ONE-MINUTE FLUENCY
SOPRIS WEST SKILL BUILDERS SERIES

SEE TO SAY

	Correct	Error
First Try		
Second Try		

READING ISOLATED SOUNDS

Vowel Sounds—Short and Long Vowels (ā – stay, a – apple)—Large Print

Directions: Say each sound.

i	ā	o	i	ē	u	a	e	ō	u	i	ā	(12)
ē	ū	a	o	a	ī	e	ī	o	ū	e	u	(24)
e	ī	u	ō	i	ā	u	a	ē	o	e	ī	(36)
ū	o	ē	a	u	e	ī	o	a	ī	u	o	(48)
u	ō	i	ē	i	ā	o	a	ū	e	o	ē	(60)
ī	a	ō	i	ē	u	a	ē	o	u	ē	u	(72)
ē	u	a	ō	a	ī	ē	i	ō	u	e	ū	(84)

ONE MINUTE FLUENCY
SOPRIS WEST SKILL BUILDERS SERIES

SEE TO SAY

READING ISOLATED SOUNDS
Consonants and Short Vowels
(c – can, g – go)—Large Print
Directions: Say each sound.

	Correct	Error
First Try		
Second Try		

a m t d i h n s o f m a (12)

z y u x d s t g v p x y (24)

f o s n h i d t m a i t (36)

m i s c e g v qu y t e c (48)

p r v m d c f n p e v qu (60)

a i o l d h s p b g o d (72)

d s r b v x a i o u i h (84)

ONE MINUTE FLUENCY
SOPRIS WEST SKILL BUILDERS SERIES

SEE TO SAY

	Correct	Error
First Try		
Second Try		

READING ISOLATED SOUNDS
Consonant Sounds—Small Print

Directions: Say each sound.

m	t	d	h	n	s	f	c	r	l	w	b	g	p	v	(15)
j	k	x	qu	y	z	t	w	g	m	z	c	n	d	s	(30)
l	r	p	b	v	k	j	qu	y	m	x	w	f	h	d	(45)
t	r	l	n	b	g	v	y	x	k	p	j	c	g	f	(60)
s	h	z	m	d	h	s	f	r	w	g	p	j	qu	y	(75)
t	n	c	l	w	b	g	p	v	j	k	qu	x	y	z	(90)
m	s	c	g	v	qu	x	y	k	p	b	l	f	n	d	(105)
t	h	r	q	j	x	d	s	r	b	v	x	l	g	j	(120)

SEE TO SAY

	Correct	Error
First Try		
Second Try		

READING ISOLATED SOUNDS

Vowel Sounds—Short and Long Vowels (ā – stay, a – apple)—Small Print

Directions: Say each sound.

i	ā	o	i	ē	u	a	e	ō	u	i	ā	o	ī	ē	(15)
ē	ū	a	o	a	ī	e	ī	o	ū	e	u	ā	o	ā	(30)
e	ī	u	ō	i	ā	u	a	ē	o	e	ī	u	ō	i	(45)
ū	o	ē	a	u	e	ī	o	a	ī	u	o	i	ē	i	(60)
u	ō	i	ē	i	ā	o	a	ū	e	o	ē	a	u	ō	(75)
ī	a	ō	i	ē	u	a	ē	o	u	ē	u	ā	o	a	(90)
ē	u	a	ō	a	ī	ē	i	ō	u	e	ū	a	ō	a	(105)
e	ī	u	o	ī	a	u	ā	e	o	ē	i	u	ō	i	(120)

ONE-MINUTE FLUENCY
SOPRIS WEST SKILL BUILDERS SERIES

SEE TO SAY

READING ISOLATED SOUNDS
Consonants and Short Vowels (c – can, g – go)—Small Print

Directions: Say each sound.

	Correct	Error
First Try		
Second Try		

a	m	t	d	i	h	n	s	o	f	m	a	a	m	t	(15)
z	y	u	x	d	s	t	g	v	p	x	y	z	y	u	(30)
f	o	s	n	h	i	d	t	m	a	i	t	f	o	s	(45)
m	i	s	c	e	g	v	qu	y	t	e	c	m	i	s	(60)
p	r	v	m	d	c	f	n	p	e	v	qu	p	r	v	(75)
a	i	o	l	d	h	s	p	b	g	o	d	a	i	o	(90)
d	s	r	b	v	x	a	i	o	u	i	h	d	s	r	(105)
qu	z	y	h	o	r	k	u	a	n	f	t	m	i	n	(120)

Blending/Reading Isolated Decodable Nonsense Words

Grades K–2; Intervention Grade 3 and Above

Scoring Note:

Nonsense words are scored as whole word units. If the student says all letter sounds in the word accurately, the word is counted as one correct response. An alternate method of scoring would be to score each individual letter/letter sound. On the teacher's or listener's copy of the fluency sheet, the listener underlines the individual letters indicating letter sounds produced correctly and scores one point for each accurate sound.

ONE MINUTE FLUENCY
SOPRIS WEST SKILL BUILDERS SERIES

SEE TO SAY

BLENDING/READING ISOLATED DECODABLE NONSENSE WORDS
VC (Short Vowel–Consonant)

Directions: These are "make-believe" words. Say each sound or word.

	Correct	Error
First Try		
Second Try		

ac	em	id	ef	ip	ig	oz	uf	(8)
al	es	um	ed	oc	ik	om	uc	(16)
ep	ad	ib	uv	ol	et	af	op	(24)
ik	ud	ej	ak	os	iv	ex	oz	(32)
ub	ab	im	en	ac	ob	ix	un	(40)
ez	ot	av	ig	ub	ag	od	ul	(48)
ut	eb	og	uj	ep	av	iz	ov	(56)
ab	ec	id	uf	ig	ak	om	ap	(64)

SEE TO SAY

BLENDING/READING ISOLATED DECODABLE NONSENSE WORDS
CVC (Consonant–Short Vowel a–Consonant)

Directions: These are "make-believe" words. Say each sound or word.

	Correct	Error
First Try		
Second Try		

bab	cac	daf	faj	gak	han	jav	kam	(8)
lan	mam	paz	rax	sas	taf	vad	wab	(16)
zac	bac	cag	dat	fap	nad	gan	hab	(24)
jad	kan	lat	mab	nax	pab	raf	sab	(32)
tav	vam	wak	yan	zat	bap	caz	faf	(40)
gaz	jat	kak	mav	pag	san	vaf	dak	(48)
haj	lac	maf	rab	yad	wat	zam	kad	(56)
gaf	kap	naz	tak	hap	dag	kab	maj	(64)

ONE MINUTE FLUENCY
SOPRIS WEST SKILL BUILDERS SERIES

SEE TO SAY

	Correct	Error
First Try		
Second Try		

BLENDING/READING ISOLATED DECODABLE NONSENSE WORDS
CVC (Consonant–Short Vowel e–Consonant)

Directions: These are "make-believe" words. Say each sound or word.

dec	neb	zec	nen	yem	leb	zep	mev	(8)
beb	pef	bej	pev	zef	mes	bex	nem	(16)
fef	ret	deg	rek	fen	nen	dev	lek	(24)
hej	sem	fec	sep	bef	pel	fet	peb	(32)
jek	tep	hed	tes	dek	rez	hef	rem	(40)
kem	ves	jeg	veb	hes	sev	jex	teg	(48)
lep	wej	kex	wev	kej	vem	kep	tev	(56)
mez	yed	mem	veb	jev	wez	lef	sed	(64)

SEE TO SAY

BLENDING/READING ISOLATED DECODABLE NONSENSE WORDS
CVC (Consonant–Short Vowel i–Consonant)

Directions: These are "make-believe" words. Say each sound or word.

	Correct	Error
First Try		
Second Try		

sif	biz	hin	dij	lic	nid	dit	tib	(8)
fim	hib	jic	nim	kig	bif	lik	vid	(16)
sij	rif	fip	nic	bim	dit	kiz	mid	(24)
vif	bip	zib	dij	wip	hiz	mib	fik	(32)
min	wid	nif	ded	piv	fim	bim	lif	(40)
riz	lig	zid	vid	zib	lif	rix	tiv	(48)
def	wif	hik	dis	kib	jik	sik	nij	(56)
tiz	fid	piv	yit	miz	pib	zix	vil	(64)

BLENDING/READING ISOLATED DECODABLE NONSENSE WORDS CVC (Consonant–Short Vowel o–Consonant)

Directions: These are "make-believe" words. Say each sound or word.

	Correct	Error
First Try		
Second Try		

fon	joz	goc	los	mog	dob	nop	hov	(8)
pob	kop	rov	cof	jod	rof	loz	bol	(16)
bot	sog	hom	moj	dom	soj	fot	joc	(24)
tob	doz	vob	kot	nos	pof	goj	cov	(32)
woz	sol	jof	gof	wot	boc	vod	kon	(40)
pog	fos	boj	sok	lof	pol	mon	poz	(48)
gog	jos	hon	toc	doj	kom	tod	vop	(56)
cos	nov	pon	jol	vom	hol	soz	fov	(64)

SEE TO SAY

BLENDING/READING ISOLATED DECODABLE NONSENSE WORDS
CVC (Consonant–Short Vowel u–Consonant)

Directions: These are "make-believe" words. Say each sound or word.

	Correct	Error
First Try		
Second Try		

duj	mub	gug	nud	cug	lum	puz	guz	(8)
luz	bup	kub	ruc	huf	suz	duv	mup	(16)
gub	sud	nuz	fub	suk	kun	nug	buc	(24)
num	duk	vuz	muc	buf	kuz	tun	fup	(32)
muv	lut	buj	suf	kug	rud	huc	sul	(40)
fuz	kud	rup	guv	nuf	fum	cuv	guf	(48)
huv	pux	tup	dup	ruk	vux	lup	wub	(56)
zud	hup	gud	kuf	mun	fud	ruv	cuf	(64)

SEE TO SAY

	Correct	Error
First Try		
Second Try		

BLENDING/READING ISOLATED DECODABLE NONSENSE WORDS
CVC Review (Consonant–Short Vowel–Consonant)

Directions: These are “make-believe” words. Say each sound or word.

bac	ded	ris	wol	tuv	pog	mab	bak	dek	(9)
lem	hik	vop	jox	fuh	nam	sot	lem	hik	(18)
kod	rin	gog	zuz	baf	sek	cak	dif	rit	(27)
def	wic	zot	tud	kux	hab	mez	dem	wik	(36)
nid	dom	soc	lus	pab	wef	tik	mip	bom	(45)
vig	ron	hup	gaf	jel	bon	zix	vit	fon	(54)
coz	muc	jat	kad	reb	dit	hob	coz	nuc	(63)
fuf	bul	sas	ned	sid	mok	roc	fuf	bul	(72)
cum	kah	teg	dif	fon	goz	vux	cum	kah	(81)
zat	beb	wem	bik	dop	hud	cac	zat	bep	(90)
dal	leb	niz	kob	sux	sut	dap	dal	beb	(99)
fes	hib	kot	mol	luv	vad	sel	fes	rij	(108)

SEE TO SAY

BLENDING/READING ISOLATED DECODABLE NONSENSE WORDS VC and CVC (Consonants and Short Vowels)

Directions: These are "make-believe" words. Say each sound or word.

	Correct	Error
First Try		
Second Try		

fut	ab	jec	nid	suf	ig	mak	vom	(8)
fap	es	lix	wot	jev	ez	kub	raf	(16)
zep	ad	mib	cuv	ol	zet	hof	rop	(24)
sev	vik	ud	tej	wak	pos	iv	bex	(32)
boz	dil	fup	hab	im	nen	gac	ob	(40)
rix	tun	ot	jez	kot	av	hig	wub	(48)
ag	jod	cul	wip	dut	eb	gog	huj	(56)
bep	dav	iz	cov	ux	ab	uf	ot	(64)

SEE TO SAY

	Correct	Error
First Try		
Second Try		

BLENDING/READING ISOLATED DECODABLE NONSENSE WORDS

Blending Consonant Teams With op, ap, od

Directions: These are "make-believe" words. Say each sound or word.

thop	shap	stap	whod	frop	trop	chod	grop	(8)
prap	spop	twop	plap	swop	glap	phop	smop	(16)
crod	snop	skop	thop	shap	stod	whod	frop	(24)
chod	grop	brop	prap	spop	twop	plap	swop	(32)
phop	smop	scop	crod	snop	skop	thop	shap	(40)
whod	frop	trop	chod	grop	brop	prap	spop	(48)
plap	swop	glod	phop	smop	scop	thop	shap	(56)
prap	spop	twop	plap	swop	glod	phop	smop	(64)

ONE MINUTE FLUENCY
SOPRIS WEST SKILL BUILDERS SERIES

SEE TO SAY

BLENDING/READING ISOLATED DECODABLE NONSENSE WORDS

Blending Sounds With Both Long and Short Vowels

Directions: These are "make-believe" words. Say each sound or word.

	Correct	Error
First Try		
Second Try		

shud	nane	flib	cate	phude	claf	chet	brin	phode	(9)
whote	plime	blox	twile	brug	thime	rollo	clak	drask	(18)
glape	snat	crend	tompt	blep	rosk	kine	quop	brap	(27)
frape	shup	shol	stos	chike	slone	dase	tite	pove	(36)
mamp	tast	thrud	flisp	stete	shope	splam	lipe	frew	(45)
shas	dife	phob	cuse	brik	spile	clift	nint	wuke	(54)
theck	grun	pleb	quat	dasp	frust	goke	phig	glid	(63)
dasp	cril	fruf	stut	snim	whave	thas	chez	mote	(72)
spip	rime	thit	frak	dresk	phop	crump	pano	whes	(81)
glish	draf	bine	vamp	chup	fune	shap	tefe	snop	(90)
phat	fluft	crend	presk	blosp	thap	whipe	glape	spift	(99)
blox	slimp	vepe	bufe	quile	rame	blep	chasp	blox	(108)

Blending/Reading Isolated Decodable Real Words

Grades K–2; Intervention Grade 3 and Above

ONE MINUTE FLUENCY
SOPRIS WEST SKILL BUILDERS SERIES

SEE TO SAY

BLENDING/READING ISOLATED DECODABLE REAL WORDS
Consonant–Short a–Consonant Words

Directions: Say each word.

	Correct	Error
First Try		
Second Try		

mat	map	tap	tam	pat	tat	Pam	man	Pat	(9)
ban	ham	hat	fat	fan	nap	nab	Nan	man	(18)
pan	tan	bat	cap	cat	can	gap	ram	rap	(27)
ran	rag	tag	bag	hag	nag	can	gab	gag	(36)
sap	Sam	sag	sad	dam	dab	Dan	jam	jab	(45)
jag	zap	wag	mad	pad	tad	bad	has	had	(54)
dad	gas	gad	cad	lap	lab	lag	lad	vat	(63)
Max	tax	sax	wax	lax	pal	gal	yam	yap	(72)
Pat	fat	man	bat	ram	tag	gab	sag	jam	(81)
ban	nap	pan	cat	rat	hag	sat	dam	Jan	(90)

SEE TO SAY

BLENDING/READING ISOLATED DECODABLE REAL WORDS
Consonant–Short e–Consonant Words

Directions: Say each word.

	Correct	Error
First Try		
Second Try		

met	pet	pep	bet	Ben	hem	men	pen	ten	(9)
hep	net	Ken	Meg	Peg	get	peg	beg	keg	(18)
bed	den	jet	Jed	wet	wed	web	fed	Ned	(27)
Deb	Tex	hex	vex	bet	Rex	vet	let	leg	(36)
led	yet	yes	yen	Ted	Jen	Les	ten	red	(45)
set	Peg	hen	Ben	yen	leg	vex	fed	jet	(54)
pen	pep	yet	vet	Tex	web	den	peg	net	(63)
pet	Ted	led	Rex	Jeb	wed	bed	get	hep	(72)
met	Jen	yen	yes	yet	led	Les	leg	let	(81)
Rex	Lex	vex	hex	Tex	deb	red	Ned	fed	(90)

	Correct	Error
First Try		
Second Try		

BLENDING/READING ISOLATED DECODABLE REAL WORDS

Consonant–Short i–Consonant Words

Directions: Say each word.

pit	Tim	tip	bit	bin	him	hip	hit	fit	(9)
nip	nib	bib	pin	tin	fib	rim	rip	pig	(18)
fig	rig	sip	sit	sin	dim	sis	dip	din	(27)
mid	bid	hid	kid	rid	did	Jim	jib	Sid	(36)
jig	wit	wig	quit	quit	vim	fix	mix	six	(45)
zip	til	lip	lit	lid	yip	pit	bin	fin	(54)
rip	sip	dip	hid	jib	wig	fix	til	Tim	(63)
nip	pig	sit	din	kid	Sid	mix	lip	tip	(72)
nib	fib	big	sin	dig	rid	his	quip	six	(81)
hit	bib	fig	dim	mid	did	jig	quit	zig	(90)

SEE TO SAY

BLENDING/READING ISOLATED DECODABLE REAL WORDS

Consonant–Short o–Consonant Words

Directions: Say each word.

	Correct	Error
First Try		
Second Try		

mop	pot	Tom	top	pop	tot	mom	bop	Bob	(9)
hot	mob	not	cop	cot	cob	rot	rob	Ron	(18)
gob	fog	hog	bog	tog	sod	sop	sob	Dot	(27)
Don	dog	pod	Tod	nod	cod	rod	jot	job	(36)
lot	log	mop	tot	hot	cot	got	tog	dot	(45)
job	pot	mom	mob	cob	gob	sod	Don	cod	(54)
Tom	bop	not	rot	fog	sop	dog	rod	lot	(63)
Bob	rob	hog	sob	pod	log	pop	hop	cop	(72)
bog	Dot	Tod	jot	pop	top	Tom	pot	mop	(81)
Bob	bop	mom	tot	cop	not	mob	hot	Ron	(90)

ONE MINUTE FLUENCY
SOPRIS WEST SKILL BUILDERS SERIES

SEE TO SAY

	Correct	Error
First Try		
Second Try		

BLENDING/READING ISOLATED DECODABLE REAL WORDS
Consonant–Short u–Consonant Words

Directions: Say each word.

tux	mum	pup	pup	hub	bum	hum	but	hut	(9)
fun	pun	nun	pub	tub	bun	cup	cut	cub	(18)
rut	rub	run	bug	tug	rug	hug	gum	Gus	(27)
gun	mug	bud	bus	sun	sup	sub	dub	dun	(36)
dug	bus	dud	jut	jug	yup	tux	lug	yum	(45)
tux	bum	fun	bun	rut	rug	gun	sup	dug	(54)
mum	hum	pun	cup	rub	hug	mug	sub	bus	(63)
pup	but	nun	cut	run	gum	bud	dub	dud	(72)
pup	hut	pub	cub	bug	Gus	bus	dun	jut	(81)
hub	nut	tub	rum	tug	gut	sun	cud	jug	(90)

ONE-MINUTE FLUENCY
SOPRIS WEST SKILL BUILDERS SERIES

SEE TO SAY

BLENDING/READING ISOLATED DECODABLE REAL WORDS
Short Vowel–Consonant Words (Random a, e, i, o, u)

Directions: Say each word.

	Correct	Error
First Try		
Second Try		

on	if	us	ag	Oz	ad	up	Ed	ax	(9)
am	ox	it	an	it	at	us	if	on	(18)
ag	ad	Ed	am	up	Oz	ax	ad	in	(27)
at	an	ox	ad	if	at	Ed	an	ag	(36)
it	ax	in	am	on	us	ox	up	Oz	(45)
ax	Oz	if	at	us	ag	on	am	up	(54)
it	an	Ed	ox	in	ad	am	if	an	(63)
Ed	ox	ad	up	ax	Oz	in	at	in	(72)
on	ag	us	if	on	in	am	Ed	ag	(81)
Oz	ax	up	ad	ox	at	us	it	an	(90)

ONE MINUTE FLUENCY
SOPRIS WEST SKILL BUILDERS SERIES

SEE TO SAY

BLENDING/READING ISOLATED DECODABLE REAL WORDS

Review Consonant–Short Vowel–Consonant Words (Random a, e, i, o, u)

Directions: Say each word.

	Correct	Error
First Try		
Second Try		

mat	pit	set	pan	run	mop	dig	mud	hem	cod	(10)
cup	ham	pop	kid	bus	bug	wet	sit	yap	mix	(20)
gob	bib	fat	nut	ran	yes	sat	quit	pep	not	(30)
vex	pub	fog	wig	wag	bud	quip	Ken	gal	rut	(40)
gas	rub	bug	wax	yum	dog	cud	jig	hep	sob	(50)
Max	fib	Rex	ram	set	run	mop	dig	mud	hem	(60)
ham	pop	did	bus	jug	wet	sit	yap	mix	bog	(70)
bib	fat	nut	ran	yes	sat	quit	pep	not	vex	(80)
pub	fog	wig	wag	bud	quip	Ken	gal	rut	gas	(90)
fib	Rex	ram	set	run	mop	dig	mud	hem	ham	(100)
kid	but	jug	wet	sit	yap	mix	gob	bib	fat	(110)
nut	ran	yes	sat	quit	pep	not	vex	pub	fog	(120)

SEE TO SAY

BLENDING/READING ISOLATED DECODABLE REAL WORDS

ee Words

Directions: Say each word.

	Correct	Error
First Try		
Second Try		

deed	feed	heed	need	seed	weed	beer	need	feed	(9)
jeer	leer	peer	deer	feel	heel	reel	deer	leer	(18)
keel	peel	feel	seek	week	peek	meek	feel	peel	(27)
reek	leek	peep	weep	keep	deep	weep	deep	peep	(36)
keep	beet	feet	meet	feet	meet	beet	keep	feet	(45)
deem	teem	seem	teem	seem	deem	reed	teem	seem	(54)
reef	reek	reel	reed	deer	deep	deed	reef	deer	(63)
seed	feed	heed	need	seed	weed	beer	deed	feed	(72)
heel	leer	peer	deer	feel	heel	reel	jeer	leer	(81)
week	peel	feel	seek	week	peek	meek	keel	peel	(90)

ONE-MINUTE FLUENCY
SOPRIS WEST SKILL BUILDERS SERIES

SEE TO SAY

	Correct	Error
First Try		
Second Try		

BLENDING/READING ISOLATED DECODABLE REAL WORDS

sh Words

Directions: Say each word.

dash	cash	gash	lash	mash	rash	sash	lash	cash	(9)
fish	dish	fish	wish	dish	gush	mush	dash	dish	(18)
shot	rush	sheep	sheet	sheer	sheen	shod	hush	rush	(27)
ship	shin	shun	shut	sheep	dash	ship	shin	shun	(36)
mash	shop	dish	gush	sheet	cash	shin	mash	shod	(45)
rash	shot	fish	mush	sheer	gash	shun	rash	fish	(54)
lash	shop	wish	hush	sheen	lash	shut	sash	shop	(63)
dash	cash	lash	mash	sash	cash	shod	dish	sheet	(72)
shot	gush	sheet	cash	shin	sheet	mash	shod	shut	(81)
rash	wish	hush	sheen	sheer	gash	shun	ship	shun	(90)

SEE TO SAY

BLENDING/READING ISOLATED DECODABLE REAL WORDS

ch, tch Words

Directions: Say each word.

	Correct	Error
First Try		
Second Try		

chap	chat	chaff	chap	chin	chip	chill	chip	chat	(9)
chill	chin	cheek	cheer	witch	chin	cheek	cheer	chill	(18)
pitch	hitch	itch	ditch	hatch	catch	match	hitch	pitch	(27)
latch	patch	much	such	rich	beech	much	catch	patch	(36)
rich	chop	hatch	chin	ditch	cheek	pitch	rich	chap	(45)
chat	catch	chip	notch	cheer	hitch	chaff	chat	catch	(54)
match	chill	beech	chop	itch	chum	latch	chop	chat	(63)
latch	beech	much	match	hatch	ditch	hitch	rich	chap	(72)
chop	rich	hatch	cheer	hitch	chaff	chap	chin	chill	(81)
chop	match	cheer	notch	catch	chill	latch	beech	patch	(90)

SEE TO SAY

	Correct	Error
First Try		
Second Try		

BLENDING/READING ISOLATED DECODABLE REAL WORDS
Review Consonant–Vowel–Consonant Words
(Short a, e, i, o, u, ch, sh)

Directions: Say each word.

six	shot	chop	man	nun	rot	hat	shut	men	chip	(10)
peg	hen	cot	get	jut	tin	cut	hub	wig	leg	(20)
bet	ship	shop	pen	bat	chin	pin	less	hag	gum	(30)
hid	cot	fib	bat	dad	jam	mat	hot	tin	cup	(40)
bet	pan	hit	wet	Ned	pet	hip	can	sob	fib	(50)
mug	Ben	beg	den	fib	mix	wed	six	shot	chop	(60)
man	nun	rot	hat	shut	men	chip	pen	hen	cot	(70)
get	jut	tin	cut	hub	wig	leg	bet	ship	shop	(80)
pen	bat	chin	pin	less	had	gum	hid	cot	bib	(90)
fib	bat	dad	jam	mat	hot	tin	cup	bet	pan	(100)
hit	wet	Ned	pet	hip	can	sob	fib	chop	man	(110)
get	jut	tin	cut	hub	wig	leg	bet	ship	shop	(120)

SEE TO SAY

BLENDING/READING ISOLATED DECODABLE REAL WORDS

oo Words (as in *moon*)

Directions: Say each word.

	Correct	Error
First Try		
Second Try		

boot	hoot	root	shoot	boon	moon	soon	boot	hoot	(9)
moon	noon	cool	fool	tool	pool	room	loom	noon	(18)
doom	boom	food	mood	roof	food	doom	food	mood	(27)
hoof	woof	roof	hoop	loop	toot	poor	hoof	woof	(36)
root	room	roof	boot	boon	noon	boom	root	fool	(45)
boot	hoot	hoof	hoop	hoof	moot	moon	noon	boot	(54)
mood	moon	boot	moon	cool	room	food	mood	moon	(63)
loop	toot	poor	doom	food	mood	hoot	root	cool	(72)
boot	hoof	hoop	moot	moon	moor	loop	hoop	roof	(81)
toot	boot	root	loop	roof	boon	moon	soon	boot	(90)

ONE-MINUTE FLUENCY
SOPRIS WEST SKILL BUILDERS SERIES

SEE TO SAY

	Correct	Error
First Try		
Second Try		

BLENDING/READING ISOLATED DECODABLE REAL WORDS

Review ee, sh, ch, oo, tch Words

Directions: Say each word.

seek	feel	leek	meet	deer	beef	shut	shod	cash	shop	(10)
cash	shop	dish	sash	sheep	gush	shot	seen	dash	meet	(20)
boom	hoop	mood	pool	roof	soon	poor	peer	feel	fool	(30)
shoot	sheet	hush	moon	feed	moon	noon	shot	deed	chat	(40)
chum	hitch	chop	catch	rich	chip	ship	cash	catch	shop	(50)
chip	ditch	seek	feel	leek	meet	deer	beef	shut	shod	(60)
cash	shop	dish	sash	sheep	gush	shot	seen	dash	meet	(70)
boom	hoop	mood	pool	roof	soon	poor	peer	feel	foot	(80)
shoot	sheet	hush	moon	feed	noon	shot	deed	chat	chum	(90)
hitch	chop	catch	rich	chip	ship	cash	catch	shop	chop	(100)
ditch	seek	feel	leek	meet	deer	beef	shut	shod	cash	(110)
boom	hoop	mood	pool	roof	soon	noon	chip	ship	poor	(120)

ONE MINUTE FLUENCY
SOPRIS WEST SKILL BUILDERS SERIES

SEE TO SAY

BLENDING/READING ISOLATED DECODABLE REAL WORDS

ay, ai Words

Directions: Say each word.

	Correct	Error
First Try		
Second Try		

bait	say	chain	gay	tail	gain	hay	vain	may	(9)
jay	gait	bail	wait	lay	ray	maid	jay	jail	(18)
hail	fail	lay	day	bay	rain	wait	way	pay	(27)
pail	chain	sail	lay	bail	nay	gay	pain	bait	(36)
wait	say	chain	gay	fail	gain	bay	vain	tail	(45)
may	gait	bail	wait	lay	ray	maid	jay	jail	(54)
hail	hay	say	day	bay	rain	wait	way	pay	(63)
fail	chain	sail	lay	bail	ray	gay	pain	bait	(72)
may	bait	say	chain	gay	vail	gain	hay	vain	(81)
jay	gait	bail	wait	hay	lay	ray	bait	say	(90)

ONE MINUTE FLUENCY
SOPRIS WEST SKILL BUILDERS SERIES

SEE TO SAY

BLENDING/READING ISOLATED DECODABLE REAL WORDS

ar Words

Directions: Say each word.

	Correct	Error
First Try		
Second Try		

bar	far	car	tar	jar	mar	par	bar	far	(9)
Bart	far	car	cart	dart	art	mart	car	far	(18)
part	card	yard	bark	hard	lard	ark	part	card	(27)
ark	park	dark	shark	arm	farm	harm	lark	park	(36)
charm	farm	yarn	barn	darn	carp	sharp	charm	farm	(45)
arch	ark	arm	art	arm	hard	mark	harm	arch	(54)
[illegible]rm	tarp	art	bar	bard	bark	barn	harm	harp	(63)
bar	far	car	tar	jar	mar	par	bar	far	(72)
tart	far	car	cart	dart	art	mart	bark	far	(81)
mark	park	dark	shark	arm	farm	harm	lark	park	(90)

ONE-MINUTE FLUENCY
SOPRIS WEST SKILL BUILDERS SERIES

SEE TO SAY

BLENDING/READING ISOLATED DECODABLE REAL WORDS
or Words

Directions: Say each word.

	Correct	Error
First Try		
Second Try		

sort	corn	port	nor	fork	or	lord	short	cord	(9)
born	for	nor	sort	pork	torn	orb	corn	lord	(18)
fort	cork	short	or	sort	corn	port	nor	fork	(27)
lord	short	cord	morn	born	for	nor	sort	pork	(36)
orb	corn	lord	horn	fort	cork	short	or	sort	(45)
port	nor	fork	or	lord	short	cord	morn	born	(54)
nor	sort	port	torn	pork	orb	born	corn	lord	(63)
fort	cork	short	or	sort	corn	port	nor	fork	(72)
orb	corn	lord	horn	fort	cork	sort	short	or	(81)
port	port	fork	or	lord	short	cord	morn	born	(90)

ONE MINUTE FLUENCY
SOPRIS WEST SKILL BUILDERS SERIES

SEE TO SAY

BLENDING/READING ISOLATED DECODABLE REAL WORDS

old Words (as in *cold*)

Directions: Say each word.

	Correct	Error
First Try		
Second Try		

old	cold	hold	told	bold	sold	old	mold	fold	(9)
bold	told	cold	hold	old	gold	fold	mold	sold	(18)
mold	cold	hold	old	fold	hold	gold	told	bold	(27)
sold	cold	told	fold	old	gold	hold	cold	bold	(36)
mold	old	cold	hold	told	bold	sold	gold	old	(45)
hold	told	bold	sold	hold	mold	fold	gold	bold	(54)
cold	hold	old	gold	fold	mold	sold	bold	mold	(63)
hold	old	fold	hold	gold	told	bold	mold	sold	(72)
told	fold	old	gold	hold	cold	bold	sold	mold	(81)
cold	hold	told	bold	sold	fold	old	cold	hold	(90)

SEE TO SAY

BLENDING/READING ISOLATED DECODABLE REAL WORDS

Review ar, or, ay, old, ai Words

Directions: Say each word.

	Correct	Error
First Try		
Second Try		

gold	or	hold	say	yarn	ark	main	told	cord	sold	(10)
chain	lay	lark	old	way	shark	ford	wait	march	hail	(20)
short	bold	maid	torn	part	tar	may	gain	fail	cold	(30)
sort	hold	day	yard	ark	rain	told	fort	sold	chain	(40)
gay	mark	old	bay	farm	wait	march	hail	short	bold	(50)
maid	torn	park	bar	may	gain	jail	fold	sort	cold	(60)
bark	arm	main	told	ford	sold	chain	hay	lark	old	(70)
bay	shark	ford	bait	hard	nail	short	mold	maid	torn	(80)
part	car	may	gain	mail	gold	for	hold	jay	far	(90)
art	pain	told	fork	sold	chain	pay	cart	old	bay	(100)
gain	sail	gold	sort	hold	dart	ark	rain	told	born	(110)
way	shark	ford	wait	card	tail	short	bold	mail	torn	(120)

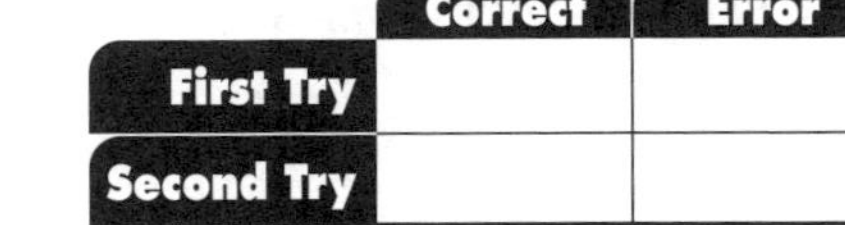

SEE TO SAY

BLENDING/READING ISOLATED DECODABLE REAL WORDS

ea Words (as in *beat*)

Directions: Say each word.

	Correct	Error
First Try		
Second Try		

beat	bean	deal	weak	leap	bead	ear	beam	beat	(9)
beach	seat	lean	heal	peak	reap	lead	hear	beach	(18)
team	reach	heat	dean	peal	peak	heap	real	rear	(27)
teach	neat	mean	seal	leak	leap	rear	seam	teach	(36)
rear	seam	teach	neat	mean	seal	leak	leap	rear	(45)
mead	dear	team	each	feat	wean	veal	beak	meat	(54)
dear	lead	near	heap	seam	peach	cheat	bean	weak	(63)
sea	cheap	bead	shear	eat	reach	beat	bean	tea	(72)
heat	bean	deal	weak	beach	team	teach	rear	meal	(81)
bean	seat	reach	neat	seam	dear	read	cheap	bean	(90)

SEE TO SAY

BLENDING/READING ISOLATED DECODABLE REAL WORDS

oa Words

Directions: Say each word.

	Correct	Error
First Try		
Second Try		

oat	oak	oar	coal	road	toad	boat	soak	roar	(9)
goal	boar	load	coat	loaf	soar	shoal	coal	road	(18)
goat	foal	boar	goal	oat	toad	moat	soak	goat	(27)
coal	moan	road	coat	road	loan	road	coax	roar	(36)
toad	coat	moat	loaf	roach	foam	soap	load	oar	(45)
load	loan	roam	oat	oar	coach	goat	oar	loaf	(54)
moan	soak	coal	roam	soar	oak	road	boat	goal	(63)
oak	goal	goat	coal	toad	load	moan	oak	loan	(72)
oar	load	boar	road	moat	roam	coal	goat	coal	(81)
goat	foal	loaf	road	roach	oar	soar	toad	moat	(90)

BLENDING/READING ISOLATED DECODABLE REAL WORDS

ck Words

Directions: Say each word.

	Correct	Error
First Try		
Second Try		

back	sack	hack	rack	tack	jack	lack	back	jack	(9)
pack	sack	chick	pick	sick	nick	kick	puck	sack	(18)
lick	tick	Dick	wick	sick	chick	rock	Rick	sick	(27)
sock	mock	dock	tock	lock	shock	hock	sock	mock	(36)
dock	sock	tuck	luck	buck	duck	muck	tuck	sock	(45)
Mick	peck	puck	neck	deck	back	pick	buck	peck	(54)
peck	tick	lock	tuck	jack	luck	shock	tick	lock	(63)
chuck	sock	lack	sick	sack	wick	deck	shack	sick	(72)
tack	beck	hack	buck	mock	rack	kick	tack	nick	(81)
muck	tock	lick	neck	back	deck	sock	muck	tick	(90)

ONE MINUTE FLUENCY
SOPRIS WEST SKILL BUILDERS SERIES

SEE TO SAY

BLENDING/READING ISOLATED DECODABLE REAL WORDS

ow, ou Words (as in *cow* or *ouch*)

Directions: Say each word.

	Correct	Error
First Try		
Second Try		

cow	now	how	vow	wow	owl	fowl	cow	pow	(9)
howl	owl	jowl	gown	down	gown	howl	owl	town	(18)
gown	pow	cow	how	now	chow	town	out	wow	(27)
pout	shout	rout	bout	tout	pout	sour	bout	shout	(36)
bound	found	hound	pouch	couch	vouch	sound	bound	found	(45)
count	cow	round	owl	shout	mound	down	found	down	(54)
loud	mount	sour	pouch	our	cow	round	loud	town	(63)
gown	rout	howl	pound	out	town	foul	bound	now	(72)
fount	now	noun	sound	couch	town	how	bound	now	(81)
out	sour	found	cow	round	owl	shout	sour	out	(90)

ONE MINUTE FLUENCY
SOPRIS WEST SKILL BUILDERS SERIES

SEE TO SAY

BLENDING/READING ISOLATED DECODABLE REAL WORDS

Review ea, oa, ck, ow, ou Words

Directions: Say each word.

	Correct	Error
First Try		
Second Try		

fear	leap	beat	weak	near	eat	foam	ear	meal	beat	(10)
road	coal	loaf	coat	loan	sea	boat	toad	coal	load	(20)
bean	oat	roach	reach	loaf	leaf	bead	heat	neat	soap	(30)
road	oak	peak	lean	roam	teach	meat	roar	goal	leak	(40)
toad	loan	back	pick	luck	rock	kick	load	moan	tack	(50)
suck	bean	sack	coat	tick	roar	leap	luck	beak	lack	(60)
cow	town	owl	howl	prow	down	out	wow	gown	fowl	(70)
loud	found	couch	tout	bout	sour	soar	pout	mound	pouch	(80)
coach	couch	heat	round	goat	now	team	coach	pouch	neat	(90)
lack	fowl	out	peach	sick	real	duck	sack	foul	count	(100)
each	muck	road	down	load	now	toad	reach	tuck	road	(110)
dear	now	tuck	goal	dock	out	peach	ream	now	tuck	(120)

SEE TO SAY

BLENDING/READING ISOLATED DECODABLE REAL WORDS

Long a, e, i, o, u With Silent Final e Words

Directions: Say each word.

	Correct	Error
First Try		
Second Try		

lake	like	Luke	male	mile	mule	bode	take	bike	(9)
kite	made	dame	dime	dome	lane	line	bite	babe	(18)
lone	pale	pile	pole	hole	hale	wide	lope	pane	(27)
wade	rode	ride	cane	cone	dive	dome	wake	robe	(36)
cape	cope	rave	rove	rake	role	ripe	came	code	(45)
rope	hike	rate	shade	made	hide	mule	nope	side	(54)
bake	tile	wine	hole	bode	chase	tone	wade	file	(63)
shine	rile	dike	rode	pine	duke	poke	shape	ripe	(72)
dive	shone	mite	cave	mute	bone	rove	zone	shine	(81)
cove	wave	rote	rope	ripe	mule	rule	cave	wave	(90)

SEE TO SAY

BLENDING/READING ISOLATED DECODABLE REAL WORDS
General Review of All Preceding Skills—Skill Sheet 1

Directions: Say each word.

	Correct	Error
First Try		
Second Try		

seek	feel	week	keep	meet	seen	feet	meek	feed	deep	(10)
weed	ship	rash	sheep	fish	cash	sheet	need	shop	rush	(20)
shot	hush	boot	loop	tool	shoot	fool	shut	dash	hoot	(30)
soon	moon	food	chat	hitch	chop	rich	noon	mood	fool	(40)
match	cheek	beech	chum	chart	part	harm	hatch	cheer	beech	(50)
march	bark	sharp	marsh	dark	say	pain	arch	lark	shark	(60)
lay	pail	say	rain	maid	nail	fork	day	pail	way	(70)
born	short	form	horn	for	fort	corn	torn	sort	dorm	(80)
old	bold	told	sold	gold	fold	mold	hold	cold	told	(90)
sad	set	men	bed	less	peg	red	shack	met	pen	(100)
beat	beach	oat	coat	back	pick	luck	bean	reach	goat	(110)
rate	mine	poke	mule	time	chase	code	date	fine	pole	(120)

BLENDING/READING ISOLATED DECODABLE REAL WORDS
General Review of All Preceding Skills—Skill Sheet 2

Directions: Say each word.

	Correct	Error
First Try		
Second Try		

gold	chin	mine	week	port	tail	horn	bold	chip	line	(10)
ship	hound	now	food	card	hole	luck	shop	found	pow	(20)
coach	seem	how	loud	tack	duke	fed	coat	seed	cow	(30)
sheep	leg	road	pay	tar	rain	mane	sheet	beg	roam	(40)
marsh	bold	way	wait	fowl	shoot	rich	harsh	told	say	(50)
sold	may	made	chain	seat	found	soap	hold	bay	wade	(60)
seam	gown	ripe	cheer	pain	rain	beef	beam	down	pipe	(70)
sash	meet	soon	jet	ditch	web	cloak	lash	beet	moon	(80)
main	lay	barn	hail	sheet	moon	catch	mail	hat	darn	(90)
wet	boat	duck	team	town	met	team	set	goat	luck	(100)
tool	shark	cow	dock	oat	meat	short	cool	sharp	how	(110)
cold	bark	tarp	fork	gear	pen	leaf	old	ark	day	(120)

ONE MINUTE FLUENCY
SOPRIS WEST SKILL BUILDERS SERIES

SEE TO SAY

BLENDING/READING ISOLATED DECODABLE REAL WORDS

Initial Consonant Blends: pl, cl, fl, bl, gl, sl Words

Directions: Say each word.

	Correct	Error
First Try		
Second Try		

play	plus	plan	plain	plum	plane	play	ploy	clock	(9)
claim	club	clap	clean	clip	clam	clan	flame	fled	(18)
flour	flog	flit	fleet	blot	blade	bless	blame	blaze	(27)
bleat	bluff	black	gloom	glass	gleam	glee	gloat	glad	(36)
glide	glen	glaze	slave	slip	slain	slide	slap	slid	(45)
slope	plod	plow	plot	plain	plea	plume	plop	plug	(54)
cloud	clash	clot	clang	clean	clip	clown	clove	flat	(63)
flag	flash	flap	flop	flake	block	bloom	blip	bleak	(72)
bleak	bloat	bleach	black	blob	bliss	gloss	glade	globe	(81)
glib	glare	glum	slit	slab	slack	slate	sled	slash	(90)

ONE-MINUTE FLUENCY
SOPRIS WEST SKILL BUILDERS SERIES

SEE TO SAY

BLENDING/READING ISOLATED DECODABLE REAL WORDS
Initial Consonant Blends: pr, cr, fr, br, gr, tr, dr Words

Directions: Say each word.

	Correct	Error
First Try		
Second Try		

prep	prowl	prim	prom	proof	pride	pray	prop	prod	(9)
crack	crush	crane	creep	crop	crab	cream	crock	crib	(18)
free	frog	Fran	fresh	brush	bred	brad	brain	brass	(27)
brood	brim	bribe	grand	groan	greet	graze	grab	grade	(36)
gruff	gray	track	trick	truck	train	tree	tray	drop	(45)
drag	drape	drip	drum	dress	drill	dream	tree	drank	(54)
preach	prime	print	prune	press	proud	prize	probe	prof	(63)
crick	crash	crate	cram	crime	crux	crown	cross	frill	(72)
frock	frail	frame	flock	braid	brand	brag	brat	bride	(81)
brave	gram	grain	grub	grain	trap	drab	drain	drive	(90)

	Correct	Error
First Try		
Second Try		

BLENDING/READING ISOLATED DECODABLE REAL WORDS

Initial Consonant Blends: sp, st, sk, sn, sm, sc, sw, tw Words

Directions: Say each word.

span	speech	spell	spill	spark	spank	spit	spin	spot	(9)
stand	stake	stain	star	stone	scab	scold	scale	scan	(18)
scowl	skate	skid	skin	small	smart	smell	smile	smog	(27)
snail	snob	sneak	sway	sweep	swim	Swiss	tweet	twin	(36)
tweed	twig	spat	speak	sped	spoke	spud	stab	stop	(45)
stack	stall	stag	stale	staff	still	Stan	stare	scar	(54)
scarf	scare	scout	skill	skip	skull	smash	smoke	smash	(63)
snap	snub	snake	snip	sneak	swag	sweet	swam	swipe	(72)
swum	twin	tweed	twig	span	star	scan	skid	smog	(81)
snob	swim	twin	spark	stand	scold	snake	sway	tweed	(90)

SEE TO SAY

BLENDING/READING ISOLATED DECODABLE REAL WORDS

Initial Consonant Blends Review: bl, br, cl, cr, dr, fl, fr, gl, gr, pl, pr, sc, sk, sl, sm, sn, sp, st, sw, tr, tw Words

Directions: Say each word.

	Correct	Error
First Try		
Second Try		

plan	plain	clash	clip	fleet	flesh	blond	blip	clap	flash	(10)
bled	gleam	globe	sleet	slay	press	prop	slam	glob	probe	(20)
cram	cream	froze	free	brag	broom	grin	crab	bran	frame	(30)
grade	trench	tray	drive	drum	spark	speak	drop	spat	trap	(40)
stack	stake	scum	scout	skin	skill	smash	stab	scab	skip	(50)
smile	snake	snug	sweet	swim	twine	twig	snake	swam	twain	(60)
plate	tweed	clasp	skill	flap	prowl	scorn	play	twin	clam	(70)
crop	blend	frail	starch	breach	gleam	grip	cross	bland	frame	(80)
spool	treat	sleeve	dress	smack	sneer	swipe	spool	treat	sleeve	(90)
plait	crab	flee	twain	skate	prick	smite	plane	crate	flop	(100)
black	stay	glass	spot	slap	swain	clown	bleach	stop	glad	(110)
snout	scan	frog	brick	groan	tray	drive	snap	scar	frock	(120)

BLENDING/READING ISOLATED DECODABLE REAL WORDS

Final Blends: ct, ft, lk, lt, mp, nt, pt, sk, sp, st Words

Directions: Say each word.

	Correct	Error
First Try		
Second Try		

punt	font	tent	count	mount	pant	hunt	paint	fount	(9)
faint	fist	bust	coast	least	toast	desk	tusk	mask	(18)
risk	dusk	brisk	frisk	lisp	wisp	crisp	rasp	clasp	(27)
gasp	grasp	damp	camp	romp	bump	lamp	dump	ramp	(36)
jump	pomp	bulk	milk	hulk	silk	bulk	sulk	bilk	(45)
welt	belt	hilt	quilt	pelt	tilt	felt	silt	pact	(54)
act	fact	sect	tact	tract	daft	lift	raft	rift	(63)
tuft	left	sift	cleft	slept	rapt	kept	crept	swept	(72)
wept	lint	bask	clump	skulk	duct	ilk	wept	rasp	(81)
runt	tusk	asp	toast	flask	mist	stamp	colt	mount	(90)

SEE TO SAY

BLENDING/READING ISOLATED DECODABLE REAL WORDS

Sound Symbols: ing Words (as in *sing*)

Directions: Say each word.

	Correct	Error
First Try		
Second Try		

sing	wing	ring	king	bring	ding	fling	sing	wing	(9)
sling	cling	fling	sting	swing	singing	winging	sling	cling	(18)
ringing	bringing	dinging	paying	wishing	farming	chaining	hooting	winging	(27)
beating	fishing	kicking	backing	packing	cheering	hushing	boating	wishing	(36)
matching	morning	arming	arming	slinging	parking	pitching	latching	morning	(45)
catching	racking	harming	sorting	saying	slaying	marching	loading	lacking	(54)
playing	raining	holding	shocking	gaining	barking	laying	paying	kicking	(63)
feeding	bringing	howling	boating	shouting	licking	waiting	seeding	tucking	(72)
steaming	howling	mocking	charming	hushing	farming	staying	meeting	hailing	(81)
dreaming	laying	shouting	gaining	barking	holding	scolding	hatching	laying	(90)

ONE-MINUTE FLUENCY
SOPRIS WEST SKILL BUILDERS SERIES

SEE TO SAY

	Correct	Error
First Try		
Second Try		

BLENDING/READING ISOLATED DECODABLE REAL WORDS
all Words (as in *ball*)

Directions: Say each word.

all	ball	tall	fall	hall	call	wall	mall	pall	(9)
hall	ball	wall	tall	stall	calling	falling	hall	ball	(18)
stalling	small	all	ball	tall	fall	hall	stalling	small	(27)
call	wall	hall	ball	wall	tall	stall	call	wall	(36)
calling	falling	stalling	mall	all	ball	tall	calling	falling	(45)
fall	hall	call	wall	hall	ball	wall	fall	hall	(54)
hall	ball	wall	tall	stall	calling	falling	hall	ball	(63)
stalling	small	tall	ball	hall	calling	fall	stalling	small	(72)
small	wall	all	calling	ball	hall	call	mall	wall	(81)
all	ball	tall	fall	hall	call	stall	pall	mall	(90)

ONE-MINUTE FLUENCY
SOPRIS WEST SKILL BUILDERS SERIES

SEE TO SAY

BLENDING/READING ISOLATED DECODABLE REAL WORDS
ight Words (as in *sight*)

Directions: Say each word.

	Correct	Error
First Try		
Second Try		

fight	might	sight	right	might	light	tight	fight	might	(9)
light	bright	fright	flight	plight	slight	light	right	bright	(18)
tight	fighting	sighting	lighting	slighting	fight	tight	fright	fighting	(27)
right	sight	night	right	flight	fighting	fright	right	sight	(36)
plight	light	slight	bright	sighting	might	fright	plight	light	(45)
fight	might	fight	might	sight	right	might	flight	might	(54)
light	tight	right	bright	fright	flight	plight	light	tight	(63)
slight	light	tight	fighting	lighting	sighting	slight	sight	light	(72)
fight	tight	right	sight	night	right	flight	fight	tight	(81)
fighting	fright	plight	light	slight	bright	sighting	fighting	fright	(90)

ONE-MINUTE FLUENCY
SOPRIS WEST SKILL BUILDERS SERIES

SEE TO SAY

	Correct	Error
First Try		
Second Try		

BLENDING/READING ISOLATED DECODABLE REAL WORDS

er, ir, ur Words (as in *her, bird, fur*)

Directions: Say each word.

her	herd	Herb	verb	per	pert	fern	her	perk	(9)
stern	perch	term	stern	her	fir	sir	stern	perch	(18)
stir	bird	girl	dirt	shirt	bird	stir	bird	birch	(27)
birch	firm	first	her	fir	bird	under	birch	firm	(36)
stir	jerk	herd	bird	birch	perch	firm	stir	stern	(45)
never	fur	burn	turn	lurch	lurk	jerk	fur	burn	(54)
curd	curb	curl	hurl	hurt	churn	curd	curb	curl	(63)
sir	Herb	girl	burst	fern	harder	smarter	sir	verb	(72)
barter	charter	cleaner	blacker	her	herd	Herb	barter	charter	(81)
verb	per	perk	fern	stern	perch	term	verb	per	(90)

ONE-MINUTE FLUENCY
SOPRIS WEST SKILL BUILDERS SERIES

SEE TO SAY

BLENDING/READING ISOLATED DECODABLE REAL WORDS
th, wh, qu Words

Directions: Say each word.

	Correct	Error
First Try		
Second Try		

them	thou	queen	quit	this	white	quack	that	than	(9)
when	quail	that	queer	wheat	with	wheel	whip	quake	(18)
quote	quest	which	thine	while	quick	than	quill	quest	(27)
lathe	thee	whale	them	bathe	quick	which	lathe	thee	(36)
quack	with	quick	quack	wheat	then	when	quiz	with	(45)
thus	thou	queer	quit	this	white	quack	thus	thou	(54)
when	quail	that	queen	wheat	with	wheel	when	quip	(63)
quote	quest	which	thine	while	quick	than	quote	quilt	(72)
lathe	thee	whale	them	bathe	quick	which	lathe	thee	(81)
quack	with	quick	quack	wheat	then	when	quack	with	(90)

SEE TO SAY

BLENDING/READING ISOLATED DECODABLE REAL WORDS

Review ing, all, ight, er, ir, ur, th, wh, qu Words

Directions: Say each word.

	Correct	Error
First Try		
Second Try		

whip	when	that	then	quack	quit	bring	whale	wham	than	(10)
sting	bright	might	ringing	queen	them	while	sling	right	light	(20)
verb	with	quake	queer	burst	fight	calling	verb	which	quiz	(30)
wheat	whip	thus	holding	plight	then	harder	wheel	which	them	(40)
quilt	small	curl	quaint	marching	call	whale	quill	mall	curt	(50)
king	quick	hall	lathe	thou	when	charter	cling	quick	stall	(60)
with	quote	stir	thee	tight	cheering	feeding	with	quote	fir	(70)
this	all	morning	tithe	tall	whip	when	this	all	morning	(80)
that	then	quack	quit	bring	sting	bright	than	then	quack	(90)
might	ringing	queen	them	while	verb	with	sight	bringing	queen	(100)
quake	queer	burst	fight	calling	wheat	whip	quake	sheer	burn	(110)
thus	holding	plight	then	harder	quilt	small	thus	scolding	plight	(120)

SEE TO SAY

	Correct	Error
First Try		
Second Try		

BLENDING/READING ISOLATED DECODABLE REAL WORDS
General Review of Preceding Skills—Skill Sheet 3

Directions: Say each word.

corn	sight	right	hound	soothe	peek	turn	horn	slight	bright	(10)
tall	made	meat	pork	catch	room	road	stall	male	seat	(20)
chain	coat	sir	pay	soon	herd	born	brain	boat	stir	(30)
saying	sing	chop	seat	that	neck	suck	playing	ring	chat	(40)
shot	when	thus	fall	raining	fir	queen	shop	when	them	(50)
quick	day	quit	paid	down	fur	such	quill	bay	quit	(60)
bold	girl	bark	shout	gun	coal	boat	sold	bird	dark	(70)
meal	not	teach	cow	match	bird	might	seal	hot	reach	(80)
shop	queen	while	town	ball	white	bout	shot	queer	whip	(90)
then	farm	seem	pool	lay	burn	pail	than	harm	seen	(100)
fight	charm	out	now	cart	king	short	flight	chart	pout	(110)
curl	call	lag	herd	hold	whip	her	curb	ball	jag	(120)

SEE TO SAY

BLENDING/READING ISOLATED DECODABLE REAL WORDS

an, in, un Words (as in *ran, pin, fun*)

Directions: Say each word.

	Correct	Error
First Try		
Second Try		

ran	ban	can	Dan	fan	man	pan	rant	ban	(9)
tan	van	Nan	can	ran	and	band	tan	van	(18)
land	hand	sand	stand	pin	tin	sin	land	hand	(27)
win	din	kin	hint	tint	hint	mint	win	din	(36)
lint	flint	run	bun	fun	nun	sun	lint	glint	(45)
gun	hunt	blunt	stunt	brunt	stunt	hunt	fun	gun	(54)
pin	pan	plan	and	land	tin	win	shin	pant	(63)
twin	fin	bin	ban	bun	hand	ran	twin	fin	(72)
run	sin	sand	fun	fan	lint	tint	runt	sin	(81)
band	hunt	sun	nun	span	gun	run	band	hunt	(90)

ONE-MINUTE FLUENCY
SOPRIS WEST SKILL BUILDERS SERIES

SEE TO SAY

BLENDING/READING ISOLATED DECODABLE REAL WORDS

en, on Words (as in *hen, pond*)

Directions: Say each word.

	Correct	Error
First Try		
Second Try		

den	Ben	ken	men	pen	ten	tend	dent	lent	(9)
bend	lend	send	mend	when	sent	bent	spend	blend	(18)
went	lent	dent	pent	on	Don	bond	went	lent	(27)
den	Don	bond	bend	con	bond	ten	dens	Ron	(36)
lent	pond	send	lend	bond	went	bend	lent	pond	(45)
lend	pent	hen	fond	pond	send	bend	lend	spent	(54)
dent	ten	pen	spent	men	Don	fond	Ben	pond	(63)
den	ten	tend	blend	went	on	mend	sent	tent	(72)
bend	lent	pond	lend	lend	bond	went	bends	lent	(81)
bend	lend	pent	Ron	fond	pond	send	men	blend	(90)

SEE TO SAY

	Correct	Error
First Try		
Second Try		

BLENDING/READING ISOLATED DECODABLE REAL WORDS
ink, ank, unk Words (as in *pink, bank, sunk*)

Directions: Say each word.

ink	wink	link	clink	blink	pink	sink	rink	slink	(9)
stink	chink	pink	sank	rank	bank	lank	blank	plank	(18)
tank	drank	prank	crank	Frank	drank	sunk	punk	slunk	(27)
chunk	junk	chink	drunk	sink	sank	sunk	chunk	junk	(36)
drank	drink	drunk	sinking	drinking	cranking	winking	crank	drink	(45)
sunk	bank	blank	blink	bank	tank	junk	bunk	bank	(54)
crank	chink	chunk	clink	sunk	drank	chink	crank	ink	(63)
tank	sink	prank	rank	stink	chunk	wink	bank	mink	(72)
drinking	pink	sinking	junk	blank	lank	sunk	drinking	pink	(81)
bank	drink	sunk	blank	winking	blink	clink	bank	wink	(90)

SEE TO SAY

BLENDING/READING ISOLATED DECODABLE REAL WORDS

Review an, in, un, en, on, ink, ank, unk Words

Directions: Say each word.

	Correct	Error
First Try		
Second Try		

ran	ban	land	pan	sand	hand	pin	bran	band	land	(10)
lint	win	sin	mint	tin	fun	bun	flint	wind	sin	(20)
sun	nun	run	gun	hen	sent	went	sun	nun	runt	(30)
send	men	bend	Don	con	fond	bond	spend	men	bend	(40)
pond	fond	ran	win	sun	went	pond	fond	rant	spin	(50)
send	sink	pink	drink	clink	blink	pink	send	pink	slink	(60)
bank	rank	crank	Frank	sand	bank	sunk	sank	blank	rank	(70)
wink	chunk	sank	drunk	link	tank	clink	wink	chunk	sank	(80)
hen	dent	tint	sank	bond	win	hunt	hen	dent	tint	(90)
clan	junk	win	blink	spin	land	hen	clan	junk	win	100)
ran	bank	ink	pink	sank	drunk	in	ran	bank	link	(110)
tin	spin	bun	gun	den	bend	van	tin	spin	bun	(120)

BLENDING/READING ISOLATED DECODABLE REAL WORDS
ing, ang, ong, ung Words

Directions: Say each word.

	Correct	Error
First Try		
Second Try		

sing	ring	bring	sting	king	bang	pang	sling	ring	(9)
gang	rang	sang	hang	clang	slang	banging	gang	rang	(18)
hanging	clanging	song	tong	strong	long	along	hanging	clanging	(27)
rung	hung	lung	rung	sung	stung	hung	rung	hang	(36)
hung	sing	sang	sung	song	stung	sting	hung	fling	(45)
ring	bring	king	bank	lung	long	longing	ring	bring	(54)
along	sing	lung	hung	rang	bring	slang	along	cling	(63)
clung	pang	gang	long	sting	pang	along	clung	pang	(72)
clang	tong	hang	ringing	bringing	singing	banging	clang	tong	(81)
sing	lung	hung	rang	bring	slang	clung	sing	lung	(90)

ONE-MINUTE FLUENCY
SOPRIS WEST SKILL BUILDERS SERIES

SEE TO SAY

BLENDING/READING ISOLATED DECODABLE REAL WORDS
and, ound, est Words

Directions: Say each word.

	Correct	Error
First Try		
Second Try		

hand	sand	land	bank	brand	sound	bound	hand	stand	(9)
round	hound	found	hand	hound	band	brand	round	hound	(18)
round	sound	sand	stand	band	bound	rest	round	sound	(27)
best	nest	chest	crest	lest	pest	quest	best	nest	(36)
test	west	grandest	chest	grand	bound	round	quest	west	(45)
roundest	zest	stand	round	best	hound	band	roundest	zest	(54)
sand	chest	brand	found	crest	sound	land	grand	chest	(63)
nest	grand	ground	round	roundest	hand	sound	vest	grand	(72)
rest	band	ground	best	sand	hound	grand	rest	band	(81)
hand	crest	nest	brand	round	chest	stand	hand	crest	(90)

ONE MINUTE FLUENCY
SOPRIS WEST SKILL BUILDERS SERIES

SEE TO SAY

BLENDING/READING ISOLATED DECODABLE REAL WORDS
all, ill, ell Words

Directions: Say each word.

	Correct	Error
First Try		
Second Try		

ball	fall	call	tall	stalling	wall	hall	ball	fall	(9)
till	mill	kill	hill	fill	gill	bill	ill	mill	(18)
chill	till	still	spill	mill	milling	rill	chill	till	(27)
bill	billing	will	willing	fill	filling	killing	bill	billing	(36)
sell	bell	tell	fell	dell	shell	well	shell	bell	(45)
Nell	sell	selling	bell	yell	selling	smelling	dell	yelling	(54)
telling	felling	bill	bell	ball	tell	till	telling	felling	(63)
tall	sell	sill	spell	wall	well	will	tall	sell	(72)
fell	fall	fill	felling	willing	swell	stall	fell	fall	(81)
still	spell	spilling	wall	willing	well	dwell	still	spelling	(90)

ONE MINUTE FLUENCY
SOPRIS WEST SKILL BUILDERS SERIES

SEE TO SAY

BLENDING/READING ISOLATED DECODABLE REAL WORDS

Review ing, ong, and, est, ill, ang, ung, ound, all, ell Words

Directions: Say each word.

	Correct	Error
First Try		
Second Try		

ring	sing	sting	sling	fling	wing	bang	bring	sing	(9)
hang	pang	gang	slang	clang	song	along	hang	pang	(18)
gong	long	tong	pong	hung	rung	lung	gong	long	(27)
hung	sung	stung	hand	and	band	brand	sung	stung	(36)
sand	stand	bound	sound	hound	found	round	sand	stand	(45)
ground	nest	best	chest	test	zest	west	ground	nest	(54)
call	fall	ball	tall	stall	wall	gill	call	fall	(63)
till	will	hill	chill	mill	well	tell	still	fill	(72)
sell	Nell	fell	shell	ground	grandest	best	sell	Nell	(81)
fill	fell	fall	roundest	still	clung	clang	fill	bill	(90)

ONE MINUTE FLUENCY
SOPRIS WEST SKILL BUILDERS SERIES

SEE TO SAY

	Correct	Error
First Try		
Second Try		

BLENDING/READING ISOLATED DECODABLE REAL WORDS
Initial Three-Letter Blends: spl, str, spr, scr Words

Directions: Say each word.

splash	spleen	split	sprang	spray	spring	strain	splat	splint	(9)
strand	street	scrap	scream	screen	strap	spleen	splinter	street	(18)
spree	scrape	split	scribe	splash	sprig	stray	spree	scrape	(27)
scrub	string	sprite	splash	spleen	split	sprang	scrub	strong	(36)
spray	spring	strain	strand	street	scrap	scream	spray	spring	(45)
screen	strap	spleen	spree	scrape	split	scribe	screen	strap	(54)
splash	sprig	stray	scrub	strong	sprite	splash	splash	sprig	(63)
spleen	split	sprang	spray	spring	strain	strand	spleen	split	(72)
street	scrap	scream	screen	strap	spleen	spree	street	scrap	(81)
scrape	split	scribe	splash	sprig	stray	scrub	scrape	split	(90)

SEE TO SAY

BLENDING/READING ISOLATED DECODABLE REAL WORDS
Review of all Blends

Directions: Say each word.

	Correct	Error
First Try		
Second Try		

plow	clam	flirt	bland	drove	trip	drive	plow	clam	flirt	(10)
speech	steal	scar	snake	sway	twin	glide	speech	steal	scar	(20)
slam	prime	crowd	frog	skill	smoke	stain	slam	prime	crowd	(30)
disk	stamp	spill	gasp	spin	toast	fast	disk	stamp	spend	(40)
trod	swept	split	spree	stroke	scrub	sprain	thrift	swept	split	(50)
strife	cramp	trust	shrink	stress	plant	dream	strife	cramp	trust	(60)
smelt	spleen	desk	twist	swell	scalp	tramp	smelt	spleen	desk	(70)
flame	stand	ground	crust	dwelt	stamp	shred	flame	stand	ground	(80)
strode	stretch	roast	strict	flinch	split	swept	strode	stretch	roast	(90)
waist	stream	plump	blond	state	trump	speak	waist	stream	plump	(100)
greet	strap	swift	starch	splash	blend	still	greet	strap	swift	(110)
flame	ground	crust	dwelt	scalp	tramp	dream	cramp	trust	roast	(120)

ONE MINUTE FLUENCY
SOPRIS WEST SKILL BUILDERS SERIES

SEE TO SAY

BLENDING/READING ISOLATED DECODABLE REAL WORDS
Short Vowel—Multisyllabic Words

Directions: Say each word.

	Correct	Error
First Try		
Second Try		

witness	bitter	matter	batter	rattle	rotten	getting	(7)
better	letter	butter	rutted	sitter	witness	bitter	(14)
matter	batter	rattle	rotten	getting	better	letter	(21)
butter	rutted	sitter	rutted	butter	letter	better	(28)
rattle	matter	sitter	witness	rutted	bitter	butter	(35)
matter	rotten	getting	rattle	better	batter	matter	(42)
sitter	rutted	butter	letter	better	getting	matter	(49)
rattle	better	letter	butter	rutted	bitter	witness	(56)
sitter	rutted	sitter	better	getting	rattle	matter	(63)
rattle	matter	letter	witness	rutted	batter	letter	(70)
sitter	rattle	better	butter	getting	matter	witness	(77)
rattle	better	rotten	witness	rutted	getting	letter	(84)

Reading High Frequency Sight Words

Any of these three different sets of Fluency Sheets can be used to build automaticity in reading high frequency sight words:

1. Dolch Words Arranged by Level of Difficulty
   These commonly taught words are organized by grade level, preprimer through third grade. Periodic review probes are included.
2. Dolch Word Lists
   The Dolch words are organized into 11 lists. Words having the greatest utility are presented on the earlier lists.
3. Isolated Words
   This sequence of high frequency words is identical to that followed in the *Basic Skill Builders Program Set Spelling* materials (Beck, Anderson, Conrad, 1998, Sopris West Educational Services, Inc.). Words are sequenced based on frequency of occurrence in student literature. This set of Fluency Sheets may be of particular value for the older student who still lacks fluency in reading familiar sight words.

Dolch Words by Level

(Grades K–3)

Dolch Words by List

(Grades K–3; Intervention Grade 3 and Above)

General High Frequency Words (Coordinated with *Basic Skill Builders Spelling*)

(Intervention Grade 2 and Above)

ONE MINUTE FLUENCY
SOPRIS WEST SKILL BUILDERS SERIES

SEE TO SAY

	Correct	Error
First Try		
Second Try		

READING HIGH FREQUENCY SIGHT WORDS
Dolch Words—Preprimer, Skill Sheet 1
(a, and, away, big, blue, can, come, down)

Directions: Say each word.

a	and	away	big	blue	can	come	down	(8)
and	come	a	down	big	can	blue	away	(16)
away	can	big	a	down	blue	and	come	(24)
blue	a	down	and	come	away	big	can	(32)
come	away	can	come	and	down	blue	a	(40)
down	big	and	blue	a	come	can	away	(48)
big	down	can	and	come	a	away	blue	(56)
a	down	and	come	away	can	blue	big	(64)

SEE TO SAY

	Correct	Error
First Try		
Second Try		

READING HIGH FREQUENCY SIGHT WORDS
Dolch Words—Preprimer, Skill Sheet 2
(find, for, funny, go, help, hers, I, in)

Directions: Say each word.

find	for	funny	go	help	hers	I	in	(8)
for	in	find	I	go	hers	help	go	(16)
go	funny	hers	in	I	find	for	help	(24)
in	find	I	go	in	for	help	funny	(32)
hers	funny	go	I	go	help	for	find	(40)
funny	go	help	find	for	I	go	hers	(48)
I	help	go	funny	find	in	hers	for	(56)
help	hers	in	for	funny	go	I	find	(64)

ONE MINUTE FLUENCY
SOPRIS WEST SKILL BUILDERS SERIES

SEE TO SAY

	Correct	Error
First Try		
Second Try		

READING HIGH FREQUENCY SIGHT WORDS
Dolch Words—Preprimer, Skill Sheet 3
(is, it, jump, little, look, make, me, my)

Directions: Say each word.

is	it	jump	little	look	make	me	my	(8)
it	little	make	my	is	jump	look	me	(16)
jump	make	is	little	me	it	look	my	(24)
little	my	look	is	make	it	jump	me	(32)
look	me	is	jump	look	make	my	it	(40)
me	is	my	look	little	jump	it	make	(48)
my	jump	make	little	look	it	me	is	(56)
make	little	it	me	is	look	my	jump	(64)

SEE TO SAY

	Correct	Error
First Try		
Second Try		

READING HIGH FREQUENCY SIGHT WORDS
Dolch Words—Preprimer, Skill Sheet 4
(not, one, play, red, run, said, see, the)

Directions: Say each word.

not	one	play	red	run	said	see	the	(8)
one	play	said	the	not	run	red	see	(16)
red	see	one	run	the	play	said	not	(24)
play	see	red	the	run	not	said	one	(32)
said	the	not	play	red	run	one	see	(40)
run	not	see	said	play	the	one	red	(48)
the	one	red	not	run	see	play	said	(56)
said	run	the	see	not	one	play	red	(64)

READING HIGH FREQUENCY SIGHT WORDS
Dolch Words—Preprimer, Skill Sheet 5
(three, to, two, up, we, yellow, you)

Directions: Say each word.

	Correct	Error
First Try		
Second Try		

three	to	two	up	we	yellow	you	to	(8)
we	yellow	three	you	two	up	yellow	three	(16)
to	up	two	you	we	three	two	we	(24)
you	to	up	yellow	to	three	up	two	(32)
yellow	we	you	yellow	you	we	two	three	(40)
to	up	two	yellow	to	we	three	you	(48)
yellow	you	we	up	two	to	three	we	(56)
two	up	yellow	you	to	we	up	three	(64)

SEE TO SAY

READING HIGH FREQUENCY SIGHT WORDS
Dolch Words—Preprimer Review

Directions: Say each word.

	Correct	Error
First Try		
Second Try		

a	and	away	big	blue	can	come	down	(8)
find	for	funny	go	help	hers	I	in	(16)
is	it	jump	little	look	make	me	my	(24)
not	one	play	red	run	said	see	the	(32)
three	to	two	up	we	yellow	you	and	(40)

ONE MINUTE FLUENCY
SOPRIS WEST SKILL BUILDERS SERIES

SEE TO SAY

	Correct	Error
First Try		
Second Try		

READING HIGH FREQUENCY SIGHT WORDS
Dolch Words—Primer, Skill Sheet 1
(all, am, are, at, ate, be, black, brown)

Directions: Say each word.

all	am	are	at	ate	be	black	brown	(8)
am	at	be	brown	all	are	ate	black	(16)
are	be	all	at	black	am	ate	brown	(24)
at	black	are	brown	ate	all	am	be	(32)
ate	all	be	are	brown	black	am	at	(40)
be	at	am	brown	all	black	are	ate	(48)
black	are	brown	at	all	ate	am	be	(56)
brown	at	black	am	be	are	ate	all	(64)

SEE TO SAY

	Correct	Error
First Try		
Second Try		

READING HIGH FREQUENCY SIGHT WORDS
Dolch Words—Primer, Skill Sheet 2
(but, came, did, do, eat, four, get, good)

Directions: Say each word.

but	came	did	do	eat	four	get	good	(8)
came	do	four	good	but	did	eat	get	(16)
did	four	but	eat	good	do	get	came	(24)
do	but	four	did	good	eat	came	get	(32)
eat	good	came	get	but	do	did	came	(40)
four	came	do	good	get	but	did	eat	(48)
get	did	eat	came	but	four	do	good	(56)
good	but	get	did	came	do	four	eat	(64)

ONE-MINUTE FLUENCY
SOPRIS WEST SKILL BUILDERS SERIES

SEE TO SAY

READING HIGH FREQUENCY SIGHT WORDS
Dolch Words—Primer, Skill Sheet 3
(has, he, into, like, must, new, no, now)

Directions: Say each word.

	Correct	Error
First Try		
Second Try		

has	he	into	like	must	new	no	now	(8)
he	like	new	now	has	into	must	no	(16)
into	new	now	into	has	no	he	must	(24)
like	no	he	must	now	into	new	has	(32)
must	like	into	he	has	now	no	new	(40)
new	he	no	into	now	like	must	has	(48)
no	must	into	has	now	new	like	he	(56)
now	like	no	into	new	has	he	must	(64)

SEE TO SAY

	Correct	Error
First Try		
Second Try		

READING HIGH FREQUENCY SIGHT WORDS
Dolch Words—Primer, Skill Sheet 4
(on, our, out, please, pretty, ran, ride, saw, say, she)

Directions: Say each word.

on	our	out	please	pretty	ran	ride	saw	(8)
say	she	on	out	pretty	ride	say	she	(16)
our	please	ran	saw	our	pretty	saw	on	(24)
please	ride	out	ran	say	she	out	our	(32)
on	she	say	saw	ride	ran	pretty	please	(40)
please	out	on	she	saw	ran	say	ride	(48)
pretty	our	ran	out	she	ride	please	on	(56)
say	saw	on	ran	out	she	our	pretty	(64)

	Correct	Error
First Try		
Second Try		

READING HIGH FREQUENCY SIGHT WORDS
Dolch Words—Primer, Skill Sheet 5
(so, soon, that, there, they, this, too, under, want)

Directions: Say each word.

so	soon	that	there	they	this	too	under	(8)
want	so	that	they	too	want	soon	there	(16)
this	under	soon	they	under	that	they	too	(24)
so	there	this	that	want	too	they	soon	(32)
under	this	there	this	there	so	want	that	(40)
soon	under	they	too	this	too	want	soon	(48)
this	there	so	they	under	that	too	want	(56)

SEE TO SAY

	Correct	Error
First Try		
Second Try		

READING HIGH FREQUENCY SIGHT WORDS

Dolch Words—Primer, Skill Sheet 6

(was, well, went, what, white, who, will, with, yes)

Directions: Say each word.

was	well	went	what	white	who	will	with	(8)
yes	was	went	white	will	with	well	what	(16)
who	yes	well	who	with	yes	went	what	(24)
will	what	was	went	what	was	well	yes	(32)
white	will	who	with	what	yes	was	with	(40)
well	who	will	white	went	who	white	was	(48)
yes	well	was	went	will	with	what	who	(56)

ONE-MINUTE FLUENCY
SOPRIS WEST SKILL BUILDERS SERIES

SEE TO SAY

READING HIGH FREQUENCY SIGHT WORDS
Dolch Words—Primer Review

Directions: Say each word.

	Correct	Error
First Try		
Second Try		

all	am	are	at	ate	be	black	brown	(8)
but	came	did	do	eat	four	get	good	(16)
has	he	into	like	must	new	no	now	(24)
on	our	out	please	pretty	ran	ride	saw	(32)
say	she	so	soon	that	there	they	this	(40)
too	under	want	was	well	went	what	white	(48)
who	will	with	yes	all	but	has	on	(56)
say	too	who	am	came	he	our	she	(64)

SEE TO SAY

	Correct	Error
First Try		
Second Try		

READING HIGH FREQUENCY SIGHT WORDS

Dolch Words—First Grade, Skill Sheet 1

(after, again, an, any, as, ask, by, could)

Directions: Say each word.

after	again	an	any	as	ask	by	could	(8)
again	any	ask	could	after	an	as	by	(16)
an	ask	after	any	by	again	could	as	(24)
any	again	could	ask	any	an	after	by	(32)
as	after	ask	an	could	any	by	again	(40)
ask	an	again	after	by	could	as	any	(48)
by	ask	could	again	after	an	any	as	(56)
could	after	an	ask	again	any	by	an	(64)

One-Minute Fluency
Sopris West Skill Builders Series

SEE TO SAY

	Correct	Error
First Try		
Second Try		

READING HIGH FREQUENCY SIGHT WORDS
Dolch Words—First Grade, Skill Sheet 2
(every, fly, from, give, going, had, has, her)

Directions: Say each word.

every	fly	from	give	going	had	has	her	(8)
fly	give	had	her	every	from	going	has	(16)
from	fly	every	her	has	had	give	going	(24)
give	has	fly	had	every	going	her	from	(32)
going	every	has	from	give	her	fly	had	(40)
had	from	her	going	fly	has	give	every	(48)
has	going	give	every	had	fly	every	from	(56)
her	every	had	going	fly	from	has	give	(64)

SEE TO SAY

	Correct	Error
First Try		
Second Try		

READING HIGH FREQUENCY SIGHT WORDS
Dolch Words—First Grade, Skill Sheet 3
(him, how, just, know, let, live, may, of)

Directions: Say each word.

him	how	just	know	let	live	may	of	(8)
how	know	live	of	him	just	let	may	(16)
just	live	him	know	may	how	let	of	(24)
know	just	how	him	of	may	live	let	(32)
let	how	may	know	live	let	of	him	(40)
live	know	him	may	let	just	how	of	(48)
may	how	of	him	live	just	let	know	(56)
of	let	may	live	know	him	just	how	(64)

SEE TO SAY

READING HIGH FREQUENCY SIGHT WORDS
Dolch Words—First Grade, Skill Sheet 4
(old, once, open, over, put, round, some, stop)

Directions: Say each word.

	Correct	Error
First Try		
Second Try		

old	once	open	over	put	round	some	stop	(8)
once	over	round	stop	old	open	put	some	(16)
open	round	old	over	some	once	stop	put	(24)
over	open	old	some	round	put	once	stop	(32)
put	some	open	old	stop	round	over	once	(40)
round	over	old	put	stop	once	open	some	(48)
some	put	old	round	stop	open	over	once	(56)
stop	over	once	open	round	old	put	some	(64)

SEE TO SAY

	Correct	Error
First Try		
Second Try		

READING HIGH FREQUENCY SIGHT WORDS

Dolch Words—First Grade, Skill Sheet 5

(take, thank, them, then, think, walk, where, when)

Directions: Say each word.

take	thank	them	then	think	walk	where	when	(8)
thank	then	walk	when	take	them	think	where	(16)
them	walk	take	then	where	thank	when	think	(24)
then	where	them	when	think	take	walk	thank	(32)
think	then	them	thank	take	when	where	walk	(40)
walk	then	thank	when	walk	them	think	take	(48)
where	then	take	walk	them	when	think	thank	(56)
when	take	where	walk	thank	them	then	think	(64)

SEE TO SAY

READING HIGH FREQUENCY SIGHT WORDS

Dolch Words—First Grade Review

Directions: Say each word.

	Correct	Error
First Try		
Second Try		

after	again	an	any	as	ask	by	could	(8)
every	fly	from	give	going	had	has	her	(16)
him	how	just	know	let	live	may	of	(24)
old	once	open	over	put	round	some	stop	(32)
take	thank	them	then	think	walk	where	when	(40)

SEE TO SAY

	Correct	Error
First Try		
Second Try		

READING HIGH FREQUENCY SIGHT WORDS
Dolch Words—Second Grade, Skill Sheet 1
(always, around, because, been, before, best, both, buy)

Directions: Say each word.

always	around	because	been	before	best	both	buy	(8)
around	been	best	buy	always	because	before	both	(16)
because	best	always	been	both	around	before	buy	(24)
been	always	best	around	both	because	buy	before	(32)
before	been	because	around	always	buy	both	best	(40)
best	been	around	buy	both	before	because	always	(48)
both	around	buy	always	before	because	been	best	(56)
buy	before	around	both	been	always	best	because	(64)

ONE-MINUTE FLUENCY
SOPRIS WEST SKILL BUILDERS SERIES

SEE TO SAY

	Correct	Error
First Try		
Second Try		

READING HIGH FREQUENCY SIGHT WORDS

Dolch Words—Second Grade, Skill Sheet 2

(call, cold, does, don't, fast, first, five, found)

Directions: Say each word.

call	cold	does	don't	fast	first	five	found	(8)
cold	don't	first	found	call	does	fast	five	(16)
does	first	call	don't	found	five	fast	cold	(24)
don't	call	first	does	found	fast	cold	five	(32)
fast	does	call	five	found	first	don't	cold	(40)
first	found	five	call	cold	does	fast	don't	(48)
five	cold	fast	does	found	first	don't	call	(56)
found	five	cll	does	fast	cold	don't	first	(64)

SEE TO SAY

	Correct	Error
First Try		
Second Try		

READING HIGH FREQUENCY SIGHT WORDS
Dolch Words—Second Grade, Skill Sheet 3
(gave, goes, green, its, made, many, off, or)

Directions: Say each word.

gave	goes	green	its	made	many	off	or	(8)
goes	its	many	or	gave	green	made	off	(16)
green	many	goes	many	gave	or	off	its	(24)
its	gave	many	off	goes	green	or	made	(32)
made	its	green	goes	or	gave	many	off	(40)
many	green	its	gave	off	made	goes	or	(48)
off	many	gave	or	goes	green	its	made	(56)
or	goes	made	off	gave	its	green	many	(64)

	Correct	Error
First Try		
Second Try		

READING HIGH FREQUENCY SIGHT WORDS

Dolch Words—Second Grade, Skill Sheet 4

(pull, read, right, sing, sit, sleep, tell, their)

Directions: Say each word.

pull	read	right	sing	sit	sleep	tell	their	(8)
read	sing	sleep	their	pull	right	sit	tell	(16)
right	sleep	pull	sing	tell	read	sit	their	(24)
sing	pull	sleep	right	tell	sit	their	read	(32)
right	read	pull	tell	their	sleep	sing	sit	(40)
sing	their	sit	sleep	right	tell	read	pull	(48)
tell	sit	sing	pull	sleep	their	right	read	(56)
their	read	sit	tell	sing	pull	sleep	right	(64)

SEE TO SAY

READING HIGH FREQUENCY SIGHT WORDS

Dolch Words—Second Grade, Skill Sheet
(these, those, upon, us, use, very, wash, which)

Directions: Say each word.

	Correct	Error
First Try		
Second Try		

these	those	upon	us	use	very	wash	which	(8)
those	us	very	which	wash	use	upon	these	(16)
upon	wash	these	us	very	which	those	use	(24)
us	those	use	these	wash	very	upon	which	(32)
use	upon	these	wash	us	those	which	very	(40)
wash	very	us	these	upon	use	which	those	(48)
very	which	those	us	wash	these	upon	use	(56)
which	upon	very	wash	these	use	those	us	(64)

ONE-MINUTE FLUENCY
SOPRIS WEST SKILL BUILDERS SERIES

SEE TO SAY

	Correct	Error
First Try		
Second Try		

READING HIGH FREQUENCY SIGHT WORDS
Dolch Words—Second Grade, Skill Sheet 6
(why, wish, work, would, write, your)

Directions: Say each word.

why	wish	work	would	write	your	wish	would	(8)
write	your	work	why	your	write	would	work	(16)
wish	why	write	wish	would	your	why	work	(24)
your	write	why	work	wish	would	write	your	(32)
would	wish	work	why	wish	work	why	would	(40)
your	write	why	your	write	wish	would	work	(48)
would	why	work	wish	why	work	wish	would	(56)
your	write	would	wish	work	why	write	would	(64)

SEE TO SAY

	Correct	Error
First Try		
Second Try		

READING HIGH FREQUENCY SIGHT WORDS
Dolch Words—Second Grade Review

Directions: Say each word.

always	around	because	been	before	best	both	buy	(8)
call	cold	does	don't	fast	first	five	found	(16)
gave	goes	green	its	made	many	off	or	(24)
pull	read	right	sing	sit	sleep	tell	their	(32)
these	those	upon	us	use	very	wash	which	(40)
why	wish	work	would	write	your	wish	would	(48)

READING HIGH FREQUENCY SIGHT WORDS

Dolch Words—Third Grade, Skill Sheet 1

(about, better, bring, carry, clean, cut, done, draw)

Directions: Say each word.

	Correct	Error
First Try		
Second Try		

about	better	bring	carry	clean	cut	done	draw	(8)
better	carry	cut	done	draw	about	bring	clean	(16)
bring	cut	about	clean	done	better	draw	carry	(24)
carry	about	cut	bring	draw	clean	better	done	(32)
clean	carry	bring	better	about	draw	done	cut	(40)
cut	bring	carry	about	better	done	clean	draw	(48)
done	better	clean	draw	bring	cut	about	carry	(56)
draw	bring	cut	about	carry	done	better	clean	(64)

SEE TO SAY

READING HIGH FREQUENCY SIGHT WORDS
Dolch Words—Third Grade, Skill Sheet 2
(drink, eight, fall, far, full, got, grow, hold)

Directions: Say each word.

	Correct	Error
First Try		
Second Try		

drink	eight	fall	far	full	got	grow	hold	(8)
eight	far	got	hold	drink	fall	full	grow	(16)
fall	got	drink	far	grow	eight	full	hold	(24)
far	drink	got	fall	grow	full	hold	eight	(32)
full	fall	drink	grow	hold	got	eight	far	(40)
got	far	eight	hold	full	grow	fall	drink	(48)
grow	full	drink	hold	fall	eight	got	far	(56)
hold	eight	full	grow	far	drink	got	fall	(64)

	Correct	Error
First Try		
Second Try		

READING HIGH FREQUENCY SIGHT WORDS

Dolch Words—Third Grade, Skill Sheet 3

(hot, hurt, if, keep, kind, laugh, light, long)

Directions: Say each word.

hot	hurt	if	keep	kind	laugh	light	long	(8)
hurt	kind	laugh	long	light	hot	if	keep	(16)
if	laugh	hot	keep	light	hurt	kind	long	(24)
keep	long	kind	hot	laugh	if	hurt	light	(32)
kind	keep	if	hurt	hot	long	light	laugh	(40)
light	kind	if	hot	long	laugh	keep	hurt	(48)
laugh	keep	hurt	if	hot	light	long	kind	(56)
long	hurt	kind	light	keep	hot	laugh	if	(64)

SEE TO SAY

READING HIGH FREQUENCY SIGHT WORDS
Dolch Words—Third Grade, Skill Sheet 4
(much, myself, never, only, own, pick, seven, shall)

Directions: Say each word.

	Correct	Error
First Try		
Second Try		

much	myself	never	only	own	pick	seven	shall	(8)
myself	only	pick	shall	seven	much	never	only	(16)
never	pick	much	own	only	seven	shall	myself	(24)
only	much	own	myself	pick	never	shall	seven	(32)
own	never	much	seven	pick	only	myself	shall	(40)
pick	shall	seven	much	myself	own	only	never	(48)
seven	shall	never	pick	myself	own	much	only	(56)
shall	myself	pick	never	seven	much	only	own	(64)

SEE TO SAY

	Correct	Error
First Try		
Second Try		

READING HIGH FREQUENCY SIGHT WORDS
Dolch Words—Third Grade, Skill Sheet 5
(show, six, small, start, ten, today, together, try, warm)

Directions: Say each word.

show	six	small	start	ten	today	together	try	(8)
warm	six	start	today	try	show	small	ten	(16)
together	show	small	warm	show	try	together	start	(24)
today	ten	six	start	small	show	try	six	(32)
together	today	warm	try	today	ten	small	show	(40)
start	together	six	warm	start	together	try	show	(48)
warm	small	show	together	ten	small	show	try	(56)
warm	six	together	small	today	start	ten	small	(64)

SEE TO SAY

READING HIGH FREQUENCY SIGHT WORDS

Dolch Words—Third Grade Review

Directions: Say each word.

	Correct	Error
First Try		
Second Try		

about	better	bring	carry	clean	cut	done	draw	(8)
drink	eight	fall	far	full	got	grow	hold	(16)
hot	hurt	if	keep	kind	laugh	light	long	(24)
much	myself	never	only	own	pick	seven	shall	(32)
show	six	small	start	ten	today	together	try	(40)
warm	about	eight	if	only	ten	better	fall	(48)

	Correct	Error
First Try		
Second Try		

READING HIGH FREQUENCY SIGHT WORDS
Dolch Words—List 1

Directions: Say each word.

the	to	and	he	a	I	you	it	(8)
of	in	was	said	his	that	she	for	(16)
on	they	but	had	and	I	the	he	(24)
to	a	it	you	of	was	his	that	(32)
she	they	had	in	said	for	but	a	(40)
the	he	and	to	I	in	of	you	(48)
it	was	she	said	that	his	for	on	(56)
had	they	but	the	and	he	a	to	(64)

SEE TO SAY

READING HIGH FREQUENCY SIGHT WORDS

Dolch Words—List 2

Directions: Say each word.

	Correct	Error
First Try		
Second Try		

at	him	with	up	all	look	is	her	(8)
there	some	out	as	be	have	go	we	(16)
am	then	little	down	at	all	with	him	(24)
up	some	is	her	look	there	out	have	(32)
go	be	as	we	down	am	little	down	(40)
there	at	some	all	look	up	her	him	(48)
is	with	out	down	as	little	be	then	(56)
have	am	go	we	at	up	with	him	(64)

ONE-MINUTE FLUENCY
SOPRIS WEST SKILL BUILDERS SERIES

SEE TO SAY

READING HIGH FREQUENCY SIGHT WORDS
Dolch Words—List 3

Directions: Say each word.

	Correct	Error
First Try		
Second Try		

do	can	could	when	did	what	so	see	(8)
not	were	get	them	like	one	this	my	(16)
would	me	will	yes	do	did	can	when	(24)
could	what	were	so	not	see	get	this	(32)
them	one	like	my	yes	would	will	me	(40)
do	were	can	not	could	so	when	see	(48)
did	what	get	yes	them	will	like	me	(56)
one	would	this	my	can	do	could	when	(64)

SEE TO SAY

READING HIGH FREQUENCY SIGHT WORDS
Dolch Words—List 4

Directions: Say each word.

	Correct	Error
First Try		
Second Try		

big	went	are	come	if	now	long	no	(8)
came	ask	very	an	over	your	its	ride	(16)
into	just	blue	red	big	if	went	come	(24)
are	now	ask	long	came	no	very	its	(32)
an	your	over	ride	red	into	blue	just	(40)
big	ask	went	came	are	no	come	long	(48)
now	if	very	red	an	blue	over	just	(56)
your	into	its	ride	big	come	are	come	(64)

READING HIGH FREQUENCY SIGHT WORDS
Dolch Words—List 5

Directions: Say each word.

	Correct	Error
First Try		
Second Try		

from	good	any	about	around	want	don't	how	(8)
know	right	put	too	got	take	where	every	(16)
pretty	jump	green	four	from	around	good	about	(24)
any	want	right	don't	know	how	put	where	(32)
too	take	got	every	four	pretty	green	jump	(40)
from	right	good	know	any	how	about	don't	(48)
around	want	put	four	too	green	got	jump	(56)
take	pretty	where	every	from	about	good	any	(64)

SEE TO SAY

READING HIGH FREQUENCY SIGHT WORDS
Dolch Words—List 6

Directions: Say each word.

	Correct	Error
First Try		
Second Try		

away	old	by	their	here	saw	call	after	(8)
well	think	ran	let	help	make	going	sleep	(16)
brown	yellow	five	six	away	here	old	by	(24)
their	saw	think	call	well	after	ran	going	(32)
help	let	make	sleep	six	brown	five	yellow	(40)
away	think	old	well	by	after	their	call	(48)
here	saw	ran	six	let	five	help	yellow	(56)
make	sleep	going	brown	old	away	their	by	(64)

	Correct	Error
First Try		
Second Try		

READING HIGH FREQUENCY SIGHT WORDS
Dolch Words—List 7

Directions: Say each word.

walk	two	or	before	eat	again	play	who	(8)
been	may	stop	off	never	seven	eight	cold	(16)
today	fly	myself	round	walk	eat	two	before	(24)
or	again	may	play	been	who	stop	eight	(32)
off	seven	never	cold	round	today	myself	fly	(40)
walk	may	two	been	or	who	before	play	(48)
eat	again	stop	round	off	myself	never	fly	(56)
seven	today	eight	cold	or	walk	two	before	(64)

SEE TO SAY

READING HIGH FREQUENCY SIGHT WORDS

Dolch Words—List 8

Directions: Say each word.

	Correct	Error
First Try		
Second Try		

tell	much	keep	give	much	first	try	new	(8)
must	start	black	white	ten	does	bring	goes	(8)
write	always	drink	once	tell	work	much	give	(24)
keep	first	start	try	must	new	black	bring	(32)
white	does	ten	goes	once	write	drink	always	(40)
tell	start	much	must	keep	new	give	try	(48)
work	first	black	once	white	drink	ten	always	(56)
does	write	bring	goes	much	keep	tell	give	(64)

ONE-MINUTE FLUENCY
SOPRIS WEST SKILL BUILDERS SERIES

SEE TO SAY

	Correct	Error
First Try		
Second Try		

READING HIGH FREQUENCY SIGHT WORDS
Dolch Words—List 9

Directions: Say each word.

soon	made	run	gave	open	has	find	only	(8)
us	three	our	better	hold	buy	funny	warm	(16)
ate	full	those	done	soon	open	made	gave	(24)
run	has	three	find	us	only	our	funny	(32)
better	buy	hold	warm	done	ate	those	full	(40)
soon	three	made	us	run	only	gave	find	(48)
open	has	our	done	better	those	hold	full	(56)
buy	ate	funny	warm	gave	soon	run	made	(64)

ONE MINUTE FLUENCY
SOPRIS WEST SKILL BUILDERS SERIES

SEE TO SAY

READING HIGH FREQUENCY SIGHT WORDS
Dolch Words—List 10

Directions: Say each word.

	Correct	Error
First Try		
Second Try		

use	fast	say	light	pick	hurt	pull	cut	(8)
kind	both	sit	which	fall	carry	small	under	(16)
read	why	own	found	use	pick	fast	light	(24)
say	hurt	both	pull	kind	cut	sit	small	(32)
which	carry	fall	under	found	read	why	own	(40)
use	both	fast	kind	say	cut	light	pull	(48)
pick	hurt	sit	found	which	own	fall	why	(56)
carry	read	small	under	fast	say	light	use	(64)

ONE MINUTE FLUENCY
SOPRIS WEST SKILL BUILDERS SERIES

SEE TO SAY

READING HIGH FREQUENCY SIGHT WORDS
Dolch Words—List 11

Directions: Say each word.

	Correct	Error
First Try		
Second Try		

wash	show	hot	because	far	live	draw	clean	(8)
grow	best	upon	these	sing	together	please	thank	(16)
wish	many	shall	laugh	wash	far	show	because	(24)
hot	live	best	draw	grow	clean	upon	please	(32)
these	together	sing	thank	laugh	wish	shall	many	(40)
wash	best	show	grow	hot	clean	because	draw	(48)
far	live	upon	laugh	these	shall	sing	many	(56)
together	wish	please	thank	wash	show	not	because	(64)

SEE TO SAY

READING HIGH FREQUENCY SIGHT WORDS
Dolch Words—Review Lists 1–4

Directions: Say each word.

	Correct	Error
First Try		
Second Try		

the	to	and	he	a	I	you	it	of	in	(10)
was	said	his	that	she	for	on	they	but	had	(20)
at	him	with	up	all	look	is	her	there	some	(30)
out	as	be	have	go	we	am	then	little	down	(40)
do	can	could	when	did	what	so	see	not	were	(50)
get	them	like	one	this	my	would	me	will	yes	(60)
big	went	are	come	if	now	long	no	came	ask	(70)
very	an	over	your	its	ride	into	just	blue	red	(80)

SEE TO SAY

READING HIGH FREQUENCY SIGHT WORDS

Dolch Words—Review Lists 5–8

Directions: Say each word.

	Correct	Error
First Try		
Second Try		

from	good	any	about	around	want	don't	how	know	right	(10)
put	too	got	take	where	every	pretty	jump	green	four	(20)
away	old	by	their	here	saw	call	after	well	think	(30)
ran	let	help	make	going	sleep	brown	yellow	five	six	(40)
walk	two	or	before	eat	again	play	who	been	may	(50)
stop	off	never	seven	eight	cold	today	fly	myself	round	(60)
tell	much	keep	give	work	first	try	new	must	start	(70)
black	white	ten	does	bring	goes	write	always	drink	once	(80)

SEE TO SAY

READING HIGH FREQUENCY SIGHT WORDS

Dolch Words—Review Lists 9–11

Directions: Say each word.

	Correct	Error
First Try		
Second Try		

soon	made	run	gave	open	has	find	only	us	three	(10)
our	better	hold	buy	funny	warm	ate	full	those	done	(20)
use	fast	say	light	pick	hurt	pull	cut	kind	both	(30)
sit	which	fall	carry	small	under	read	why	own	found	(40)
wash	show	hot	because	far	live	draw	clean	grow	best	(50)
upon	these	sing	together	please	thank	wish	many	shall	laugh	(60)
soon	our	made	run	hold	gave	buy	open	funny	has	(70)
better	warm	find	ate	only	full	us	those	three	done	(80)

SEE TO SAY

READING HIGH FREQUENCY SIGHT WORDS

Dolch Words—Review Lists 1–3 (Small Print)

Directions: Say each word.

	Correct	Error
First Try		
Second Try		

the	to	and	he	a	I	you	it	of	in	(10)
was	said	his	that	she	for	on	they	but	had	(20)
at	him	with	up	all	look	is	her	there	some	(30)
out	as	be	have	go	we	am	then	little	down	(40)
do	can	could	when	did	what	so	see	not	were	(50)
get	them	like	one	this	my	would	me	will	yes	(60)
the	had	to	but	and	they	he	on	a	for	(70)
I	she	you	that	it	his	of	said	in	was	(80)
at	down	him	little	with	then	up	all	am	we	(90)
look	out	some	go	is	there	have	as	her	be	(100)
do	my	did	yes	can	would	when	will	could	me	(110)
what	get	were	this	so	them	not	one	see	like	(120)

SEE TO SAY

	Correct	Error
First Try		
Second Try		

READING HIGH FREQUENCY SIGHT WORDS
Dolch Words—Review Lists 1–5 (Small Print)

Directions: Say each word.

the	to	and	he	a	I	you	it	of	in	(10)
was	said	his	that	she	for	on	they	but	had	(20)
at	him	with	up	all	look	is	her	there	some	(30)
out	as	be	have	go	we	am	then	little	down	(40)
do	can	could	when	did	what	so	see	not	were	(50)
get	them	like	one	this	my	would	me	will	yes	(60)
big	went	are	come	if	now	long	no	came	ask	(70)
very	an	over	your	its	ride	into	just	blue	red	(80)
from	good	any	about	around	want	don't	how	know	right	(90)
put	too	got	take	where	every	pretty	jump	green	four	(100)

SEE TO SAY

READING HIGH FREQUENCY SIGHT WORDS
Dolch Words—Review Lists 6–11 (Small Print)

Directions: Say each word.

	Correct	Error
First Try		
Second Try		

away	old	by	their	here	saw	call	after	well	think	(10)
ran	let	help	make	going	sleep	brown	yellow	five	six	(20)
walk	two	or	before	eat	again	play	who	been	may	(30)
stop	off	never	seven	eight	cold	today	fly	myself	round	(40)
tell	much	keep	give	work	first	try	new	must	start	(50)
black	white	ten	does	bring	goes	write	always	drink	once	(60)
soon	made	run	gave	open	has	find	only	us	three	(70)
our	better	hold	buy	funny	warm	ate	full	those	done	(80)
use	fast	say	light	pick	hurt	pull	cut	kind	both	(90)
sit	which	fall	carry	small	under	read	why	own	found	(100)
wash	show	hot	because	far	live	draw	clean	grow	best	(110)
upon	these	sing	together	please	thank	wish	many	shall	laugh	(120)

SEE TO SAY

READING HIGH FREQUENCY SIGHT WORDS
Dolch Phrases—Skill Sheet 1

Directions: Say each phrase.

	Correct	Error
First Try		
Second Try		

is coming	her mother	I was	to go	you were	can run	we were	I am	(16)
with us	to stop	they are	went away	he was	was made	must be	will go	(32)
at school	has made	some bread	was found	will think	from home	will walk		(46)
my father	it is	went down	could eat	would like	to stop	with us	I am	(62)
we were	can run	you were	to go	I was	her mother	is coming	some bread	(78)
has made	at school	will go	must be	was made	he was	went away	I was	(94)
they are	would like	could eat	went down	it is	my father	will walk		(108)
from home	will think	was found	is coming	her mother	I was	to go		(122)
you were	can run	we were	I am	with us	to stop	they are	went away	(138)
was found	will think	from home	will walk	my father	it is	went down		(152)
could eat	would like	to stop	with us	I am	we were	can run	you were	(168)
to go	I was	her mother	is coming	some bread	has made	at school	I am	(184)

	Correct	Error
First Try		
Second Try		

READING HIGH FREQUENCY SIGHT WORDS
Dolch Phrases—Skill Sheet 2

Directions: Say each phrase.

his sister	my brother	has found	can fly	your sister	could make	for them		(14)
so much	all day	can live	would want	will look	at once	is going	about it	(30)
too soon	at home	can play	her father	at three	down there	so long	up there	(46)
they were	will buy	for him	some cake	so much	for them	could make	your sister	(62)
can fly	has found	my brother	his sister	at home	too soon	about it	is going	(78)
at once	will look	would want	can live	all day	will buy	they were	up here	(94)
up there	so long	down there	at three	her father	can play	has found	can fly	(110)
your sister	could make	for them	so much	some cake	for him	his sister		(124)
my brother	has found	can fly	so much	all day	can live	would want	will look	(140)
at once	is going	about it	too soon	at home	can play	her father	at three	(156)
down there	so long	up there	up here	they were	will buy	for him	some cake	(172)
so much	for them	could make	your sister	can fly	has found	my brother		(186)

SEE TO SAY

READING HIGH FREQUENCY SIGHT WORDS
Dolch Phrases—Skill Sheet 3

Directions: Say each phrase.

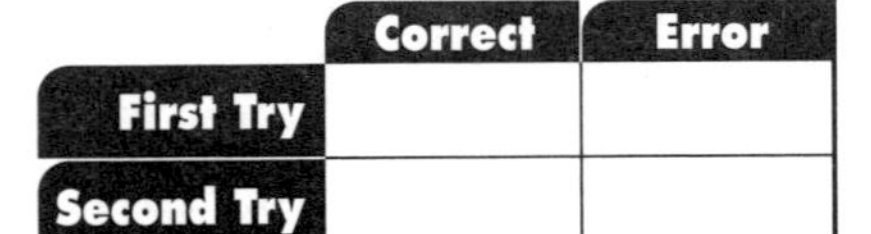

	Correct	Error
First Try		
Second Try		

all night   he is   must go   too little   we are   with more   it was   about him   (16)

will read   you are   his brother   down here   your mother   he would do   when I can   (32)

down the hill   on the chair   a pretty picture   you will like   if I may   what I want   (50)

if you can   on the floor   by the house   the old men   for the baby   did not go   you are   (70)

will read   the funny rabbit   about him   it was   with more   we are   too little   (85)

must go   he is   all night   on the chair   down the hill   when I can   he would do   (103)

your mother   down here   his brother   by the house   on the floor   if you can   it was   (120)

what I want   if I may   you will like   a pretty picture   about him   will read   you are   his brother   (140)

down here   your mother   he would do   when I can   down the hill   on the chair   it was   (158)

a pretty picture   you will like   if I may   what I want   if you can   on the floor   (176)

SEE TO SAY

READING HIGH FREQUENCY SIGHT WORDS
Dolch Phrases—Skill Sheet 4

Directions: Say each phrase.

	Correct	Error
First Try		
Second Try		

to the nest	a pretty home	the yellow cat	in the garden	the old man	the black horse	(18)
the yellow ball	the red apple	I may go	in the box	has run away	in the grass	(36)
the small boy	the white sheep	the black bird	a new hat	you will do	by the tree	(54)
the little children	a new book	to the barn	a big horse	as I said	the new coat	(72)
for the girl	when I wish	to the school	then he said	the black horse	the old man	(90)
in the garden	the yellow cat	a pretty home	to the nest	the small boy	in the grass	(108)
has run away	in the box	I may go	the red apple	the yellow ball	by the tree	(126)
the little children	you will do	a new hat	the black bird	the white sheep	as I said	(144)
when I wish	for the girl	the new coat	as I said	a big horse	to the barn	(162)
a new book	to the nest	a pretty home	the yellow cat	in the garden	the old man	(180)
the black horse	the yellow ball	the red apple	I may go	in the box	has run away	(198)
in the grass	the small boy	the white sheep	the black bird	a new hat	you will do	(216)

SEE TO SAY

READING HIGH FREQUENCY SIGHT WORDS

Dolch Phrases—Skill Sheet 5

Directions: Say each phrase.

	Correct	Error
First Try		
Second Try		

the little chickens	then he came	if you wish	as he did	to the farm	as he said	(18)
when you come	as I do	the small boat	the new doll	the little pig	the white duck	(36)
in the water	I may get	did not fall	the little dog	what I say	has come back	(54)
if I must	to the house	in the barn	he would try	down the street	I will come	(72)
in the window	the funny man	from the tree	a big house	the red cow	from the farm	(90)
when you know	when you come	as he said	to the farm	as he did	if you wish	(108)
then he came	the little chickens	I may get	in the water	the white duck	as I do	(126)
in the barn	to the house	if I must	has come back	what I say	the little dog	(144)
did not fail	the funny man	in the window	I will go	I will come	down the street	(162)
he would try	when you come	from the farm	when you know	the red cow	a big house	(180)
from the tree	I may get	the little chickens	then he came	if you wish	as he did	(198)
in the barn	as I do	the small boat	the new doll	the little pig	the white duck	(216)

READING HIGH FREQUENCY SIGHT WORDS
Dolch Sentences—Skill Sheet 1

Directions: Say each word.

	Correct	Error
First Try		
Second Try		

The See-Saw

Jane was going to the store. She went down the street. She saw a boy and a little dog. (19)

The boy said, "Come and play with me. You may play with my dog." (33)

Jane said, "I will play with you. What can the dog do? He is not very big." (50)

"He is a good dog," said the boy. "He can run and jump. And he can ride a see-saw." (70)

"Oh, I want to see him ride," said Jane. "Where is the see-saw?" (84)

"I have it here," the boy said. (91)

He said to the dog. "Go find the see-saw. We will have a ride." (106)

The dog ran to the see-saw. (113)

"Do you like to ride?" said the boy. "Say 'yes'." (123)

The dog said, "Bow-wow!" (128)

"Look at this," said the boy. "I am up and he is down. He is up and I am down." (148)

"What a funny ride for a dog!" said Jane. (157)

Did you ever see a dog ride a see-saw? (167)

SEE TO SAY

READING HIGH FREQUENCY SIGHT WORDS
Dolch Sentences—Skill Sheet 2

Directions: Say each word.

	Correct	Error
First Try		
Second Try		

Camping Out

Some boys went camping. They were going to sleep in a brown tent. They put it up by a tree. Two of the (23)
boys went into the tent to make the beds. They had put up the tent too fast, and it soon came down on them. (47)
The boys were under it. They could not get out. The other three boys began to laugh. The boys began to call, (69)
"Help, Help! Stop laughing and give us some help! This is no fun!" (82)

After the tent was up, they made the beds. Then they all went for a walk. There were so many pretty (103)
flowers they picked some to take home. The flowers were red and blue and white. They saw some green (122)
and black berries, but they were not good to eat. They saw an old woman. One of the boys gave his flower (144)
to her. She was very pleased at that. She said to him, "Thank you for your flowers." (161)

After supper, one boy said, "Who has to do the dishes while we are away from home?" (178)

"We will all do dishes now," said another boy. (187)

"Yes, and then we will read and sing until bedtime." (197)

SEE TO SAY

READING HIGH FREQUENCY SIGHT WORDS
Dolch Passage

Directions: Say each word.

	Correct	Error
First Try		
Second Try		

The Best Thing in The World

Once upon a time there were four brothers who lived in a far away land. Their father was an old king. (21)
One day he said, "I will not live long now. Today you must start out into the world. In a year, bring back (44)
something you have found. The one who can pick the best thing shall be the new king." (61)

The first brother said, "I will look in every city or town. I will buy the best thing I can find for my father." (85)

The next two brothers said, "We will both go on fast ships over the sea. We will find something better." (105)

The last brother said, "I am going to ask the people here in our own land to tell me the best thing." The (128)
other three began to laugh. (133)

"Then you will never be king!" they said. (141)

The last brother started off. When he had gone about six miles, he met a man. (157)

"What do you carry in those big bags?" he asked. (167)

"The best thing in the world," said the man. "Those bags are full of the good nuts that fall from my five (189)
nut trees." (191)

"I don't think that will work," said the brother to himself. "I must try again." (206)

The brother went on another seven miles. He found a small brown bird. It had been hurt so he put it in (228)
his coat where it could keep warm. As he went on, he saw a little girl crying. He ran to meet her. (250)

READING HIGH FREQUENCY SIGHT WORDS
Dolch Passage (continued)

	Correct	Error
First Try		
Second Try		

"Why are you crying?" he asked. (256)

"I want to get some water from the well," she said. "We use so much. We drink cold water. We wash (277)
the clothes clean with hot water. But I do not know how to pull it up. Please show me." (296)

The brother said, "Hold this bird and I will help you. It does not fly around anymore because its (315)
wing is hurt." (318)

"Thank you. What a pretty bird!" she said. "I wish you would give it to me. If you will let me keep it, I will (343)
always be very kind to it. I will take care of it myself. I will make it grow well again." (363)

"Yes, you may have it," said the brother. So he gave her the bird and went on. (380)

At night, he went to sleep under a round yellow hay stack. When it was light again he walked on. (400)
Everyday he would walk eight or ten miles. He asked the people about the best thing in the world. (419)
Some said it was best to sing. Some said it was best to run and jump and play. Some said the green (441)
grass was best. Some liked the red and blue and white flowers best. One man said the best thing was to (462)
ride a black horse. (466)

The brother always stopped to help people who needed it. Soon he made many friends. All the people began (485)
to like him. They would say, "See, there goes the king's son. He would be just the right kind of a king for us." (509)

READING HIGH FREQUENCY SIGHT WORDS
Dolch Passage (continued)

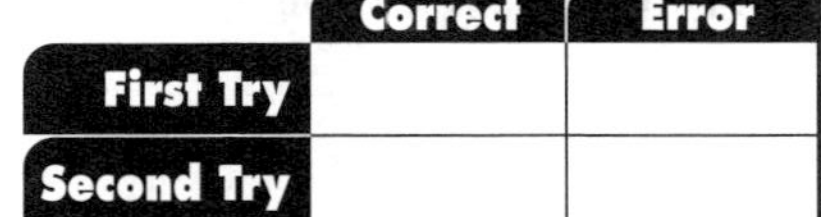

	Correct	Error
First Try		
Second Try		

Every door was open to him. The people would call to him to stop. They would ask him to come and (530)
eat with them. After he ate, he would sit down and read to the children. After he read, he showed them (551)
how to draw and write. (556)

Months went by. He still had no beautiful thing to take to his father. Just before the year was done he (577)
went home again. (580)

The time came when the king called his sons together. (590)

"What did you bring?" he asked. (596)

The other brothers had many beautiful things. (603)

"And what do you bring?" said the king to the last brother. (615)

"This is too funny!" said the other brothers. "He has nothing." (626)

"I bring only the friendship of your people," said the last brother. (638)

"And that is the best thing!" cried his father. "You shall be the new king." (653)

SEE TO SAY

READING HIGH FREQUENCY SIGHT WORDS
Isolated Words—Skill Sheet 1

Directions: Say each word.

	Correct	Error
First Try		
Second Try		

the	to	a	and	I	you	of	in	(8)
it	that	I	the	a	to	and	you	(16)
in	of	that	it	and	a	the	to	(24)
it	that	of	you	in	I	that	a	(32)
and	the	you	in	to	of	I	it	(40)
you	a	and	to	the	it	in	of	(48)
that	I	to	of	you	and	that	the	(56)
a	it	in	I	of	in	to	and	(64)
I	you	the	it	that	it	you	the	(72)
to	and	it	a	that	of	in	I	(80)

ONE MINUTE FLUENCY
SOPRIS WEST SKILL BUILDERS SERIES

SEE TO SAY

READING HIGH FREQUENCY SIGHT WORDS
Isolated Words—Skill Sheet 2

Directions: Say each word.

	Correct	Error
First Try		
Second Try		

for	on	was	he	at	with	but	are	(8)
not	this	but	on	this	was	are	at	(16)
for	with	he	not	are	at	he	this	(24)
but	not	for	was	with	on	this	he	(32)
at	but	with	are	not	was	for	on	(40)
for	are	not	but	at	this	he	was	(48)
with	on	are	this	but	not	with	for	(56)
he	at	on	was	he	are	on	not	(64)
this	was	at	with	for	but	not	with	(72)
are	he	this	was	on	for	at	but	(80)

SEE TO SAY

READING HIGH FREQUENCY SIGHT WORDS

Isolated Words—Skill Sheet 3

Directions: Say each word.

	Correct	Error
First Try		
Second Try		

had	all	they	she	so	his	is	if	(8)
up	were	so	had	is	she	all	his	(16)
they	if	were	up	all	they	had	is	(24)
if	were	so	his	she	up	is	all	(32)
his	if	she	up	had	so	they	were	(40)
up	had	his	all	they	if	she	is	(48)
were	so	if	up	his	had	is	so	(56)
she	they	all	were	is	all	his	had	(64)
if	she	up	so	they	were	up	she	(72)
all	his	had	is	were	if	so	they	(80)

ONE-MINUTE FLUENCY
SOPRIS WEST SKILL BUILDERS SERIES

SEE TO SAY

READING HIGH FREQUENCY SIGHT WORDS
Isolated Words—Skill Sheet 4

Directions: Say each word.

	Correct	Error
First Try		
Second Try		

as	my	have	by	would	we	be	me	(8)
them	said	me	would	be	by	we	said	(16)
would	have	as	them	my	me	have	be	(24)
by	as	them	said	we	as	said	my	(32)
me	we	would	be	have	them	as	by	(40)
have	them	be	my	me	said	would	we	(48)
as	by	said	we	by	be	them	would	(56)
we	me	my	have	them	my	me	have	(64)
be	would	by	my	said	as	have	me	(72)
said	be	we	as	my	would	by	them	(80)

SEE TO SAY

READING HIGH FREQUENCY SIGHT WORDS
Isolated Words—Skill Sheet 5

Directions: Say each word.

	Correct	Error
First Try		
Second Try		

get	him	see	just	from	your	like	when	(8)
will	can	just	like	your	when	him	from	(16)
see	get	can	will	like	get	just	him	(24)
when	can	will	your	see	from	when	like	(32)
see	get	from	him	just	will	your	can	(40)
just	your	like	when	get	can	him	will	(48)
from	see	your	from	just	him	can	see	(56)
like	will	get	when	him	just	get	like	(64)
your	from	when	see	can	will	when	get	(72)
him	just	your	like	will	see	from	can	(80)

ONE-MINUTE FLUENCY
SOPRIS WEST SKILL BUILDERS SERIES

SEE TO SAY

	Correct	Error
First Try		
Second Try		

READING HIGH FREQUENCY SIGHT WORDS
Isolated Words—Skill Sheet 6

Directions: Say each word.

now	do	there	no	where	or	what	come	(8)
some	big	no	now	what	do	where	there	(16)
or	come	some	big	no	now	come	what	(24)
do	where	big	there	or	some	no	now	(32)
there	or	do	where	come	what	big	some	(40)
where	now	or	do	big	there	some	no	(48)
come	what	now	or	do	no	there	big	(56)
what	some	where	come	no	or	now	do	(64)
some	big	come	what	there	where	do	where	(72)
big	there	what	no	now	come	some	or	(80)

ONE MINUTE FLUENCY
SOPRIS WEST SKILL BUILDERS SERIES

SEE TO SAY

READING HIGH FREQUENCY SIGHT WORDS
Isolated Words—Skill Sheet 7

Directions: Say each word.

	Correct	Error
First Try		
Second Try		

about	out	way	away	here	well	got	think	(8)
long	time	here	about	away	out	way	long	(16)
got	think	time	well	got	here	about	away	(24)
out	way	well	time	long	think	time	here	(32)
away	well	about	way	out	long	think	got	(40)
way	here	long	got	time	away	well	about	(48)
think	out	away	long	well	about	here	way	(56)
time	got	think	out	way	got	long	well	(64)
here	away	out	think	about	time	out	long	(72)
well	about	got	here	think	way	away	time	(80)

ONE MINUTE FLUENCY
SOPRIS WEST SKILL BUILDERS SERIES

SEE TO SAY

READING HIGH FREQUENCY SIGHT WORDS
Isolated Words—Skill Sheet 8

Directions: Say each word.

	Correct	Error
First Try		
Second Try		

went	back	much	other	an	their	take	make	(8)
every	dog	other	take	much	make	every	an	(16)
back	went	much	their	take	dog	make	back	(24)
much	other	their	back	every	take	an	dog	(32)
other	their	went	much	dog	an	their	every	(40)
take	much	an	every	their	other	back	went	(48)
their	an	dog	went	back	every	much	other	(56)
make	back	every	other	an	went	dog	much	(64)
an	make	take	dog	went	back	other	their	(72)
dog	every	back	an	other	much	went	take	(80)

SEE TO SAY

	Correct	Error
First Try		
Second Try		

READING HIGH FREQUENCY SIGHT WORDS
Isolated Words—Skill Sheet 9

Directions: Say each word.

call	came	saw	old	when	very	turn	after	(8)
letter	her	old	after	her	when	saw	turn	(16)
came	call	very	her	saw	after	letter	old	(24)
after	old	saw	came	letter	call	when	saw	(32)
saw	came	when	turn	very	letter	old	after	(40)
when	very	after	letter	call	came	turn	very	(48)
old	when	turn	very	came	turn	call	letter	(56)
very	saw	letter	call	after	old	came	when	(64)
turn	after	came	when	turn	saw	after	call	(72)
when	letter	call	saw	old	turn	very	her	(80)

ONE-MINUTE FLUENCY
SOPRIS WEST SKILL BUILDERS SERIES

SEE TO SAY

READING HIGH FREQUENCY SIGHT WORDS
Isolated Words—Skill Sheet 10

Directions: Say each word.

	Correct	Error
First Try		
Second Try		

how	then	say	day	ran	man	let	first	(8)
house	home	day	let	how	first	say	home	(16)
then	let	home	man	first	day	house	say	(24)
ran	how	then	say	home	house	man	day	(32)
home	say	let	then	man	ran	how	house	(40)
man	ran	first	house	day	say	then	man	(48)
say	day	man	first	then	how	ran	home	(56)
first	house	ran	home	how	then	say	let	(64)
day	man	say	how	house	let	home	then	(72)
let	first	house	ran	say	home	day	how	(80)

SEE TO SAY

READING HIGH FREQUENCY SIGHT WORDS
Isolated Words—Review Skill Sheets 1–10

Directions: Say each word.

	Correct	Error
First Try		
Second Try		

the	to	a	and	I	you	of	in	(8)
it	that	for	on	was	he	at	with	(16)
but	are	not	this	had	all	they	she	(24)
so	his	is	if	up	were	as	my	(32)
have	by	would	we	be	me	them	said	(40)
get	him	see	just	from	your	like	when	(48)
will	can	now	do	there	no	where	or	(56)
what	come	some	big	about	out	way	away	(64)
here	well	got	think	long	time	went	back	(72)
much	other	an	their	take	make	every	dog	(80)
call	came	saw	old	when	very	turn	after	(88)
letter	her	how	then	say	day	ran	man	(96)
let	first	house	home	said	was	were	is	(104)

ONE MINUTE FLUENCY
SOPRIS WEST SKILL BUILDERS SERIES

SEE TO SAY

READING HIGH FREQUENCY SIGHT WORDS
Isolated Words—Skill Sheet 11

Directions: Say each word.

	Correct	Error
First Try		
Second Try		

help	thought	go	side	good	has	any	many	(8)
use	more	good	many	help	side	use	go	(16)
thought	any	more	has	go	any	good	help	(24)
has	side	thought	use	many	more	help	thought	(32)
go	many	has	good	side	use	more	any	(40)
side	help	use	go	thought	good	has	more	(48)
any	many	side	help	any	go	thought	good	(56)
use	has	many	more	use	help	side	has	(64)
good	go	any	thought	more	many	go	side	(72)
more	good	help	any	has	thought	use	many	(80)

ONE-MINUTE FLUENCY
SOPRIS WEST SKILL BUILDERS SERIES

SEE TO SAY

READING HIGH FREQUENCY SIGHT WORDS
Isolated Words—Skill Sheet 12

Directions: Say each word.

	Correct	Error
First Try		
Second Try		

which	know	our	am	work	could	did	made	(8)
been	up	could	which	been	am	up	know	(16)
did	work	know	our	made	did	could	work	(24)
am	our	been	up	know	which	work	up	(32)
know	which	did	made	could	been	our	did	(40)
could	am	up	know	did	work	made	which	(48)
our	made	which	did	up	know	am	been	(56)
did	could	am	work	our	made	been	am	(64)
made	been	work	could	which	up	know	our	(72)
work	did	made	been	am	our	which	could	(80)

ONE-MINUTE FLUENCY
SOPRIS WEST SKILL BUILDERS SERIES

SEE TO SAY

READING HIGH FREQUENCY SIGHT WORDS
Isolated Words—Skill Sheet 13

Directions: Say each word.

	Correct	Error
First Try		
Second Try		

each	other	over	these	people	order	yours	into	(8)
look	may	each	into	other	yours	over	order	(16)
other	these	people	may	each	look	into	people	(24)
over	look	yours	each	into	other	these	over	(32)
may	people	other	yours	over	each	order	look	(40)
these	order	into	other	yours	may	look	each	(48)
people	yours	look	order	these	into	other	may	(56)
order	over	may	people	look	these	each	people	(64)
yours	into	order	over	may	people	these	other	(72)
into	each	these	look	order	over	may	yours	(80)

ONE MINUTE FLUENCY
SOPRIS WEST SKILL BUILDERS SERIES

SEE TO SAY

READING HIGH FREQUENCY SIGHT WORDS
Isolated Words—Skill Sheet 14

Directions: Say each word.

	Correct	Error
First Try		
Second Try		

who	before	write	read	listen	find	number	send	(8)
glad	part	find	who	send	write	read	write	(16)
before	who	send	listen	part	glad	send	listen	(24)
find	write	glad	before	who	listen	who	part	(32)
write	number	listen	part	glad	before	who	find	(40)
read	send	part	write	before	number	find	who	(48)
listen	glad	before	number	find	read	write	send	(56)
part	read	number	send	write	listen	before	read	(64)
number	find	who	glad	read	send	part	before	(72)
send	listen	read	find	number	part	glad	number	(80)

ONE MINUTE FLUENCY
SOPRIS WEST SKILL BUILDERS SERIES

SEE TO SAY

READING HIGH FREQUENCY SIGHT WORDS
Isolated Words—Skill Sheet 15

Directions: Say each word.

	Correct	Error
First Try		
Second Try		

oil	water	please	thanks	receive	name	same	minute	(8)
hour	thanks	oil	same	please	hour	minute	receive	(16)
water	same	name	hour	minute	same	oil	please	(24)
thanks	hour	water	receive	oil	minute	same	water	(32)
please	receive	thanks	name	hour	water	please	thanks	(40)
minute	oil	same	minute	name	thanks	receive	oil	(48)
receive	please	hour	water	same	minute	name	hour	(56)
same	minute	hour	please	thanks	oil	water	name	(64)
name	hour	thanks	oil	water	please	same	minute	(72)
oil	name	water	same	hour	receive	thanks	please	(80)

ONE-MINUTE FLUENCY
SOPRIS WEST SKILL BUILDERS SERIES

SEE TO SAY

READING HIGH FREQUENCY SIGHT WORDS
Isolated Words—Skill Sheet 16

Directions: Say each word.

	Correct	Error
First Try		
Second Try		

again	book	upon	horse	family	swimming	game	mad	(8)
night	right	swimming	again	game	right	horse	book	(16)
upon	mad	night	family	book	upon	right	swimming	(24)
family	horse	again	mad	night	game	family	again	(32)
book	upon	mad	swimming	horse	night	game	right	(40)
swimming	again	book	right	upon	family	night	mad	(48)
horse	game	upon	night	again	swimming	book	horse	(56)
right	family	game	mad	night	book	again	upon	(64)
game	swimming	family	game	mad	horse	upon	night	(72)
mad	right	horse	book	swimming	again	mad	family	(80)

ONE-MINUTE FLUENCY
SOPRIS WEST SKILL BUILDERS SERIES

SEE TO SAY

READING HIGH FREQUENCY SIGHT WORDS
Isolated Words—Skill Sheet 17

Directions: Say each word.

	Correct	Error
First Try		
Second Try		

room	another	brother	only	why	asked	sister	father	(8)
eat	cat	why	father	room	brother	only	another	(16)
asked	eat	sister	cat	only	another	eat	sister	(24)
why	brother	father	room	asked	cat	brother	room	(32)
another	asked	only	sister	eat	why	cat	father	(40)
only	room	cat	another	sister	eat	asked	brother	(48)
father	why	eat	brother	why	room	another	only	(56)
cat	sister	asked	father	another	sister	why	asked	(64)
brother	only	room	eat	cat	father	room	cat	(72)
sister	father	another	only	brother	asked	eat	why	(80)

SEE TO SAY

	Correct	Error
First Try		
Second Try		

READING HIGH FREQUENCY SIGHT WORDS
Isolated Words—Skill Sheet 18

Directions: Say each word.

also	car	I'm	through	always	ride	small	around	(8)
bear	found	ride	around	I'm	bear	car	through	(16)
found	always	also	small	around	found	I'm	ride	(24)
car	small	through	always	also	bear	always	car	(32)
ride	I'm	bear	around	small	through	found	also	(40)
I'm	bear	car	also	through	always	around	small	(48)
found	ride	small	I'm	car	ride	also	always	(56)
bear	through	around	found	ride	small	through	I'm	(64)
always	car	found	bear	around	also	small	found	(72)
through	also	always	car	bear	I'm	ride	around	(80)

READING HIGH FREQUENCY SIGHT WORDS
Isolated Words—Skill Sheet 19

Directions: Say each word.

	Correct	Error
First Try		
Second Try		

called	ever	never	run	something	sometimes	place	more	(8)
play	girl	ever	place	never	more	called	run	(16)
girl	something	play	sometimes	run	something	ever	never	(24)
sometimes	place	called	more	girl	play	more	sometimes	(32)
run	never	something	ever	play	called	girl	place	(40)
ever	run	place	never	sometimes	girl	play	more	(48)
something	called	girl	play	ever	never	run	called	(56)
place	more	sometimes	something	called	run	something	ever	(64)
never	sometimes	more	girl	place	play	sometimes	girl	(72)
more	place	run	called	play	ever	never	something	(80)

ONE MINUTE FLUENCY
SOPRIS WEST SKILL BUILDERS SERIES

SEE TO SAY

READING HIGH FREQUENCY SIGHT WORDS
Isolated Words—Skill Sheet 20

Directions: Say each word.

	Correct	Error
First Try		
Second Try		

fell	gave	money	should	knew	last	bed	best	(8)
left	next	knew	fell	bed	gave	should	money	(16)
best	last	next	left	should	best	fell	knew	(24)
next	bed	gave	last	money	left	next	bed	(32)
money	fell	should	best	left	knew	gave	last	(40)
gave	should	best	bed	fell	money	last	left	(48)
knew	next	left	money	best	should	next	gave	(56)
last	bed	fell	knew	next	fell	best	should	(64)
left	money	knew	gave	last	bed	money	best	(72)
next	left	bed	should	gave	last	knew	fell	(80)

ONE MINUTE FLUENCY
SOPRIS WEST SKILL BUILDERS SERIES

SEE TO SAY

READING HIGH FREQUENCY SIGHT WORDS
Isolated Words—Review Skill Sheets 11–20

Directions: Say each word.

	Correct	Error
First Try		
Second Try		

help	thought	go	side	good	has	any	many	(8)
use	more	which	know	our	am	work	could	(16)
did	made	been	up	each	other	over	these	(24)
people	order	yours	into	look	may	who	before	(32)
write	read	listen	find	number	send	glad	part	(40)
oil	water	please	thanks	receive	name	same	minute	(48)
hour	again	book	upon	horse	family	swimming	game	(56)
mad	night	right	room	another	brother	only	why	(64)
asked	sister	father	eat	cat	also	car	I'm	(72)
through	always	ride	small	around	bear	found	called	(80)
ever	never	run	something	sometimes	place	more	play	(88)
girl	fell	gave	money	should	know	last	bed	(96)
best	left	next	thought	which	could	receive	another	(104)

ONE-MINUTE FLUENCY
SOPRIS WEST SKILL BUILDERS SERIES

SEE TO SAY

READING HIGH FREQUENCY SIGHT WORDS
Isolated Words—Skill Sheet 21

Directions: Say each word.

	Correct	Error
First Try		
Second Try		

soon	because	started	still	told	food	need	put	(8)
really	tree	food	need	soon	still	put	because	(16)
tree	really	told	started	food	need	really	soon	(24)
told	still	put	because	tree	started	still	food	(32)
need	soon	tree	really	because	told	put	started	(40)
still	need	soon	told	put	because	food	really	(48)
started	tree	because	need	still	soon	started	told	(56)
tree	really	put	food	need	put	because	still	(64)
really	started	tree	soon	told	food	need	tree	(72)
because	told	still	put	started	really	soon	food	(80)

ONE-MINUTE FLUENCY
SOPRIS WEST SKILL BUILDERS SERIES

SEE TO SAY

READING HIGH FREQUENCY SIGHT WORDS
Isolated Words—Skill Sheet 22

Directions: Say each word.

	Correct	Error
First Try		
Second Try		

fire	didn’t	don’t	tell	more	gave	give	live	(8)
love	morning	more	fire	gave	didn’t	morning	don’t	(16)
give	tell	love	live	don’t	morning	fire	more	(24)
live	gave	didn’t	love	give	tell	gave	didn’t	(32)
tell	don’t	morning	more	fire	live	love	give	(40)
morning	more	fire	gave	tell	love	didn’t	live	(48)
don’t	give	tell	don’t	morning	fire	more	love	(56)
didn’t	live	gave	give	love	more	didn’t	fire	(64)
gave	morning	don’t	live	morning	tell	give	love	(72)
live	fire	love	morning	didn’t	give	tell	don’t	(80)

SEE TO SAY

READING HIGH FREQUENCY SIGHT WORDS
Isolated Words—Skill Sheet 23

Directions: Say each word.

	Correct	Error
First Try		
Second Try		

going	fun	while	than	fish	gone	heard	most	(8)
nice	tried	than	most	going	tried	fun	fish	(16)
while	nice	heard	gone	fun	than	heard	going	(24)
fish	most	gone	while	tried	nice	fish	while	(32)
gone	nice	fun	tried	than	going	most	heard	(40)
fun	than	most	going	nice	fish	while	gone	(48)
tried	heard	fish	most	while	fun	going	than	(56)
nice	gone	tried	heard	gone	most	than	nice	(64)
tried	going	heard	fun	fish	while	gone	fun	(72)
than	while	going	fish	heard	most	tried	nice	(80)

ONE MINUTE FLUENCY
SOPRIS WEST SKILL BUILDERS SERIES

SEE TO SAY

READING HIGH FREQUENCY SIGHT WORDS
Isolated Words—Skill Sheet 24

Directions: Say each word.

	Correct	Error
First Try		
Second Try		

happy	last	want	thing	move	head	lot	new	(8)
through	oh	move	happy	head	last	oh	want	(16)
thing	lot	through	new	thing	move	happy	head	(24)
oh	new	last	lot	through	want	move	oh	(32)
want	happy	head	through	new	thing	last	lot	(40)
last	move	thing	new	happy	head	want	through	(48)
lot	oh	happy	move	through	oh	thing	last	(56)
head	want	lot	new	oh	happy	head	thing	(64)
move	thing	through	want	last	lot	new	happy	(72)
thing	head	oh	last	want	through	lot	move	(80)

ONE MINUTE FLUENCY
SOPRIS WEST SKILL BUILDERS SERIES

SEE TO SAY

READING HIGH FREQUENCY SIGHT WORDS
Isolated Words—Skill Sheet 25

Directions: Say each word.

	Correct	Error
First Try		
Second Try		

door	until	under	woods	correct	wrong	yes	want	(8)
wanted	walk	correct	want	wrong	door	wanted	until	(16)
yes	under	walk	want	woods	wanted	want	correct	(24)
woods	door	wrong	wanted	until	yes	walk	under	(32)
correct	wanted	walk	door	want	under	wrong	woods	(40)
until	yes	want	correct	wanted	woods	walk	door	(48)
under	wrong	until	yes	door	correct	until	wrong	(56)
want	walk	woods	under	yes	wanted	door	yes	(64)
wrong	woods	want	until	walk	correct	under	wanted	(72)
wanted	correct	door	walk	under	until	woods	want	(80)

ONE MINUTE FLUENCY
SOPRIS WEST SKILL BUILDERS SERIES

SEE TO SAY

READING HIGH FREQUENCY SIGHT WORDS
Isolated Words—Review Skill Sheets 21–25

Directions: Say each word.

	Correct	Error
First Try		
Second Try		

soon	because	started	told	food	need	put	really	(8)
tree	fire	didn't	don't	more	gave	give	love	(16)
morning	going	while	than	gone	heard	most	nice	(24)
tried	happy	want	thing	move	head	new	through	(32)
oh	door	until	under	woods	correct	wrong	walk	(40)
want	wanted	still	live	fun	fish	last	lot	(48)
yes	because	need	heard	don't	door	woods	still	(56)
love	fun	through	put	most	more	until	correct	(64)
want	morning	soon	oh	really	nice	gave	under	(72)
wrong	thing	going	fish	started	tree	tried	give	(80)
live	walk	move	while	last	yes	told	happy	(88)
because	lot	want	head	than	really	fire	food	(96)
heard	under	didn't	wanted	new	gone	through	didn't	(104)

ONE MINUTE FLUENCY
SOPRIS WEST SKILL BUILDERS SERIES

SEE TO SAY

READING HIGH FREQUENCY SIGHT WORDS
Isolated Words—Number Words, Skill Sheet 26 (Zero–Nine)

Directions: Say each word.

	Correct	Error
First Try		
Second Try		

zero	one	two	three	four	five	six	seven	(8)
eight	nine	six	two	zero	eight	four	one	(16)
three	seven	nine	five	one	six	nine	two	(24)
four	eight	three	seven	five	zero	seven	five	(32)
one	zero	two	six	nine	four	eight	three	(40)
two	four	seven	nine	six	one	three	zero	(48)
five	eight	one	three	two	five	six	four	(56)
eight	seven	zero	nine	four	two	zero	eight	(64)
six	three	five	one	seven	nine	one	six	(72)
nine	five	four	zero	eight	three	two	seven	(80)

ONE MINUTE FLUENCY
SOPRIS WEST SKILL BUILDERS SERIES

SEE TO SAY

	Correct	Error
First Try		
Second Try		

READING HIGH FREQUENCY SIGHT WORDS
Isolated Words—Number Words, Skill Sheet 27 (Ten–Nineteen)

Directions: Say each word.

ten	eleven	twelve	thirteen	fourteen	fifteen	sixteen	seventeen	(8)
eighteen	nineteen	fourteen	eighteen	nineteen	thirteen	seventeen	twelve	(16)
eleven	ten	sixteen	fifteen	seventeen	twelve	nineteen	fourteen	(24)
fifteen	thirteen	eighteen	ten	sixteen	eleven	fourteen	eleven	(32)
twelve	seventeen	ten	sixteen	fifteen	nineteen	eighteen	thirteen	(40)
sixteen	eleven	fifteen	fourteen	eighteen	seventeen	nineteen	ten	(48)
thirteen	twelve	thirteen	eleven	ten	nineteen	twelve	fifteen	(56)
seventeen	sixteen	nineteen	eighteen	twelve	eighteen	ten	sixteen	(64)
fourteen	fifteen	seventeen	thirteen	eleven	nineteen	thirteen	seventeen	(72)
nineteen	fourteen	eleven	twelve	fifteen	ten	sixteen	eighteen	(80)

SEE TO SAY

READING HIGH FREQUENCY SIGHT WORDS

Isolated Words—Number Words, Skill Sheet 28
(Twenty, Thirty, . . . Hundred, Thousand, etc.)

Directions: Say each word.

	Correct	Error
First Try		
Second Try		

twenty	thirty	forty	fifty	sixty	seventy	eighty	ninety	(8)
hundred	thousand	sixty	twenty	ninety	thousand	forty	eighty	(16)
thirty	seventy	fifty	hundred	eighty	twenty	sixty	seventy	(24)
forty	ninety	hundred	thousand	fifty	thirty	ninety	sixty	(32)
fifty	hundred	thirty	forty	twenty	eighty	seventy	thousand	(40)
sixty	twenty	eighty	hundred	forty	ninety	thousand	fifty	(48)
seventy	thirty	ninety	sixty	hundred	fifty	twenty	forty	(56)
eighty	thousand	seventy	thirty	seventy	sixty	fifty	thirty	(64)
ninety	forty	twenty	eighty	thousand	hundred	thirty	twenty	(72)
thousand	fifty	seventy	ninety	sixty	forty	eighty	hundred	(80)

SEE TO SAY

READING HIGH FREQUENCY SIGHT WORDS

Isolated Words—Review Number Words, Skill Sheets 26–28

Directions: Say each word.

	Correct	Error
First Try		
Second Try		

zero	one	two	three	four	five	six	seven	(8)
eight	nine	ten	eleven	twelve	thirteen	fourteen	fifteen	(16)
sixteen	seventeen	eighteen	nineteen	twenty	thirty	forty	fifty	(24)
sixty	seventy	eighty	ninety	hundred	thousand	three	eighteen	(32)
five	twelve	twenty	seven	forty	sixteen	two	thirteen	(40)
seventy	nine	thousand	hundred	zero	ten	sixty	eight	(48)
fourteen	eighty	one	nineteen	fifteen	ninety	thirty	seventeen	(56)
six	fifty	eleven	four	twelve	fifteen	eight	three	(64)
forty	ten	two	seventy	nineteen	four	twenty	fourteen	(72)
seven	eighty	seventeen	fifty	one	eleven	ninety	sixty	(80)
hundred	nine	thousand	five	eighteen	thirty	six	thirteen	(88)
zero	sixteen	six	eight	zero	five	eleven	thirteen	(96)
seven	two	ten	one	twelve	three	fourteen	four	(104)

ONE MINUTE FLUENCY
SOPRIS WEST SKILL BUILDERS SERIES

SEE TO SAY

READING HIGH FREQUENCY SIGHT WORDS
Isolated Words—Color Words, Skill Sheet 29

Directions: Say each word.

	Correct	Error
First Try		
Second Try		

color	red	blue	yellow	green	orange	purple	brown	(8)
white	black	green	orange	yellow	purple	color	blue	(16)
red	brown	black	white	purple	black	green	orange	(24)
brown	yellow	white	blue	red	color	yellow	purple	(32)
blue	orange	brown	color	white	green	red	black	(40)
yellow	color	red	black	blue	brown	white	green	(48)
orange	purple	yellow	brown	orange	red	black	white	(56)
green	blue	color	purple	black	blue	brown	yellow	(64)
white	green	purple	red	color	orange	white	red	(72)
purple	orange	black	green	brown	yellow	blue	color	(80)

SEE TO SAY

	Correct	Error
First Try		
Second Try		

READING HIGH FREQUENCY SIGHT WORDS
Isolated Words—Days of Week, Skill Sheet 30

Directions: Say each word.

Sunday	Monday	Tuesday	Wednesday	Thursday	Friday	Saturday	week	(8)
weekend	weekday	Wednesday	Sunday	Friday	week	Monday	weekend	(16)
Tuesday	Thursday	Saturday	weekday	Monday	Saturday	weekend	Sunday	(24)
week	Wednesday	Friday	Thursday	Tuesday	weekday	Wednesday	Monday	(32)
weekend	Saturday	week	Tuesday	weekday	Sunday	Friday	Thursday	(40)
Monday	Friday	weekday	Saturday	Sunday	Wednesday	week	Tuesday	(48)
Thursday	weekend	Thursday	week	Saturday	weekend	Sunday	weekday	(56)
Wednesday	Tuesday	Friday	Monday	week	Tuesday	Thursday	Wednesday	(64)
weekday	Friday	Sunday	weekend	Saturday	Monday	weekday	Tuesday	(72)
Thursday	Sunday	Wednesday	Saturday	weekend	Friday	Monday	week	(80)

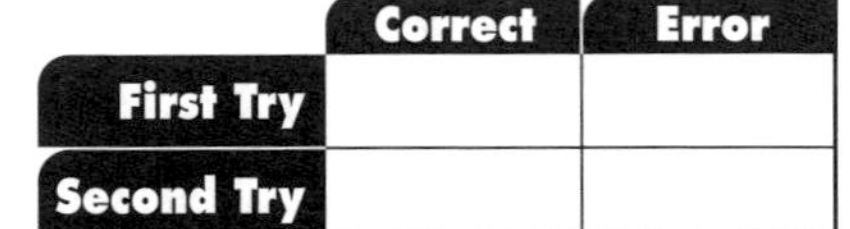

SEE TO SAY

READING HIGH FREQUENCY SIGHT WORDS
Isolated Words—Months of Year and Seasons, Skill Sheet 31

Directions: Say each word.

	Correct	Error
First Try		
Second Try		

January	February	March	April	May	June	July	August	(8)
September	October	November	December	winter	spring	summer	fall	(16)
autumn	months	year	calendar	February	November	March	months	(24)
June	April	spring	October	May	fall	January	July	(32)
winter	June	calendar	September	December	July	May	August	(40)
February	year	September	January	summer	October	autumn	April	(48)
June	winter	fall	September	January	November	July	February	(56)
December	March	months	spring	August	calendar	October	year	(64)
summer	May	June	April	November	autumn	May	August	(72)
December	months	winter	March	spring	January	fall	summer	(80)

ONE MINUTE FLUENCY
SOPRIS WEST SKILL BUILDERS SERIES

SEE TO SAY

READING HIGH FREQUENCY SIGHT WORDS
Isolated Words—Review Skill Sheets 30–31

Directions: Say each word.

	Correct	Error
First Try		
Second Try		

Monday	January	winter	August	Friday	May	calendar	December	(8)
spring	Tuesday	February	week	September	Saturday	June	summer	(16)
weekend	fall	Wednesday	March	years	October	Sunday	July	(24)
autumn	weekday	months	Thursday	April	November	Friday	winter	(32)
February	summer	September	Sunday	March	spring	December	June	(40)
autumn	Monday	fall	October	Tuesday	years	May	Saturday	(48)
months	weekend	January	weekday	November	April	week	July	(56)
Thursday	August	calendar	Wednesday	May	Monday	June	Tuesday	(64)
years	Wednesday	November	Thursday	fall	summer	Friday	autumn	(72)
Saturday	weekday	July	calendar	April	weekend	December	October	(80)
August	spring	years	January	week	winter	October	months	(88)
March	September	February	Sunday	October	January	June	February	(96)
Sunday	April	spring	autumn	winter	fall	summer	calendar	(104)

Beginning Reading—Isolated Words and Sentences

Grades K–2

ONE MINUTE FLUENCY
SOPRIS WEST SKILL BUILDERS SERIES

SEE TO SAY

	Correct	Error
First Try		
Second Try		

BEGINNING READING—ISOLATED WORDS AND SENTENCES

Isolated Words—High Frequency Words, Preprimer Level
(is, the, in, go, will, not, on, he, and, I, to, we, you, it, a)

Directions: Say each word.

a	and	the	will	you	in	it	is	(8)
I	to	he	not	we	You	go	it	(16)
Will	to	and	is	on	I	the	We	(24)
On	a	In	you	I	Go	we	will	(32)
not	he	to	and	Is	We	In	On	(40)
Go	He	the	it	to	I	will	A	(48)
and	in	Is	will	you	on	the	go	(56)
We	not	a	he	to	we	not	In	(64)
Will	it	Go	and	He	I	the	On	(72)
A	on	will	In	It	he	we	You	(80)
Will	it	Go	and	He	I	the	On	(88)
We	not	a	he	to	we	not	In	(96)
and	in	Is	will	you	on	the	go	(104)

SEE TO SAY

BEGINNING READING—ISOLATED WORDS AND SENTENCES

Rebus Sentences—15 Basic High Frequency Words

Directions: Say each word.

	Correct	Error
First Try		
Second Try		

He is on the . We will not go. Go to the . He and I will go . A is (21)

in it. The will not go. The is in a . I will go in the . It is (42)

in the . The is in a . He will not go. He is in the . The (62)

is in the . You will not go. Is the in the ? He and I will go. Is the (84)

in the ? I will go. The is in the . I will not go in. He is on the . (106)

Go in the . He will go. The is in it. The will not go. Go in the . (127)

The is in the . Is the in the ? The is on the . The will (148)

not go. Will the go? The is not in the . The will not go in. (167)

Go to the . I will not go. He will go in a . He and I will go. He (187)

is in the . I will go in the . A is in it. He and I will go. It is in the . (212)

It is in the . You will go in the . The will not go. It is in the . (233)

ONE-MINUTE FLUENCY
SOPRIS WEST SKILL BUILDERS SERIES

SEE TO SAY

	Correct	Error
First Try		
Second Try		

BEGINNING READING—ISOLATED WORDS AND SENTENCES

Rebus Sentences—15 Basic High Frequency Words (plus get, no, yes)

Directions: Say each word.

He is in the  . (5)

The 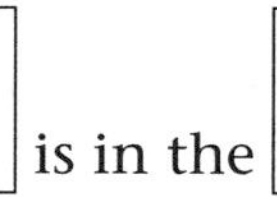 is in the . (11)

The is in the  . (17)

We will go in it and get the  . (26)

The is on the  . (32)

We will go on the  . (38)

Will you go on the ? (44)

No, I will not go. (49)

The 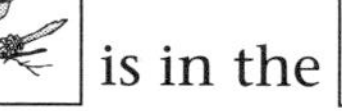 is in the  . (55)

The is in the  . (61)

The is not in the  . (68)

He is in the . (73)

I will not go in. (78)

Will you go in the  ? (84)

Yes, I will go in. (89)

No, the is not on the  . (97)

BEGINNING READING—ISOLATED WORDS AND SENTENCES

Rebus Sentences—High Frequency and Color Words, Skill Sheet 1 (red, yellow, blue)

Directions: Say each word.

	Correct	Error
First Try		
Second Try		

The will go in the red . (8)

The will go in the red . (16)

We will get a red . (22)

We will go to the red . (29)

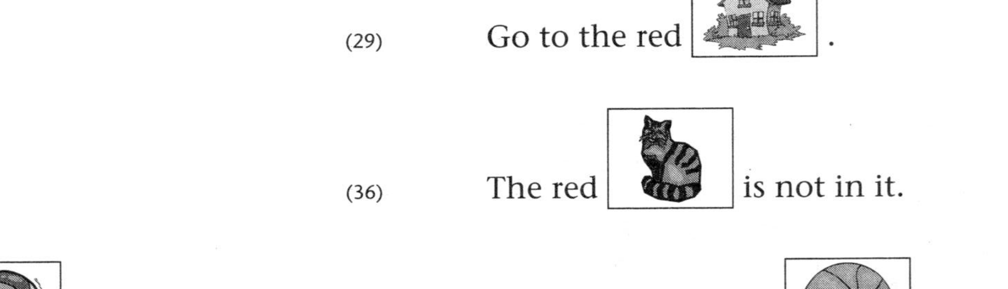

The is on the red . (36)

The will not get the red . (44)

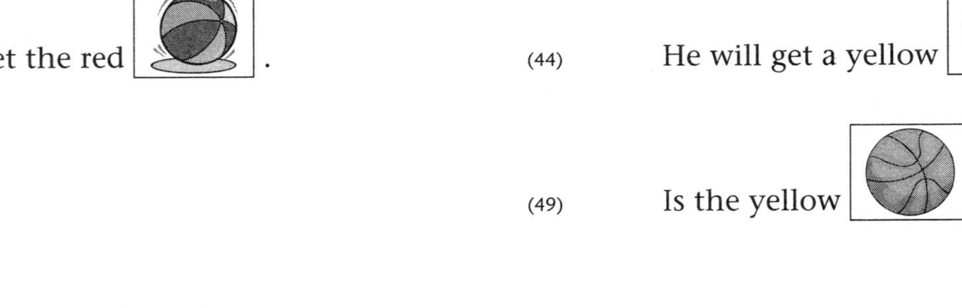

You will get a . (49)

I will get a . (54)

The is red. (58)

The is not yellow. (63)

We will get a yellow . (69)

Go to the red . (74)

The red is not in it. (81)

He will get a yellow . (87)

Is the yellow in the blue ? (95)

No, it is in the yellow . (102)

SEE TO SAY

BEGINNING READING—ISOLATED WORDS AND SENTENCES

Rebus Sentences—High Frequency and Color Words, Skill Sheet 2

Directions: Say each word.

	Correct	Error
First Try		
Second Try		

Go to the green  . (5)

A brown will go to the green . (14)

The brown will get an orange . (22)

He will go on the brown . (29)

The brown will go in a blue . (38)

The black is in the brown . (46)

I will get a brown  . (52)

He is in a green 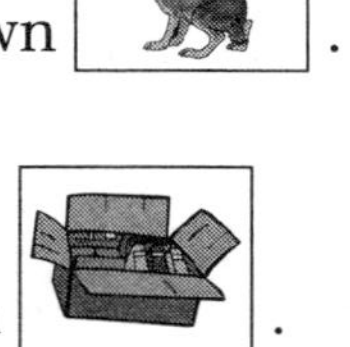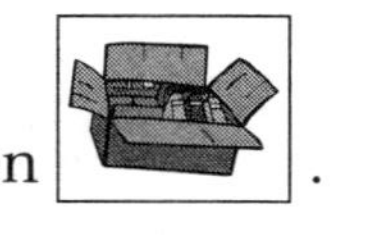 . (58)

We will get a red 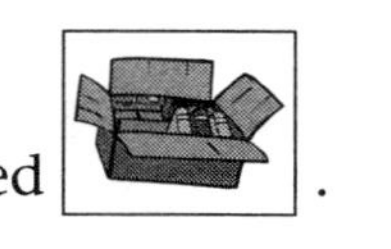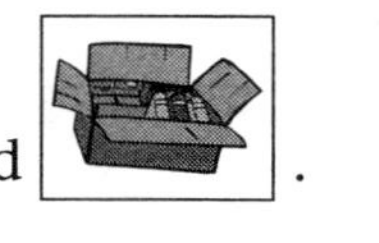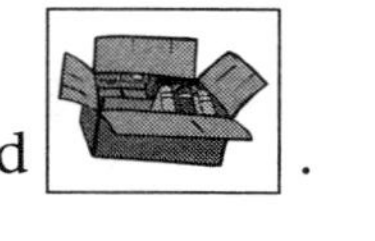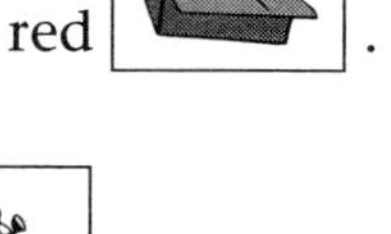 . (64)

A black 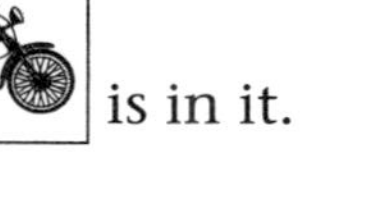 is in it. (70)

The black  will get an orange and a blue . (82)

The brown 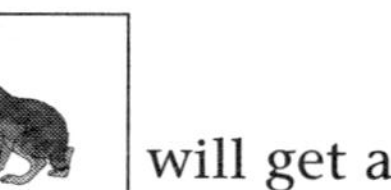 will get a yellow and purple  . (92)

SEE TO SAY

BEGINNING READING—ISOLATED WORDS AND SENTENCES

Rebus Sentences—High Frequency and Color Words, Skill Sheet 3

Directions: Say each word.

	Correct	Error
First Try		
Second Try		

Is the blue [ ] in the yellow [ ] ? (8)

No, he is in the blue  [ ] . (15)

Go get the blue  [ ] . (20)

He and I will go in the purple  [ ] . (29)

Will the purple  [ ] go? (34)

No, the purple  [ ] will not go. (41)

Go to the red  [ ] . (46)

The purple  [ ] is in it. (52)

The purple  [ ] is not on the blue [ ] . (61)

It is not on a purple 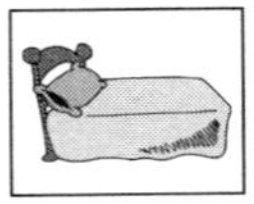 [ ] . (68)

It is on an orange 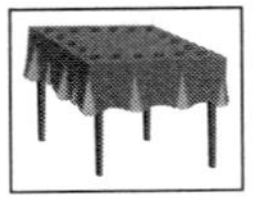 [ ] . (74)

Get the purple  [ ] . (78)

I will get an orange  [ ] . (84)

I will go to a green  [ ] . (91)

I see the orange  [ ] . (96)

It is by a green  [ ] . (102)

A blue  [ ] is in the green [ ] . (110)

The blue  [ ] is not in the red [ ] . (119)

SEE TO SAY

	Correct	Error
First Try		
Second Try		

BEGINNING READING—ISOLATED WORDS AND SENTENCES

Rebus Sentences—High Frequency, Color and Number Words (One–Six)

Directions: Say each word.

I will get one black [ ] . (6)

You can get three red  [ ] . (12)

He will get two yellow  [ ] . (18)

We will have six red and yellow  [ ] . (26)

I go to a green  [ ] . (32)

I see six orange [ ] . (37)

You get three orange  [ ] . (42)

One orange  [ ] is in a green [ ] . (50)

Will you get one green  [ ] ? (56)

No, I can not get one green  [ ] . (64)

I can get four purple cats. (70)

He will get three brown cats. (76)

We will have four purple cats and three brown cats. (86)

You can get five [ ] . (91)

The five  [ ] will be blue. (97)

Will the five blue  [ ] go? (103)

Yes, the five blue  [ ] will go. (110)

We will have five blue cars. (116)

SEE TO SAY

	Correct	Error
First Try		
Second Try		

BEGINNING READING—ISOLATED WORDS AND SENTENCES
Rebus Sentences—High Frequency, Color and Number Words (One–Ten)

Directions: Say each word.

We have six 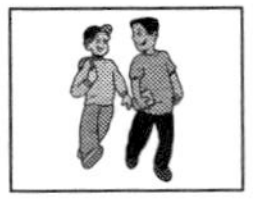 in a brown 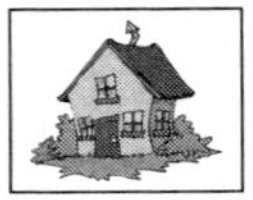 . (8)

We have seven 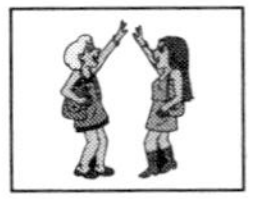 in a yellow 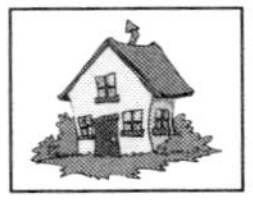 . (16)

The six 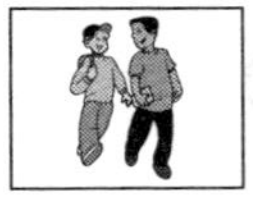 go in one black 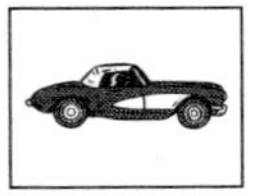 . (24)

Will the seven 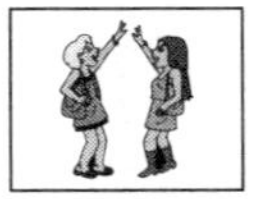 go in a yellow 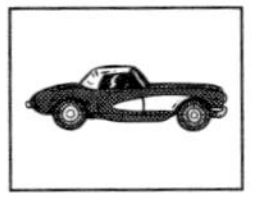 ? (33)

No, the seven 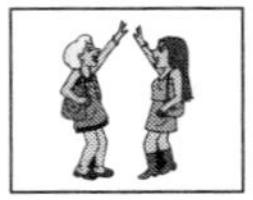 will go in two yellow 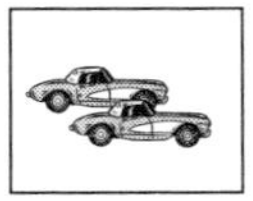 . (43)

Seven and one will be eight. ●●●●●●●● (49)

Four and four will be eight. (55)

Five and three will be eight. (61)

Six and two will be eight. (67)

You will be eight. (71)

Eight and one will be nine. ▲▲▲▲▲▲▲▲▲ (77)

Five and four will be nine. (83)

Six and three will be nine. (89)

Seven and two will be nine. (95)

Will you be nine? (99)

No, I will be ten. (104)

Five and five will be ten. ○○○○○○○○○○ (110)

Six and four will be ten. (116)

Will seven and three be ten? (122)

Yes, seven and three will be ten. (129)

BEGINNING READING—ISOLATED WORDS AND SENTENCES

Sentences—Preprimer Level

Directions: Say each word.

	Correct	Error
First Try		
Second Try		

1. I have a ball. (4)

2. Father and I can go. (9)

3. The ball is blue. (13)

4. Father is big. (16)

5. The blue ball is big. (21)

6. I can jump. (24)

7. Come and see father. (28)

8. I can go down. (32)

9. See father go. (35)

10. I can run for the ball. (41)

SEE TO SAY

BEGINNING READING—ISOLATED WORDS AND SENTENCES

Sentences—Primer Level 1

Directions: Say each word.

	Correct	Error
First Try		
Second Try		

1. We all are in the boat. (6)

2. I will go to the birthday. (12)

3. Father and I are boys. (17)

4. Mother is at the house. (22)

5. I will run away. (26)

6. I have a birthday. (30)

7. The boat is red. (34)

8. The boy is in the boat. (40)

9. I see the boy in the boat. (47)

10. I can run, but father can not. (54)

SEE TO SAY

	Correct	Error
First Try		
Second Try		

BEGINNING READING—ISOLATED WORDS AND SENTENCES
Sentences—Primer Level 2

Directions: Say each word.

1. I came to the farm. (5)
2. Did the boy have fun? (10)
3. Do you want to play? (15)
4. The dog is at the farm. (21)
5. My doll is in the box. (27)
6. The duck will eat at the farm. (34)
7. The farm is fun. (38)
8. Did you find my ball? (43)
9. My doll is fun to play with. (50)
10. I will eat the duck. (55)

SEE TO SAY

BEGINNING READING—ISOLATED WORDS AND SENTENCES

Sentences—Primer Level 3

Directions: Say each word.

	Correct	Error
First Try		
Second Try		

1. The blue dog is funny. (5)

2. I am a good girl. (10)

3. The boy has a kitten. (15)

4. He is a funny kitten. (20)

5. Can you help mother? (24)

6. I want to go home. (29)

7. The kitten is fun. (33)

8. Do you know my name? (38)

9. The dog is good. (42)

10. I like to laugh. (46)

SEE TO SAY

BEGINNING READING—ISOLATED WORDS AND SENTENCES

Sentences—Primer Level 4

Directions: Say each word.

	Correct	Error
First Try		
Second Try		

1. Do you like my hat? (5)
2. Mr. Dog is my name. (10)
3. My mother said no. (14)
4. I will go now. (18)
5. He is on the boat. (23)
6. Mother has one boy and one girl. (30)
7. Father is out at the farm. (36)
8. I have a kitten for a pet. (43)
9. Please find the boy. (47)
10. Put the doll in the box. (53)

SEE TO SAY

BEGINNING READING—ISOLATED WORDS AND SENTENCES

Sentences—First Grade, Skill Sheet 1

Directions: Say each word.

	Correct	Error
First Try		
Second Try		

1. The garden is about green. (5)

2. I will go after the baby. (11)

3. Mother is after me again. (16)

4. The animal is around the barn. (22)

5. Would you like an apple? (27)

6. The boy ran around the house. (33)

7. She is as funny as a monkey. (40)

8. I will ask if I can go. (47)

9. The baby is in the bed. (53)

10. The cow is back in the barn. (60)

SEE TO SAY

BEGINNING READING—ISOLATED WORDS AND SENTENCES

Sentences—First Grade, Skill Sheet 2

Directions: Say each word.

	Correct	Error
First Try		
Second Try		

1. I put the doll in a brown bag. (8)
2. The barn is by the hill. (14)
3. I will be in the barn. (20)
4. The brown bear ran fast. (25)
5. We began to look at the book. (32)
6. The dog is black. (36)
7. I like to look at books. (42)
8. My kitten is brown. (46)
9. The bear is by the house. (52)
10. Can you call me? (56)

SEE TO SAY

BEGINNING READING—ISOLATED WORDS AND SENTENCES

Sentences—First Grade, Skill Sheet 3

Directions: Say each word.

	Correct	Error
First Try		
Second Try		

1. Can you run fast? (4)
2. We have two feet. (8)
3. I was first to see the bear. (15)
4. Do you like to fish? (20)
5. A fish can not fly. (25)
6. The girl has four animals. (30)
7. The boy is my friend. (35)
8. I ran from the bear. (40)
9. Can you see the garden? (45)
10. I gave the cow to him. (51)

SEE TO SAY

BEGINNING READING—ISOLATED WORDS AND SENTENCES

Sentences—First Grade, Skill Sheet 4

Directions: Say each word.

	Correct	Error
First Try		
Second Try		

1. Give me a brown cow. (5)

2. Can you guess my name? (10)

3. I saw a green bear. (15)

4. The cow had to run. (20)

5. My mother is happy to see me. (27)

6. The animal has a brown head. (33)

7. I heard the boat go by. (39)

8. I said "Hello" to the children. (45)

9. The hen and the cow ate the apple. (53)

10. Her feet are cold. (57)

SEE TO SAY

BEGINNING READING—ISOLATED WORDS AND SENTENCES

Sentences—First Grade, Skill Sheet 5

Directions: Say each word.

	Correct	Error
First Try		
Second Try		

1. The horse ran up the hill. (6)

2. Go after him! (9)

3. His friend could give him a book. (16)

4. How did you find the door? (22)

5. I like to see her horse. (28)

6. If you hurry, I will let you go. (36)

7. I will let the horse go to the barn. (45)

8. The baby can go to the door. (52)

9. The children can live in the house. (59)

10. Ask the baby if he can color. (66)

BEGINNING READING—ISOLATED WORDS AND SENTENCES
Sentences—First Grade, Skill Sheet 6

Directions: Say each word.

	Correct	Error
First Try		
Second Try		

1. The man gave him a monkey. (6)

2. May I go to the door? (12)

3. I met the bear at the barn. (19)

4. I put my mitten on the bed. (26)

5. The monkey is fun to see. (32)

6. I like to get up in the morning. (40)

7. Mrs. May is her name. (45)

8. I have many dogs. (49)

9. I must go home. (53)

10. Do you like my name? (58)

	Correct	Error
First Try		
Second Try		

BEGINNING READING—ISOLATED WORDS AND SENTENCES
Sentences—First Grade, Skill Sheet 7

Directions: Say each word.

1. I will never find my mitten. (6)

2. The new doll is in the box. (13)

3. I live next to the garden. (19)

4. I go to bed at night. (25)

5. My nose gets cold in the morning. (32)

6. The dog is old. (36)

7. Can you open the door? (41)

8. I can go if mother will let me. (49)

9. I like the other kitten. (54)

10. Our house is on the other hill. (61)

SEE TO SAY

BEGINNING READING—ISOLATED WORDS AND SENTENCES

Sentences—First Grade, Skill Sheet 8

Directions: Say each word.

	Correct	Error
First Try		
Second Try		

1. The cow jumped over the house. (6)

2. I like to paint with blue paint. (13)

3. My birthday party was fun. (18)

4. Will you give me a penny? (24)

5. My mother is pretty. (28)

6. The rabbit has a white nose. (34)

7. Rain, rain, go away. (38)

8. The rabbit can hop down the road. (45)

9. I sat up all night. (50)

10. You must go to school. (55)

SEE TO SAY

BEGINNING READING—ISOLATED WORDS AND SENTENCES
Sentences—First Grade, Skill Sheet 9

Directions: Say each word.

	Correct	Error
First Try		
Second Try		

1. I have a brown shoe. (5)

2. I like to sleep at night. (11)

3. Snow is white. (14)

4. Go to sleep so I can go to sleep. (23)

5. I have some rabbits. (27)

6. Rain makes a splash on the road. (34)

7. Stay in bed if you must sleep. (41)

8. I will open the store the next morning. (49)

9. Mother will tell me a story. (55)

10. My friend lives on my street. (61)

SEE TO SAY

BEGINNING READING—ISOLATED WORDS AND SENTENCES
Sentences—First Grade, Skill Sheet 10

Directions: Say each word.

	Correct	Error
First Try		
Second Try		

1. Tell me about the new store. (6)

2. I think that is a funny story. (13)

3. Did you think about the party? (19)

4. Morning is a good time of day. (26)

5. Father took me to school. (31)

6. Tell me the thing you like to do best. (40)

7. The green tree is tall. (45)

8. I have two old shoes. (50)

9. The monkey is under the bed. (56)

10. Mrs. Rabbit told us a story. (62)

SEE TO SAY

BEGINNING READING—ISOLATED WORDS AND SENTENCES

Sentences—First Grade, Skill Sheet 11

Directions: Say each word.

	Correct	Error
First Try		
Second Try		

1. He is a very good boy. (6)

2. The red wagon sat next to the road. (14)

3. We will walk down the street. (20)

4. Rain gives us new water. (25)

5. When did the woman go to work? (32)

6. I will wish for a rabbit. (38)

7. I can find the way to school. (45)

8. Mother and I were at the store. (52)

9. I will sleep when it is night. (59)

10. When I work, I get a penny. (66)

SEE TO SAY

BEGINNING READING—ISOLATED WORDS AND SENTENCES
Sentences—Second Grade, Skill Sheet 1

Directions: Say each word.

	Correct	Error
First Try		
Second Try		

1. The man is running across the yard. (7)
2. I am afraid to ride on the train. (15)
3. I ran along the back of the house. (23)
4. She is always the one at the door. (31)
5. I gave him an apple. (36)
6. Can you have him go another way? (43)
7. Is there any candy in the bag? (50)
8. No, I ate all the candy. (56)
9. I want a big, yellow balloon. (62)
10. The basket will be full of toys. (69)

SEE TO SAY

BEGINNING READING—ISOLATED WORDS AND SENTENCES
Sentences—Second Grade, Skill Sheet 2

Directions: Say each word.

	Correct	Error
First Try		
Second Try		

1. The hills are beautiful. (4)
2. I was the first one in bed. (11)
3. I have been to the farm. (17)
4. I can get to the house before you can. (26)
5. Who is that behind the barn? (32)
6. I heard the bell ring. (37)
7. This is the best balloon there is. (44)
8. Did you see the red and yellow bird? (52)
9. I will see if I can do better. (60)
10. The wind can blow the tree over. (67)

SEE TO SAY

BEGINNING READING—ISOLATED WORDS AND SENTENCES
Sentences—Second Grade, Skill Sheet 3

Directions: Say each word.

	Correct	Error
First Try		
Second Try		

1. Both mother and father came to the play. (8)

2. I will bring you a green balloon. (15)

3. She brought us a basket with toys in it. (24)

4. I will build a house. (29)

5. Don't put your hand on it, it will burn. (38)

6. I like to ride on the bus. (45)

7. I was so busy that I missed the bus. (54)

8. I brought an animal for the cage. (61)

9. Mother can buy me a new toy. (68)

10. Did you see the bee buzz in the house? (77)

SEE TO SAY

BEGINNING READING—ISOLATED WORDS AND SENTENCES
Sentences—Second Grade, Skill Sheet 4

Directions: Say each word.

	Correct	Error
First Try		
Second Try		

1. I always like to buy a new coat. (8)

2. The red cookie was the best. (14)

3. I can take care of the corn in the garden. (24)

4. You live in the city and I live in the country. (35)

5. Did you cry when the ball hit you? (43)

6. Come to my house and we will cut the cake. (53)

7. Wash your hands before you come to dinner. (61)

8. Does your dog like to eat his dinner? (69)

9. I can dress in the morning. (75)

10. Each of us will go to the circus. (83)

SEE TO SAY

BEGINNING READING—ISOLATED WORDS AND SENTENCES
Sentences—Second Grade, Skill Sheet 5

Directions: Say each word.

	Correct	Error
First Try		
Second Try		

1. I saw an elephant at the circus. (7)

2. Did you ever see a yellow bird? (14)

3. We have a fence in the back yard. (22)

4. There is a fence around the field. (29)

5. Every time it rains, I run to the house. (38)

6. The fire will burn you if you put your hand in it. (50)

7. He gave me five balloons for my birthday. (58)

8. I had to clean the floor in my room. (67)

9. I found the bird in the cage. (74)

10. It is a fine day to go to the country. (84)

SEE TO SAY

BEGINNING READING—ISOLATED WORDS AND SENTENCES

Sentences—Second Grade, Skill Sheet 6

Directions: Say each word.

	Correct	Error
First Try		
Second Try		

1. The front yard is better to play in. (8)

2. What game do you like best? (14)

3. I am glad you brought me a dog. (22)

4. The goat ate all the clothes. (28)

5. Mother has gone to get my coat. (35)

6. We got to go to the city to see the circus. (46)

7. I like to see the corn grow in my garden. (56)

8. My mitten will keep my hand warm. (63)

9. Can you see that hat on the dog? (71)

10. The bell is high on the shelf. (78)

SEE TO SAY

BEGINNING READING—ISOLATED WORDS AND SENTENCES
Sentences—Second Grade, Skill Sheet 7

Directions: Say each word.

	Correct	Error
First Try		
Second Try		

1. I am so hungry I could eat a cow. (9)
2. The fence will keep the elephant in the yard. (18)
3. She knew the best book to read. (25)
4. I am afraid of the large dog. (32)
5. She brought me the last cookie. (38)
6. I like to get a letter. (44)
7. It is always fun to play the game. (52)
8. Can you build a chimney? (57)
9. Before you go, put your coat on. (64)
10. Can I have another cookie? (69)

Reading Passages

Note: Pre-First and Second Grade Level reading passages are reproduced with permission from Hofmeister, *Isseesam* series.

READING PASSAGES

Pre-First Grade Level—Skill Sheet 1

Directions: Say each word. If you finish before the end of the timing, go back to the beginning and start over.

	Correct	Error
First Try		
Second Try		

I see Sam. (3)

See! See! (5)

I see. I see. (9)

Sam? (10)

I see Sam. I see. (15)

Sam! Sam! (17)

Sam! Sam! See Sam! (21)

See Sam? (23)

I see. I see Sam! (28)

See Sam. (30)

I see Sam! I see Sam! (36)

	Correct	Error
First Try		
Second Try		

READING PASSAGES

Pre-First Grade Level—Skill Sheet 2

Directions: Say each word. If you finish before the end of the timing, go back to the beginning and start over.

See Sam. I see Sam. (5)

Sam! Sam! (7)

See! Sam. Sam. See. See. (12)

I am Sam! I am Sam! (18)

Sam. Sam. (20)

I am Sam. See! (24)

Sam! I see. I see. (29)

See! (30)

See, Sam, see! (33)

I see Sam. See! See! (38)

	Correct	Error
First Try		
Second Try		

READING PASSAGES

Pre-First Grade Level—Skill Sheet 3

Directions: Say each word. If you finish before the end of the timing, go back to the beginning and start over.

Mat. (1)

I am Mat. See me. (6)

I see Sam. (9)

See me, Sam. (12)

See Mat. See Sam. (16)

I see Mat. (19)

See me. See me, Sam! (24)

I am Sam. See me! (29)

I see! See Mat. See Sam. (35)

I see Mat! See, Mat. See Mat. (42)

See Mat. See Sam. (46)

READING PASSAGES

Pre-First Grade Level—Skill Sheet 4

Directions: Say each word. If you finish before the end of the timing, go back to the beginning and start over.

	Correct	Error
First Try		
Second Try		

Meet Mit. (2)

See Sam. Meet Mit. (6)

Meet me, Sam. I am Mit. (12)

Meet me, Sis. I am Mit. (18)

Sis, meet Sam. (21)

Sam, Sam! Meet Sis. Meet Sis, Sam. (28)

See Mit. See Sis. See Sam. (34)

See Sam. (36)

I am Sam! I am Sam! (42)

Sam, Sam. Sam, meet Sis. (47)

Sis, meet Sam. See Sam. See Sis. (54)

ONE MINUTE FLUENCY
SOPRIS WEST SKILL BUILDERS SERIES

	Correct	Error
First Try		
Second Try		

READING PASSAGES

Pre-First Grade Level—Skill Sheet 5

Directions: Say each word. If you finish before the end of the timing, go back to the beginning and start over.

See me. (2)

Meet me. Meet me. I am Mit. (9)

See me. I sit on it. (15)

I am Sis. (18)

I sit in it. See me sit in it. (27)

See Mat. See Mit sit in it. See Sis sit in it. (39)

See me. See me sit in it. (46)

See! See! See it. See it on Sam. (54)

See me on it. See Sis on it. (62)

See Mat on it. See Sam on it. (70)

SEE TO SAY

READING PASSAGES

Pre-First Grade Level—Skill Sheet 6

Directions: Say each word. If you finish before the end of the timing, go back to the beginning and start over.

	Correct	Error
First Try		
Second Try		

Sam sat. (2)

I sit in it. (6)

Sit in it, Mat. Sit in it. (13)

I sat in it. I see it on Mat. (22)

Mat sat in it. See me sit in it. (31)

Sam sat in it. See Mat. See Sam. (39)

I sit in it. I sit in it. (47)

Mat sat in it. Sam sat in it. (55)

I am Sam. I sit in it. Sit on me, Mat. (66)

Sam sat on it. Mat sat on Sam. (74)

	Correct	Error
First Try		
Second Try		

READING PASSAGES

Pre-First Grade Level—Skill Sheet 7

Directions: Say each word. If you finish before the end of the timing, go back to the beginning and start over.

I am Ann. See me. Ann sat. (7)

I am Nan. Meet me. Meet me. I am Mit. (17)

Mit and Nan sit. See. See this, Nan. (25)

Nan and Mit see it. See this on me, Nan. (35)

Nan is in it. Nan and Mit see Ann. (44)

Ann, Ann. See this! It is on me. (52)

Ann and Mit and Nan sit. (58)

SEE TO SAY

READING PASSAGES

Pre-First Grade Level—Skill Sheet 8

Directions: Say each word. If you finish before the end of the timing, go back to the beginning and start over.

	Correct	Error
First Try		
Second Try		

This is Mit. See that on me. (7)

I am Sam. See that, Sis. Is that Sam? I am mad! (19)

Is that Sam? I am mad! (25)

I am Sam. See me. See me. (32)

I am Sam. That is Mit. I am mad. (41)

I am mad. See Mit. See that. (48)

Mit is mad. See that on Sam. (55)

See that on me. That is Sam. See Sam. (64)

ONE MINUTE FLUENCY
SOPRIS WEST SKILL BUILDERS SERIES

SEE TO SAY

	Correct	Error
First Try		
Second Try		

READING PASSAGES

Pre-First Grade Level—Skill Sheet 9

Directions: Say each word. If you finish before the end of the timing, go back to the beginning and start over.

Who am I? I am Nell. See me. Meet me. Am I (12)
Nell? Yes, I am. (16)
See this. What is it? See me in this. Who am I? (28)
What is this? Who is this? Is it Nell? Yes, it is. (40)
See the hat on me. I run and run. This is fun. See (53)
the feet run. (56)
What is that? Is it the sun? Yes, it is the sun. (68)
Nell fell. See the feet. Who fell? Is it Nell? Yes, (79)
it is. (81)
Who am I? I am Nell. What am I? I am a mess. (94)

ONE-MINUTE FLUENCY
SOPRIS WEST SKILL BUILDERS SERIES

SEE TO SAY

READING PASSAGES

Pre-First Grade Level—Skill Sheet 10

Directions: Say each word. If you finish before the end of the timing, go back to the beginning and start over.

	Correct	Error
First Try		
Second Try		

We will run. Sam will run. Nell will run. Who (10)

will run with them? (14)

Let me! Let me! I will run. It is fun! (24)

We will run. It is fun! (30)

See the feet? The feet will run. The feet will run (41)

on this. The feet will run on that. (49)

See Sam? Sam runs well. (54)

See Nell? She runs well. (59)

See Mit? Mit runs with them. Is it fun? (68)

Sam runs. Nell runs. Mit runs with them. It is fun. (79)

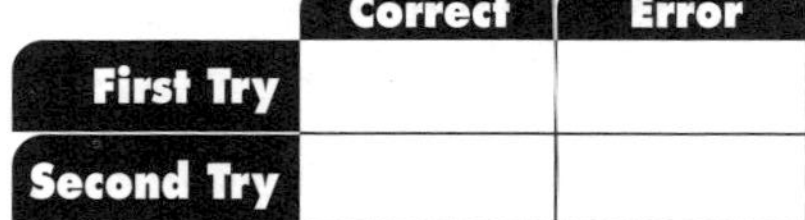

READING PASSAGES

First Grade Level—Skill Sheet 1

Directions: Say each word. If you finish before the end of the timing, go back to the beginning and start over.

Tim and Ed and Meg met a big, fat red hen. (11)

Can Tim pet the hen? Will the hen let him? Yes, Tim (23)

can. The hen let him. (28)

Meg fed the red hen. The hen let Meg. (37)

Ed let the big red hen get on his lap. Yes, he did. (50)

Ed and Tim and Meg got to pat the red hen. (61)

The red hen is a pet. (67)

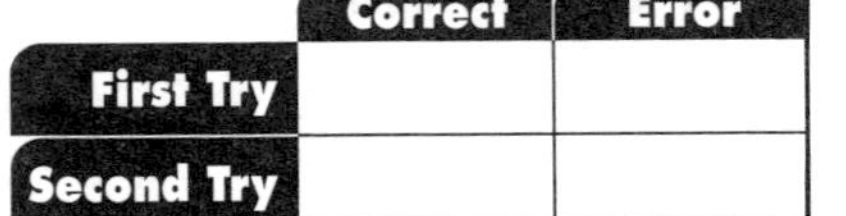

SEE TO SAY

READING PASSAGES

First Grade Level—Skill Sheet 2

Directions: Say each word. If you finish before the end of the timing, go back to the beginning and start over.

	Correct	Error
First Try		
Second Try		

The sun is up. It is hot, hot, hot. (9)

Pug is a pig. Pug is in the sun and is hot, hot, hot. (23)

He is big and hot. (28)

Mud is in a big tin tub. Pug can run and go get into (42)

the tub. He can go rub in the mud. The mud is not hot. (56)

The sun is hot, but Pug is not. The mud is fun. (68)

Pug is a fun pig. (73)

ONE MINUTE FLUENCY
SOPRIS WEST SKILL BUILDERS SERIES

SEE TO SAY

	Correct	Error
First Try		
Second Try		

READING PASSAGES
First Grade Level—Skill Sheet 3

Directions: Say each word. If you finish before the end of the timing, go back to the beginning and start over.

The sun is hot. Pug the pig is hot, but Meg is not hot. (14)

Meg is in the sun but she is not hot. She is on a (28)
wet jet. The jet is red. (34)

Tim is not hot. Tim is wet. He is on a wet jet. (47)

Let it rip, Tim. Let it zip and let it dip. (58)

Meg can jet up to Tim. Tim can jet up to Meg. It is (72)
fun to jet. It is fun to get wet. (81)

Pug is not on a jet, but Pug is not hot. Pug can sip (95)
pop. Yum. (97)

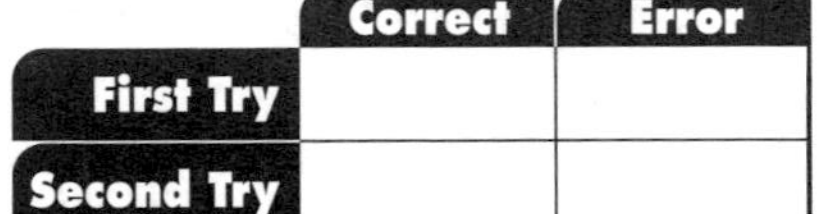

SEE TO SAY

READING PASSAGES
First Grade Level—Skill Sheet 4

Directions: Say each word. If you finish before the end of the timing, go back to the beginning and start over.

	Correct	Error
First Try		
Second Try		

Big Jim had a big red rig. The big rig had to dig a big pit. (16)

Jim is big. Did Big Jim fit in the big rig? Yes, the big (30)

man did fit in his cab. (36)

Dig, Jim, dig. Dig a big pit. (43)

Tim is a pal to Jim. Jim let Tim sit in the big rig. Tim (58)

can dig. Tim can dig in the pit. (66)

Dig, Tim, dig. Dig a big pit. (73)

ONE MINUTE FLUENCY
SOPRIS WEST SKILL BUILDERS SERIES

SEE TO SAY

READING PASSAGES
First Grade Level—Skill Sheet 5

Directions: Say each word. If you finish before the end of the timing, go back to the beginning and start over.

	Correct	Error
First Try		
Second Try		

Dot is a sick tot. Dot is sad and sick. (10)

Mom can rock Dot. Mom can pat Dot on the back and (22)
tuck Dot into bed. (26)

But Dot can not nap. Dot is mad and sick and sad. (38)

Can Dad pick up the sad tot? Yes, he can. Dad can rock (51)
Dot. Dad can pat Dot on the back. Dad can tuck Dot (63)
into bed. (65)

Dad is in luck! Dot can nap. Dot can get well. (76)

ONE MINUTE FLUENCY
SOPRIS WEST SKILL BUILDERS SERIES

SEE TO SAY

	Correct	Error
First Try		
Second Try		

READING PASSAGES
First Grade Level—Skill Sheet 6

Directions: Say each word. If you finish before the end of the timing, go back to the beginning and start over.

The duck can peck. It can peck on the rock. It can peck (13)

on the dock. (16)

The duck can dip in and get wet. (24)

Yuck! Yuck! What bad luck! The duck got in the mud (35)

and muck! (37)

Look! Look! The duck got a big cod. Quack, quack! (47)

Ick! Ick! What bad luck. The duck got a sock. Yuck! (58)

Peck, peck, peck. The duck can peck. What will it get? (69)

	Correct	Error
First Try		
Second Try		

READING PASSAGES

First Grade Level—Skill Sheet 7

Directions: Say each word. If you finish before the end of the timing, go back to the beginning and start over.

Zap is a dog. He is at the pond. A fish is in the pond. (15)
Zap has a wish. He must get the fish! (24)
Zap will jump on the fish. Splash! The fish can dash. (35)
Zap is not as fast as the fish. (43)
Zap will rush to the fish. Splash! The fish can shimmy. (54)
Zap is not as fast as the fish. (62)
What will Zap do? Zap will sit still. He will not dash (74)
and he will not rush. He will hush. Shhh. (83)
The fish will rest. Hush. (88)
Dash! Zap gets the fish. He gets his wish—fresh fish! (99)

ONE MINUTE FLUENCY
SOPRIS WEST SKILL BUILDERS SERIES

SEE TO SAY

READING PASSAGES
First Grade Level—Skill Sheet 8

Directions: Say each word. If you finish before the end of the timing, go back to the beginning and start over.

	Correct	Error
First Try		
Second Try		

A bobcat is a big cat. It is not a pet and it is not a pal. (17)

A bobcat bit a dog. It bit a big hog. A hog is a big pig. (33)

Zap is not a bobcat. Zap is a tomcat. He is a pet. Mom (47)

and Dad can pat him. (52)

Zap can hop onto the cot. Zap can hop onto Mom's lap. (64)

A tomcat is a pal. A bobcat is not a pal. (75)

ONE MINUTE FLUENCY
SOPRIS WEST SKILL BUILDERS SERIES

SEE TO SAY

READING PASSAGES
First Grade Level—Skill Sheet 9

Directions: Say each word. If you finish before the end of the timing, go back to the beginning and start over.

	Correct	Error
First Try		
Second Try		

Meg dug in the mud. Meg set a seed into the mud. The (13)
sun got hot. Meg had a fun job. Meg had to get the (26)
seed wet. (28)

Look at the plant. The plant got a bit big in the hot sun. (42)
Meg set a rod into the mud. The plant can run up the rod. (56)
It can hug the rod. (61)

The plant got big. Meg got a big cup. Met set ten seed (74)
pods into the cup. Mom got the cup and Meg got a (86)
big hug. (88)

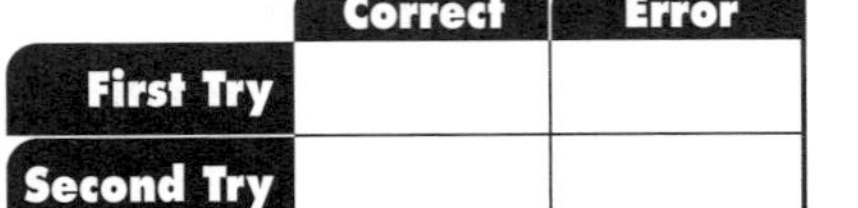

SEE TO SAY

READING PASSAGES

First Grade Level—Skill Sheet 10

Directions: Say each word. If you finish before the end of the timing, go back to the beginning and start over.

	Correct	Error
First Try		
Second Try		

The sun felt hot. Tim, Nick, and Pug, the pig, went to (12)
the pond. (14)

Tim dug his hand into the sand. Nick dug his cup into (26)
the sand. (28)

Pug just sat on his back in the damp sand. (38)

The kids dug and dug. Tim dug just as fast as Nick. (50)

Nick dug a big ramp. Tim set up a dock at the end. (63)

Nick and Tim had fun at the pond. Pug had a nap at (76)
the pond. (78)

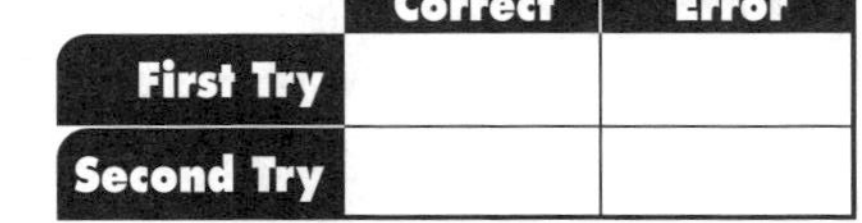

SEE TO SAY

	Correct	Error
First Try		
Second Try		

READING PASSAGES
First Grade Level—Skill Sheet 11

Directions: Say each word. If you finish before the end of the timing, go back to the beginning and start over.

Tim has a pen and a big pad. On his pad, he can make (14)
a big hulk. His hulk is as big as a van. (25)

The hulk has a fat neck and a tusk. He has a big hump (39)
on his back. (42)

Bump, bump, bump. His hulk can bump and jump (51)
and hit. He can go fast. He can run as fast as (63)
the wind. (65)

He can lift up a fat log. He can bend a big rock. He (79)
can hunt on the land and in the pond. He is just a (92)
big hulk. (94)

ONE MINUTE FLUENCY
SOPRIS WEST SKILL BUILDERS SERIES

SEE TO SAY

READING PASSAGES
First Grade Level—Skill Sheet 12

Directions: Say each word. If you finish before the end of the timing, go back to the beginning and start over.

	Correct	Error
First Try		
Second Try		

Meg is happy. She has a gift. What is it? (10)
The gift is a pet. It is a fuzzy bunny. The bunny (22)
is Dizzy. (24)

Dizzy is not big. She is just itty-bitty. She can fit into (36)
a hat. Hop, hop, hop. The Dizzy is in the hat and the (49)
hat can hop. (52)

Dizzy is silly! Dizzy can twist fast. She can spin and (63)
get dizzy. She is a silly, funny bunny! (71)

Meg can let her pet on her lap. She can pat Dizzy. The (84)
itty-bitty bunny is happy. What fun! (90)

SEE TO SAY

READING PASSAGES

First Grade Level—Skill Sheet 13

Directions: Say each word. If you finish before the end of the timing, go back to the beginning and start over.

	Correct	Error
First Try		
Second Try		

Meg's bed is bumpy and lumpy. Dizzy, the itty-bitty (9)
bunny, is in the bed. (14)

Off, Dizzy! Off the bed! No pets in bed. (23)

Dot's crib is lumpy and bumpy. Zap is a kitty. The (34)
kitty is in the crib. Off, Zap, off the crib! No pets (46)
in bed. (48)

Pug is in Tim's bed. Tim's bed is muddy and dusty. (59)
Pug is a pig. (63)

Get off, Pug! Get the pig off the bed! No pets in bed. (76)
No lumpy, bumpy, dusty, pets in bed! (83)

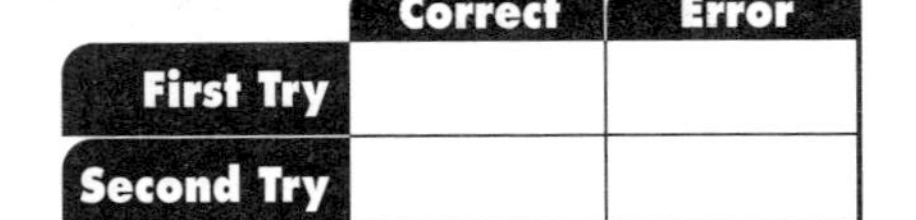

SEE TO SAY

READING PASSAGES
First Grade Level—Skill Sheet 14
Directions: Say each word. If you finish before the end of the timing, go back to the beginning and start over.

	Correct	Error
First Try		
Second Try		

It is sunny. Dizzy is Meg's bunny. Meg will let (10)
Dizzy hop up the hill. The bunny will nip the dill on (22)
the hill. She will nip the mint as well. (31)

Yummy! Dizzy is happy. (35)

Hiss! Hiss! Oh, no! It is a bobcat! The big cat is (47)
hidden in the grass. A bobcat can kill a bunny. Run, (58)
Dizzy! Run back to Meg. Go fast! Huff and puff. (68)

Meg yells to Dad. She picks up the upset bunny. She (79)
hugs Dizzy. (81)

Dad sets grass and mint in the pen. Meg sets Dizzy (92)
in the pen. Dizzy fills her tummy. Dizzy is lucky and (103)
happy and well. (106)

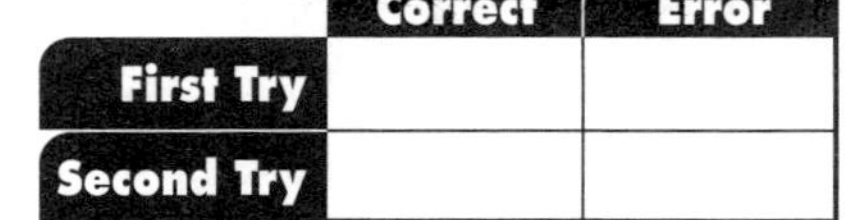

	Correct	Error
First Try		
Second Try		

READING PASSAGES
First Grade Level—Skill Sheet 15

Directions: Say each word. If you finish before the end of the timing, go back to the beginning and start over.

It can sing. It can sing a song. What is it? (11)
It is a finch in a nest. The finch can sing a song. (24)
What is this? It can hang. It can swing on a branch. (36)
What is it? (39)
It is a bat on a long branch. The bat has wings (51)
and fangs. (53)
What is this? It can ring. Ring-a-ling-ling. The finch (62)
will not sing its song. The bat will not hang on the (74)
branch. What is it? (78)
It is a cat with a bell! Ding-a-ling-ling. If the bell rings, (90)
the finch will not sing. If the bell rings, the bat will not (103)
hang. If the bell rings, Zap the cat is getting into things. (115)

SEE TO SAY

READING PASSAGES
First Grade Level—Skill Sheet 16

Directions: Say each word. If you finish before the end of the timing, go back to the beginning and start over.

	Correct	Error
First Try		
Second Try		

Stan can flip on the grass. He can flip and twist and (12)
spin. Do not trip, Stan. Do not slip. (20)

Fran can toss a rock on the grid. Fran can stand on the (33)
top of the rock. Stand still, Fran. Do not trip. (43)

Tip can jump. She can jump up past the stick. She can (55)
jump up past the flag. Do not slip, Tip. (64)

Meg must sit. She has a cast and cannot skip and jump. (76)
She cannot flip, but she can clap. Meg claps as Stan (87)
flips and Fran hops and Tip jumps. (94)

Stan can print on Meg's cast. Fran and Tip can print (105)
on Meg's cast. (108)

Meg is glad. She claps. What fun! (115)

	Correct	Error
First Try		
Second Try		

READING PASSAGES

First Grade Level—Skill Sheet 17

Directions: Say each word. If you finish before the end of the timing, go back to the beginning and start over.

Big Bob and his buddy Jimmy were ganging up on Tim. Big (12)
Bob was hitting Tim. (16)

Wes was Tim's buddy. "Stop it!" he said to Big Bob and (28)
Jimmy. The kids did not stop. Wes went running to get (39)
Mr. Ling. (41)

Mr. Ling was the boss. He ran fast to help Tim. Mr. Ling (54)
ran yelling, "Stop!" He was telling Jimmy and Big Bob to (65)
back off. (67)

Mr. Ling had Jimmy and Big Bob sit on the bench. He said, (80)
"Do not get off the bench." (86)

Big Bob and Jimmy felt sad. Mr. Ling said, "No kicking and (98)
no punching!" Jimmy and Big Bob said, "Yes, Mr. Ling." (108)

ONE MINUTE FLUENCY
SOPRIS WEST SKILL BUILDERS SERIES

SEE TO SAY

READING PASSAGES
First Grade Level—Skill Sheet 18

Directions: Say each word. If you finish before the end of the timing, go back to the beginning and start over.

	Correct	Error
First Try		
Second Try		

Tim went with Beth and Pug the pig to the pond. The (12)
pals went on a path to the pond. (20)

The path was wet. It was wet with thick mud. Rush! (31)
Dash! Pug went fast on the wet path. Thud! He fell in (43)
the thick muck. Pug was just a mucky mess. (52)

At the pond, Pug had a bath. The pond was his bathtub! (64)
He had a bath with a lot of fish. (73)

Tim had a sack of fish food. Tim and Beth fed the fish (86)
a bit of food. (90)

Tim had lots of fun at the pond with Pug and Beth. (102)

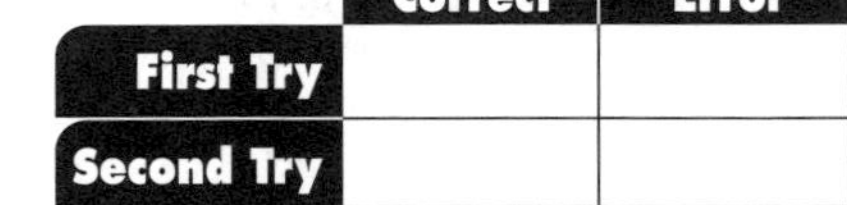

SEE TO SAY

	Correct	Error
First Try		
Second Try		

READING PASSAGES
First Grade Level—Skill Sheet 19

Directions: Say each word. If you finish before the end of the timing, go back to the beginning and start over.

At sunset, the children were all resting in bed. At sunset, the ten (13)
thin bats were hanging on a branch. The skinny bats were hungry. (25)

Ten bugs went past. Buzzy, buzzy, buzz. The silly bugs (35)
were buzzing. (37)

Zip! The bats went to get the bugs. The ten thin bats were (50)
winging. The bats were zinging. The silly bugs were dashing. (60)
The silly bugs were rushing. (65)

The lucky bats were catching all the bugs. The lucky bats (76)
were munching. (78)

At sunset, all the children were resting in bed. At sunset, ten (90)
fat bats were hanging on a branch. The fat bats were happy (102)
and were resting. (105)

	Correct	Error
First Try		
Second Try		

READING PASSAGES

First Grade Level—Skill Sheet 20

Directions: Say each word. If you finish before the end of the timing, go back to the beginning and start over.

As Zap the cat slept, mommy finch sat on a bunch of eggs. (13)
She kept the eggs hot. It was such a big job. Mommy finch (26)
did not get off the nest. The eggs did not get chilly. Mommy (39)
did not get much lunch. (44)

Crack! Mommy felt an egg chip and hatch. It was an (55)
itty-bitty finch. It was fuzzy and skinny. Mommy finch (64)
went to get lunch. The chick sat on the eggs. The itty-bitty (76)
chick kept the eggs hot. (81)

Crack! Chip! The chick felt an egg hatch. (89)

Mommy went back to the nest with lunch. She fed the (100)
thin chicks. (102)

And Zap? He was not a problem, not for the finch. (113)

READING PASSAGES

Second Grade Level—Skill Sheet 1

Directions: Say each word. If you finish before the end of the timing, go back to the beginning and start over.

	Correct	Error
First Try		
Second Try		

Star and Storm had lots of jobs to do. Star raked the yard and cut the grass. Star (18)
did all the hard jobs. All Storm did was play. (28)

Star wanted to play, but she still had a job to do. She went down to the fishpond (46)
to fish. (48)

She sat down on the bank. Then her fishing pole fell into the fishpond. It sank. (64)
She bent down to try to get it. (72)

“I cannot get the fishing pole back,” Star said. “I do not want to go home without (89)
it. I am upset. I must get it back.” (98)

Star jumped into the fishpond. She sank far, far down. Just then the Pond King (113)
swam by. (115)

“I'm upset,” Star said to him. “My fishing pole fell into this fishpond. I cannot (130)
go home without it.” (134)

“Do not be upset,” said the Pond King. “I'll get the pole for you. You must do (151)
lots of jobs for me. First, rake my yard.” (160)

“I'll be glad to,” said Star. She did all the things the Pond King asked. Then the (177)
Pond King said, “Thank you,” and gave Star her fishing pole. (188)

SEE TO SAY

READING PASSAGES

Second Grade Level—Skill Sheet 2

Directions: Say each word. If you finish before the end of the timing, go back to the beginning and start over.

	Correct	Error
First Try		
Second Try		

Kim, Jack, Jill, and Russ went for a hike in the park. All of them hiked to the hilly part (20)
of the park. They ran up and down the hills. The time went by fast. It was getting late. The (40)
sky started turning dark. (44)

"We must go home now!" Jill said. "We must not be out late." (57)

"Let's go up this big hill." Russ said. "It's a shortcut. In a short time we'll be at home." (76)

"It's getting stormy," said Jill. "It's not safe to go up a hill in a storm. Let's take the path." (96)

"But that will make us later," said Russ. "Let's try the hilly shortcut. The storm will not (113)
get us." (115)

All of them started up the steep hill. "This hill is getting steeper and steeper," said (131)
Kim. "This is a tricky hike." (137)

"And it's getting late. It's getting later and later," said Jill. (148)

The sky turned darker. Then the storm started. In a short time the storm had made the (165)
hill muddy. (167)

Jill, Jack, and Kim made it to the top. Russ did not. Russ had slipped down the muddy (185)
hill. He was stuck! They all helped him to the top of the hill. Russ was dirty, but he (204)
was safe. (206)

	Correct	Error
First Try		
Second Try		

READING PASSAGES
Second Grade Level—Skill Sheet 3

Directions: Say each word. If you finish before the end of the timing, go back to the beginning and start over.

When Russ woke up, he jumped out of bed. He went to see his mom and dad. (17)

"Get up, Mom and Dad," he yelled. "Today is the day we go on the hay ride." (34)

"Maybe," said Mom, "but I'm tired. Let me stay in bed a while longer." (48)

"But it's very nice outside today," said Russ. "Say yes, Mom!" (59)

Then Jill came in. "Mom," she asked, "is today the day we go on the hay (75)
ride?" Jill asked. (78)

"I had hoped to stay home," Dad said. "I am tired, also." (90)

"Go with us, Dad. Go with us!" yelled Jill and Russ. (101)

"I do not think I want to go," said Dad. "Hay rides are fun, but hay makes (118)
me sneeze." (120)

"It will be fun," said Mom. "Be a sport and go with us. We can stay all day at (139)
the lake. We can get a mule and cart there. What do you say to that?" (155)

"Yes," said Dad, "I'll go. First, let's pack a big lunch." (166)

All of them helped make the lunch. They all went on the hay ride and had a (183)
great time. (185)

SEE TO SAY

	Correct	Error
First Try		
Second Try		

READING PASSAGES
Second Grade Level—Skill Sheet 4

Directions: Say each word. If you finish before the end of the timing, go back to the beginning and start over.

It was a hot day in Ant Land. All the ants were by the pond. They were resting (18)
in the grass when a huge beast jumped out of a tree. It came down to the pond. (36)

"Quick! Quick!" yelled an ant. "We must hide." (44)

The ants ran in back of a rock. The beast bent down by the pond and had a (62)
drink. Then he picked out a place to rest and sat down. He sat on top of the ant (81)
hill. Soon he started to snore. (87)

All the ants were upset. "What a bad place for him to be!" said an ant. "If he (105)
stays there, we can't get into the ant hill." (114)

Soon, Moony the ant came by with her cart. Moony did not see the beast. (129)
Moony drove up onto the beast and stopped. "This is funny," she said. "What (143)
is this big hill doing here?" (149)

The ants came out from the back of the rock. "Get down, get down!" they (164)
yelled. "You are on top of a huge beast, and he is on top of the ant hill." (182)

"Well he can't stay here on the ant hill. He must go," said Moony. "I'll make (198)
him go." She rang the bell on her cart and woke the beast up. He woke up. Then (216)
he jumped up and ran away. All the ants ran to thank Moony for her help. They (233)
made her queen of all the ants. (240)

SEE TO SAY

READING PASSAGES
Second Grade Level—Skill Sheet 5

Directions: Say each word. If you finish before the end of the timing, go back to the beginning and start over.

	Correct	Error
First Try		
Second Try		

On a hot day in May, Timmy went to the pond to fish. As he was sitting on the (19)
bank fishing, he spotted an old teddy bear next to a tree. Timmy picked up the (35)
big bear. He played with teddy bear for a while. (45)

Soon it was time to eat lunch. Timmy had packed a lunch and the spread from (61)
his bed. He put down his spread and sat down to eat. (73)

He ate lots and lots of bread. Timmy wanted to give bread to the bear, but the (90)
bear did not take it. He just sat there, for he was just a teddy bear. (106)

Timmy jumped up and picked a pear from a nearby tree. "Maybe my bear wants (121)
a pear," said Timmy. He gave the pear to the bear. Of all things, the bear ate it! (139)

When the bear ate the pear, he sat up slowly. The pear must have had magic in it. (157)
Soon he was running in the grass. Timmy jumped up and down. He was glad to (173)
have the bear play with him. (179)

Timmy and the bear ran up the path. The path went up a steep hill. It was hard, (197)
but they made it. At the top they stopped to rest before going home. (211)

SEE TO SAY

	Correct	Error
First Try		
Second Try		

READING PASSAGES
Second Grade Level—Skill Sheet 6

Directions: Say each word. If you finish before the end of the timing, go back to the beginning and start over.

There was an old woman who made soup on cold days. She made the best (15)
soup in all the land. She was glad to give out soup to the small birds and (32)
beasts that stopped by her place. They said her soup was the best. (45)

The birds and beasts told of the old woman's soup to all they met from far (61)
and near. All of them wanted to try it, too. (71)

When the first snows fell, they came to the old woman's home. Big beasts and (86)
small beasts came from far and near to try the old woman's soup. The giants (101)
came, the bears came, and the birds came. So did the ants and all kinds of bugs. (118)

The woman looked up from her sink. She saw the beasts waiting for soup. (132)
"There are a lot of beasts out there," she said. "I do not think I can give all of (151)
them soup, but I will try." (157)

All that day she made soup for the beasts. By the next day she had run out. (174)
There were still lots and lots of beasts who wanted soup. "What will I do?" (189)
asked the woman. "They want to eat, but I cannot keep up with them." (203)

Just then a fly came and landed next to the woman. The fly said, "I can help (220)
you. Make a bowl of soup. Then put a whole sack of salt in it. No beasts or (238)
birds or bugs will want to eat your soup. It will be too salty." (252)

	Correct	Error
First Try		
Second Try		

READING PASSAGES

Second Grade Level—Skill Sheet 7

Directions: Say each word. If you finish before the end of the timing, go back to the beginning and start over.

Nip and Pop were hungry, so they went to town to look for something to eat. By (17)
and by they came to a shop. There were lots of things to play with in the shop. (35)

"This shop looks like fun," said Nip. "Let's see what things we can find in (50)
here." Pop and Nip went into the shop. The shop was run by a jolly giant. He (67)
made things for all the giants in town. (75)

"My!" said Nip. "Look how big all the things are. It will take a long time to (92)
see them." (94)

Pop wanted to play with a truck, and Hip wanted to try a drum. Just as they (111)
were ready to start, the giant came into the room. Nip and Pop hid in back of a (129)
teddy bear. The giant did not see them. (137)

"I'm hungry and the icebox is empty," he said. "I think I'll go out and get (153)
some food to make a sandwich. It will take a lot to fill me up." Soon the giant (171)
was out of the shop. (176)

Nip said, "We have had a long walk. Let's take a nap." They jumped on a huge (193)
top and took a nap. (198)

SEE TO SAY

	Correct	Error
First Try		
Second Try		

READING PASSAGES
Second Grade Level—Skill Sheet 8

Directions: Say each word. If you finish before the end of the timing, go back to the beginning and start over.

Ana, Rosa, and Carlos went to see Uncle Ray. They took a bus to his home at the edge (19)
of town. Ana rang the bell and Uncle Ray came out. (30)

"We have come to see your horse," said Carlos. (39)

"I'll be glad to show her to you," said Uncle Ray. "Come with me and I'll take you to (58)
see her." (60)

They all walked out to the backyard. A big brown horse stood looking at them from the (77)
edge of the fence. (81)

"What a nice horse," said Ana as they stood nearby. (91)

"Her name is Fudge," said Uncle Ray. "She is a good and gentle horse." (105)

Rosa reached into her lunch sack and pulled out a pear. "May I give Fudge something (121)
to eat?" she asked. (125)

"Give her some of your pear," said Uncle Ray. "She will like that." (138)

"May we have a ride on Fudge, Uncle Ray?" Carlos asked. (149)

"Since I am here, you may each have a turn to ride," said Uncle Ray. "She is a gentle (168)
horse, but you must be careful." (174)

First, it was Rosa's turn to ride on Fudge. Uncle Ray helped her into the saddle while (191)
Ana and Carlos sat on the fence. Rosa let Fudge walk slowly up and down the riding ring. (209)
Then she hopped off the horse and it was Ana's turn to ride. (222)

SEE TO SAY

	Correct	Error
First Try		
Second Try		

READING PASSAGES

Second Grade Level—Skill Sheet 9

Directions: Say each word. If you finish before the end of the timing, go back to the beginning and start over.

Gail put her face next to the window. She looked out at the falling rain. She was trying (18)
to see if her horse, Candy, was in the pen. (28)

"Zack Brown's mom just called," said Gail's mom, walking into the room. "Zack's cold (42)
is bad, so I'll have to go over there. Gail, why are you looking out the window?" (59)

"I'm trying to see if Candy is okay," said Gail. "I wanted to ride her, but now I'm afraid (78)
it is going to rain all day." (85)

"Well, today is not a good day for riding. It's raining too hard for you to go outside," (103)
said Mom. "Stay inside and paint. If the rain stops, then you can go out." (118)

Gail sat down and started to paint a small, gray ship with a tall sail. She worked very (136)
carefully and very slowly. Suddenly she stopped. She put down her paints and walked (150)
to the window. She looked out and saw Candy. Then she spotted some mud sliding (165)
down a nearby hill. The mud was heading for Candy's pen! She had to do something fast. (182)

Gail raced outside to the pen. She pulled the gate back. "Hurry!" said Gail to Candy. "Get (199)
out of the pen." (203)

Candy raced out of the pen and into the backyard. Both Candy and Gail were safe. (219)

SEE TO SAY

	Correct	Error
First Try		
Second Try		

READING PASSAGES
Second Grade Level—Skill Sheet 10

Directions: Say each word. If you finish before the end of the timing, go back to the beginning and start over.

Sue and her mom had an old home in town. One day Sue's mom called to her while she (19)
was sitting on the front lawn. (25)

"Sue," she said. "It's time we fixed some things around here. Let's take down this old (41)
fence and put up a new one. You pull down the old fence, and I'll get the wood to make (61)
a new one." (64)

"I'll try," said Sue. "But this old fence may be hard to pull down. The ground around it (82)
is hard and rocky." (86)

"Just do your best," said her mom. Then she left to get the new wood. (101)
As soon as her mom was gone, Sue started to pull down the fence. She pushed on it (119)
but nothing happened. She pulled on it, and still the old fence did not come out of (136)
the ground. (138)

"What can I do?" said Sue as she threw a rock at the fence. "I can't get this old fence (158)
out of the way." She sat down on the grass to think. "I can paint it!" she said. "I can (178)
make it look just like new if I paint it. I think I'll paint it blue." (194)

Sue went inside to get the paint. She saw a big blue can. She took the can outside, took (213)
off the lid, and threw the lid on the ground. Then she went to work on the fence. Soon (232)
the fence was covered with thick blue paint. (240)

	Correct	Error
First Try		
Second Try		

READING PASSAGES
Second Grade Level—Skill Sheet 11

Directions: Say each word. If you finish before the end of the timing, go back to the beginning and start over.

Willy the Walrus was good at many things, like floating on his back and swimming. But (16)
Willy wasn't very good at telling time. Each day Willy went outside to play with his (32)
friends. And each day his mom told him when to come home. But Willy was always (48)
late. His mom was very upset with him. (56)

"If you do not come home on time," said his mom, "I will not let you go outside at all. (76)
I worry when you are late." (82)

"I do not want to be late," said Willy. "I just do not know what time it is." (100)

"Well, if you want to go outside," said Mom, "you need to find a way to keep track of (119)
the time." (121)

That afternoon Willy sat down to see a TV show. When the show came on, he saw a (139)
seal holding a watch. (143)

"Good afternoon to all my friends," said the seal. "Today I'm selling a wonderful watch. (158)
This watch works under water. It's made just for creatures of the sea. You can wear it (175)
while you swim! You can wear it while you wash! Hurry, get yours today!" (189)

The very next day Willy got the watch. He took it out of the box and put it on. Now he (210)
could go outside and not come home late. (218)

READING PASSAGES
Second Grade Level—Skill Sheet 12

Directions: Say each word. If you finish before the end of the timing, go back to the beginning and start over.

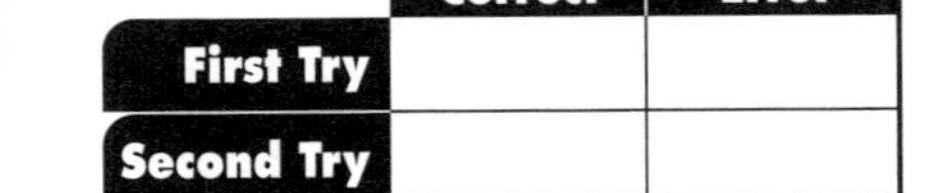

	Correct	Error
First Try		
Second Try		

Kim the Tiger had a baby. All the creatures in the jungle came to visit her. (16)
"Let's see the new tiger," the anteater said to Kim. "He must be big and strong. If he's (34)
at all like his mom, he'll be king of the jungle." (45)
Kim showed the baby tiger to all her friends. "I'm going to call him Tiny," she told them. (63)
"He's still very small but he's just a few days old." (74)
Time went by, but Tiny the Tiger didn't get bigger. Tiny ate the right foods, sipped lots (91)
of water, and rested each afternoon. But nothing helped. He stayed as tiny as a toy. Tiny (108)
was still the tiniest tiger in the jungle. (116)
Tiny walked alone in the jungle one day. He came across some creatures playing by a (132)
pond. They would not play with him because they said he was too small. (146)
Then Tiny saw a spider sitting near some tulips. She was just a little smaller than Tiny. (163)
She had brown and gray spots on her back and her name was Lucky. From that day on, (181)
Tiny no longer had to play alone. Each day Tiny and Lucky ran around the jungle. They (198)
became best friends. (201)

SEE TO SAY

	Correct	Error
First Try		
Second Try		

READING PASSAGES
Second Grade Level—Skill Sheet 13

Directions: Say each word. If you finish before the end of the timing, go back to the beginning and start over.

March first was Vicky Brown's birthday. Her friends showed up to wish her a (14)
happy birthday. After playing games outside, Vicky and her friends went inside (26)
to eat some cake and to open birthday gifts. As they walked down the hall, they (42)
saw a sign on a door: KEEP OUT! Doctor Brown at work. (54)

"Who is Doctor Brown?" asked one of Vicky's friends. "Is it your dad or (68)
your mom?" (70)

"They are both called Doctor Brown," answered Vicky. (78)

"What kind of an invention are your mom and dad working on this time?" (92)
the boys and girls asked. (97)

"I think they're trying to shrink things in the work room," said Vicky. "They (111)
put things under a big green box to shrink them. When they turn a knob on the (128)
wall, the things become very tiny." (134)

Vicky and her friends listened at the door. They could hear Vicky's dad (147)
walking around. "Poor Skippy," he said aloud. "I wish I could find you. By (161)
now you must be the size of an ant." (170)

"Oh no," Vicky said. "Dad must have put our dog, Skippy, under the green (184)
box to shrink him. A dog the size of an ant isn't much fun to play with." (201)

SEE TO SAY

	Correct	Error
First Try		
Second Try		

READING PASSAGES
Second Grade Level—Skill Sheet 14

Directions: Say each word. If you finish before the end of the timing, go back to the beginning and start over.

Most of the time, the king of the castle was happy. However, sometimes he became (15)
very angry. He was often angry at dinner time. (24)

"What's wrong with the cooks in this town?" he would scream. "No one in this town (40)
knows how to make a good bowl of soup." (49)

The king was right. The soup in that town tasted just like water. (62)

Cook after cook came and went. Still the soup tasted like water. The king didn't know (78)
what to do. Finally, he went into the town and called out loudly for everyone to hear, (95)
"Who can make a bowl of soup that tastes good? You will become the soup cook (111)
for the castle." (114)

William, the castle dishwasher, was in the town. "I think I'll try to make some soup for (131)
the king," he said. "Being the soup cook in the castle would be a lot more fun than (149)
washing dishes!" (151)

William went back to the castle and began to make some soup. He took a few things (168)
down from the shelf and started to add them to a large pot of water. (183)

When the cook walked in, she made him stop. She told him to start washing dishes. (199)
Slowly he walked over to the sink to wash the dishes. He was sad that he would not get (218)
to be the soup cook for the castle. (226)

SEE TO SAY

READING PASSAGES
Second Grade Level—Skill Sheet 15

Directions: Say each word. If you finish before the end of the timing, go back to the beginning and start over.

	Correct	Error
First Try		
Second Try		

Carter lived on a farm. One day, he was sawing some wood when a boy from town rode (18)
up on his bike. The boy stopped to watch Carter for a little while. At last the boy (36)
said, "My name is David. What you're doing looks fun to me. Do you mind if I try it?" (55)

"How can sawing wood be fun?" Carter thought to himself. "I think I will get this boy to (73)
do all my work for me." (79)

Carter looked at David and said, "Sawing wood is lots of fun. Here, you may try it if (97)
you would like to." He handed David the saw. (106)

David sawed and sawed. "I like working on a farm," he said in a happy voice. (122)

"Great!" said Carter. "I'll let you saw the rest of this wood by yourself." (136)

"That's real friendship," said David. (141)

Carter sat down in a pile of hay, and soon he was fast asleep. He did not get up until (161)
David finished sawing all the wood by himself. (169)

"Now show me what I can do next," said David. (179)

All day long David worked around the farm picking pumpkins, catching fish, and (192)
putting the cut wood into a big pile. At last he said, "I've had a good time on your farm, (212)
but I need to go home now." (219)

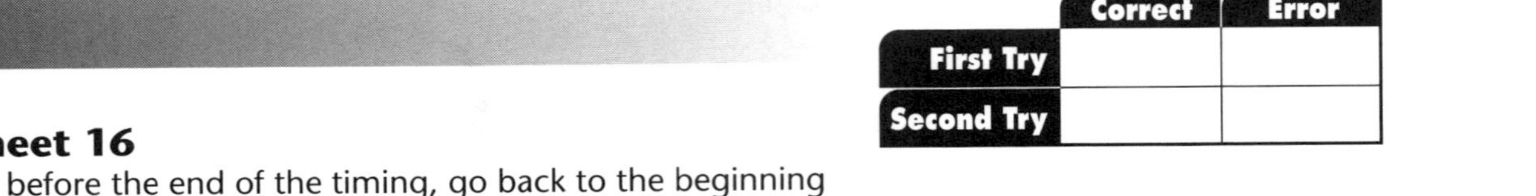

READING PASSAGES

Second Grade Level—Skill Sheet 16

Directions: Say each word. If you finish before the end of the timing, go back to the beginning and start over.

	Correct	Error
First Try		
Second Try		

"Look out, Mom!" Rob yelled as he rolled a ball of brown thread toward (14)
her. "Here comes a mean spider!" (20)

"A spider!" yelled his mom. (25)

Rob stood in the middle of the room and grinned. (35)

"That's not a real spider," said Rob. "That's just some harmless brown (47)
thread. I thought it would be fun to scare you with it." (59)

Rob's mom bent down to get a better look at the thread. (71)

"Rob," she said as she picked up the thread, "when are you ever going to (86)
stop playing tricks?" (89)

"I don't think I'll ever want to stop," Rob said as he ran out the door. "I like (107)
to play tricks." (110)

Rob saw his older brother sitting in the yard. Rob took a play bug out of his (127)
pocket and walked up behind his brother. Without making a sound, he set the (141)
play bug down by his brother. Then he walked back over to the porch. (155)

"Watch out!" Rob called. "There's a hairy bug right next to you." (167)

Rob's brother turned and saw the bug. He jumped up and hit the bug with his (183)
sneaker. Then he saw that the bug was not real and could not hurt him. (198)

SEE TO SAY

READING PASSAGES
Second Grade Level—Skill Sheet 17

Directions: Say each word. If you finish before the end of the timing, go back to the beginning and start over.

	Correct	Error
First Try		
Second Try		

Kim had a new camera and was getting ready to snap a picture of her friend Craig. (17)
"Come on, Craig, don't make a silly face this time," said Kim. "I want this to be a (35)
nice picture." (37)
As Kim snapped the picture, her friend Jill came by. "Wow, where did you get that (53)
camera?" asked Jill. (56)
"My aunt gave it to me for my birthday," answered Kim. "Let me take your picture." (72)
Before Kim could get the camera ready, Jill stood on her head. "Now what did you do (89)
that for?" asked Kim. "You'll wreck the picture!" (97)
"If I have to be in a picture, this is the way I want to look," Jill said. "It's a lot more (119)
fun to be in action shots than to just stand still." (130)
"I didn't think of that," Kim said. "Hold still and I'll take your picture." Kim took (146)
the picture. (148)
"I think we should try some more pictures like that," said Craig. (160)
"I still have a few shots left in my camera, so let's think of something to do that will (179)
make a good action picture," said Kim. (186)
Craig scratched his head. "How about playing ball?" he said. "Let's pretend we have (200)
a ball and bat. That should make a good picture." (210)

SEE TO SAY

READING PASSAGES

Second Grade Level—Skill Sheet 18

Directions: Say each word. If you finish before the end of the timing, go back to the beginning and start over.

	Correct	Error
First Try		
Second Try		

Buddy was a one-man band. With one hand he slid a spoon across a washboard, and with (17)
the other hand he played a trumpet. His left foot tapped a small drum while his right foot (35)
pressed a loud fog horn. (40)

Buddy had one big problem. He could not play a tune. The music he made was terrible. (57)
He always played with a rattle, crack, whistle, squeak, bang, puff, puff! Everyone ran (71)
the other way when he played. (77)

One day, Buddy went for a walk with his drum and washboard on his back. He had his (95)
fog horn under his arm, and he was playing his trumpet. He looked very funny as he (112)
walked along. (114)

It was a nice day to be outside, but soon the walk and fresh air made Buddy hungry. He (133)
went to Mrs. Martin's store to get some fruit. He picked out some fat pears. As Buddy (150)
went to the front to pay for his pears, he saw a robber. "I have to do something to help (168)
Mrs. Martin!" he said. "I know what I can do." (178)

Buddy set up his washboard and drum and began to play. The robber had just pulled the (197)
money out of the safe when he heard a rattle, crack, whistle, squeak, bang, puff, puff! (213)
The robber was so surprised that he jumped up and ran away. (225)

SEE TO SAY

READING PASSAGES

Second Grade Level—Skill Sheet 19

Directions: Say each word. If you finish before the end of the timing, go back to the beginning and start over.

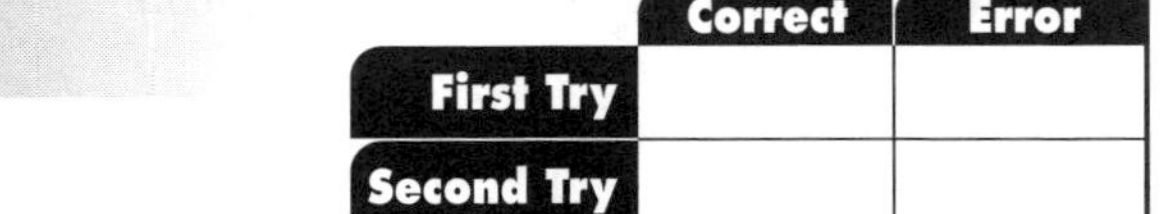

	Correct	Error
First Try		
Second Try		

Ken and Jan walked down the beach to do some fishing. They spotted something large (15)
that had washed up on the beach. (22)

"That looks like an old shipwreck," said Ken. "The rainstorm last night must have washed (37)
it up. I bet this is the beach called Ship's Graveyard." (48)

"Why is it called Ship's Graveyard?" asked Jan. (56)

"A lot of old shipwrecks are here under the sand," Ken said. "New ones turn up after (73)
every storm, but it doesn't take long for the wind and sea and sand to cover them back (91)
up again." (93)

Jan and Ken decided to run over to the wreck and look around. (106)

"This ship must be very old," Jan said. "Just look at these cannons." (119)

"Let's look inside," said Ken. (124)

Jan followed Ken into the wreck. It was full of sand and smashed boards. They noticed (140)
something sticking out of the sand. (146)

"It looks like part of an old trunk," Ken said. (156)

Jan began scooping away the sand. Ken threw down his fishing pole and box and began (172)
to dig, too. It was an old trunk, but before they could dig it out, big waves washed up on (192)
the beach. Jan and Ken had to run up to a high place. They had to leave the trunk. (211)

SEE TO SAY

	Correct	Error
First Try		
Second Try		

READING PASSAGES
Second Grade Level—Skill Sheet 20

Directions: Say each word. If you finish before the end of the timing, go back to the beginning and start over.

Chester was the Mouse Town jail keeper. He put his feet under his desk and sat back in (18)
his chair. He stared out the window with tired eyes. (28)

Chester had stayed up all night. He had been talking to some worried mice from town. (44)
They were worried about the Mouse Town well. It was just about empty. If they didn't (60)
get a new well, Mouse Town would soon be out of water. (72)

Just then Chester heard someone shouting in the street. "Sounds like trouble," he (85)
thought. "It looks like I won't be getting any rest today." (96)

Chester jumped up and ran to the door. When he got to the door, he saw Miss Cook (114)
running toward him. (117)

"A terrible thing has happened," said Miss Cook as she tried to catch her breath. (132)
"Someone broke into my cheese shop and took all my cheese." (143)

"How did the robber get in?" asked Chester. "Wasn't the door locked?" (155)

"The robber didn't use the door," answered Miss Cook. "The robber made a tunnel and (170)
came up through the floor." (175)

When Chester looked at the hole in Miss Cook's floor, he knew right away who the (191)
robber was. No one but a mole could have tunneled in so quickly and so quietly. (207)

SEE TO SAY

READING PASSAGES

Third Grade Level—Skill Sheet 1 (Science: Plants)

Directions: Say each word. If you finish before the end of the timing, go back to the beginning and start over.

Everything is quiet in the bog, or almost everything. A tiny black fly buzzes around, looking for (17)
food. All of a sudden, it smells nectar, a sugary juice that plants make. The sweet smell is coming (36)
from a strange plant growing flat against the ground. (45)

The fly lands near the plant and crawls toward a leaf. Closer, closer, closer. (59)

SNAP! (60)

The leaf slams shut, squishing the fly between two green walls. (71)

The fly tries to get out but can't. The fly will never escape. This plant will eat it alive! (90)

How can a plant eat a fly? (97)

It's easy for the Venus flytrap. (103)

The Venus flytrap is just one of more than six hundred kinds of plants that eat insects and other tiny (123)
animals. These plants are called carnivorous. This word means "meat eating." Carnivorous plants (136)
are the T. rexes of the plant world. (144)

Eating bugs might seem like a strange thing for a plant to do. But insect-eating plants grow in (162)
very poor soil. They make up for this by eating bugs. (173)

Meat-eating plants hunt very differently than meat-eating animals. (181)

Unlike animals, plants don't have legs. So they can't move around and hunt their prey like animals (198)
can. Plants don't have claws and sharp teeth either. But they can still catch food. (213)

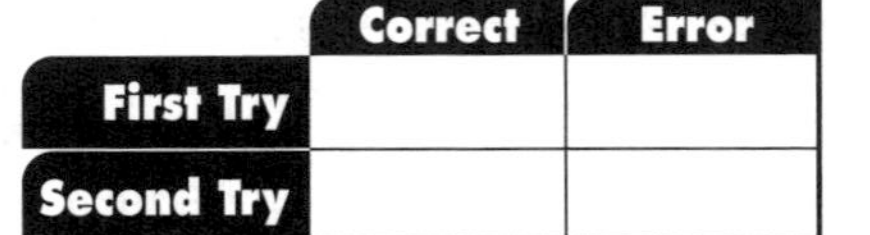

	Correct	Error
First Try		
Second Try		

READING PASSAGES

Third Grade Level—Skill Sheet 2 (Science: Plants)

Directions: Say each word. If you finish before the end of the timing, go back to the beginning and start over.

Carnivorous plants have different kinds of traps. Some, like the Venus flytrap, are active. This (15)
means that part of the plant moves to catch its meal. The Venus flytrap is active because its (33)
leaves snap shut. (36)

The leaves of this meat-eating plant are really small traps with spines along the edges. Many (52)
traps are no larger than a dime. The biggest are about the size of a half-dollar. A Venus flytrap (71)
has about seven leaf traps. (76)

On each leaf is a red spot. Insects like red, and they head toward it. The spot is covered with (96)
sweet nectar that lures the insect like fish to bait. But it's a trick. Instead of finding food, the (115)
insect becomes food for a hungry plant. (122)

When a fly crawls onto a Venus flytrap leaf, it touches a tiny hair. These little hairs are triggers. (141)
When two trigger hairs are touched, the leaf trap suddenly snaps shut. The two sides of the leaf (159)
close around the insect. Like the bars of a cage, the spines keep the bug from escaping. (176)

The Venus flytrap leaf can open and close about seven times. This means it can eat about seven (194)
insect meals. Then the leaf opens as wide as it can and just acts like a regular leaf. But the plant (215)
still has other leaf traps ready to catch its next victim. (226)

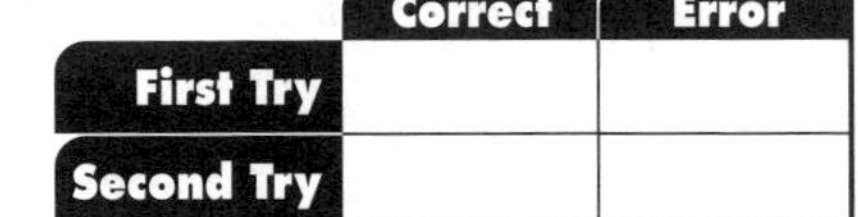

	Correct	Error
First Try		
Second Try		

READING PASSAGES

Third Grade Level—Skill Sheet 3 (Science: Plants)

Directions: Say each word. If you finish before the end of the timing, go back to the beginning and start over.

Another type of insect-eating plant is the bladderwort. It is also an active trap. There (15)
are more than two hundred kinds of bladderworts. Some have beautiful flowers that (28)
look like orchids. But quicker than you can blink your eye, bladderworts suck up (42)
their prey. (44)

The bladderwort's traps are tiny pouches shaped like little eggs. Most bladderworts (56)
grow in ponds or lakes. The plant's stem and flower grow above the water, but the (72)
traps are underwater. When tiny water animals swim by, they touch a trigger hair on (87)
the plant's trapdoor. In less than half a second, the pouch opens, sucking the water (102)
and the animal inside—just as you'd suck juice through a straw. It takes about one (118)
hour for the plant to reset the trap. Then it's ready to catch another passing bug. (134)

SEE TO SAY

	Correct	Error
First Try		
Second Try		

READING PASSAGES
Third Grade Level—Skill Sheet 4 (Science: Plants)

Directions: Say each word. If you finish before the end of the timing, go back to the beginning and start over.

Like a small helicopter, a bee whizzes in for a landing on the edge of a plant. The (18)
bee smells nectar and wants a sip. It crawls inside the plant and quickly loses its (34)
footing. The plant walls are slippery. The bee begins to slide. It tries as hard as it (51)
can to climb out, but tiny downward-pointing hairs keep it from crawling back up. (65)
Down, down, down the bee slides. It can't stop. At the bottom of the plant is a pool (83)
of water. (85)

SPLASH! The bee falls. It can't get out. Soon the bee drowns. The chemicals in the (101)
water help the plant digest the bee just as chemicals inside your stomach help you (116)
digest your food. (119)

The unlucky bee fell into a pitcher plant, another kind of carnivorous plant. Unlike (133)
Venus flytraps and bladderworts, pitcher plants don't move. So they are called (145)
passive traps. (147)

They, too, use nectar to bait insects. But they just sit still and wait for their victims (164)
to fall inside. (167)

There are many different kinds of pitcher plants. Some grow on long vines in tropical (182)
countries where it is hot all year round. Many tropical pitcher plants grow in (196)
rainforests on mountains thousands of feet high. (203)

SEE TO SAY

	Correct	Error
First Try		
Second Try		

READING PASSAGES
Third Grade Level—Skill Sheet 5 (Science: Plants)

Directions: Say each word. If you finish before the end of the timing, go back to the beginning and start over.

Tropical pitcher plants look like hanging pouches. The plant's pitcher is really a leaf that grows (16)
in an unusual shape. The opening is the pitcher's mouth. The pouch is its stomach. (31)

Some have stems more than sixty feet long that snake along the ground or hang from trees. Some (49)
are big enough to trap a tree frog or a small bird. (61)

Most tropical pitcher plants are climbing vines that usually have two types of pitchers. Lower (76)
pitchers are shaped sort of like cans. Because they are closer to the ground, lower pitchers catch (93)
crawling insects. Upper pitchers are shaped like funnels. Upper pitchers catch mostly flying insects (107)
such as honeybees, flies, and hornets. (113)

Above the plant's mouth is a hood that acts like a little umbrella. It keeps the pitcher from filling (132)
up with rainwater. Flying insects use the hood as a landing pad. (144)

The pitcher doesn't always get a chance to eat every bug it catches. Sometimes it is robbed by a (163)
food thief. A diving spider can dive into the pitcher and steal a bug that plant has trapped. Diving (182)
spiders can get out of pitcher plants without being trapped. They crawl up a silk thread that they (200)
spin from their bodies. The thread acts like a safety line. (211)

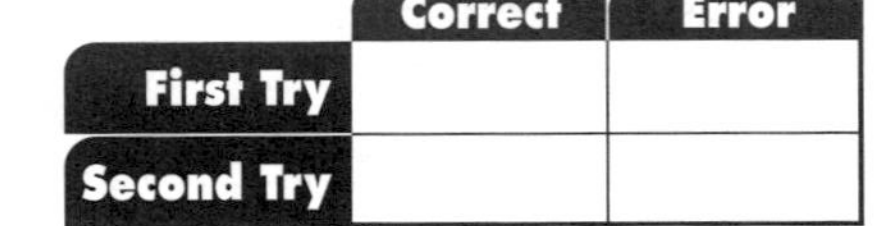

	Correct	Error
First Try		
Second Try		

READING PASSAGES
Third Grade Level—Skill Sheet 6 (Science: Plants)

Directions: Say each word. If you finish before the end of the timing, go back to the beginning and start over.

Sundews are some of the prettiest bug-eating plants around. But don't let that fool (14)
you. They are also pretty deadly. (20)

Each sundew has tentacles that grow on its leaves. Sundews get their name from the (35)
little gluey balls that look like dewdrops on their tentacles. (45)

When a beetle flies over the plant, it smells the plant's nectar and lands to take a (62)
sip. Then it gets stuck to the gooey balls. The beetle tries to pull its legs free. But it's (81)
no use. The harder the beetle tries to escape, the more glue the sundew makes. (96)

Then this passive trap becomes very active. The sticky tentacles slowly wrap around (109)
the insect's body, squeezing it so hard that it can't breathe. The sundew's tentacles (123)
make an acid that turns the beetle into beetle juice. The plant feeds on its "insect (139)
slurpy" for several days. (143)

Sundews come in all sizes. The pygmy sundew is not bigger than a penny. The (158)
staghorn sundew may have as many as twelve branches and spread two feet across. (172)
It can catch larger bugs, like butterflies and moths. (181)

The great British scientist Charles Darwin was fascinated by sundews. He thought they had (195)
a stronger sense of taste and touch than any animal he had studied. He spent twenty years (212)
studying insect-eating plants. In 1875, he wrote an entire book about them. (224)

	Correct	Error
First Try		
Second Try		

READING PASSAGES
Third Grade Level—Skill Sheet 7 (Social Science: Great Depression)

Directions: Say each word. If you finish before the end of the timing, go back to the beginning and start over.

Eleven-year-old Evelina Lopez was leaving her family for the first time. She struggled to hold (15)
back her tears as she said good-bye. (22)

Her mother held her a long time. She then said, "Be brave my sweet child. We will all be together (42)
someday. I promise." (45)

Her mother, Eva Cruz Lopez, had faced an impossible decision—to part with her oldest (61)
daughter. Eva Lopez was raising three children by herself. In ordinary years that is hard to do, (79)
but in the years of the Great Depression it had become a hopeless task. (91)

Worried about her children's future, Eva Lopez decided to send Evelina to New York City. She (107)
would live with Eva's older sister who had recently married. They had no children yet and were (124)
willing to take Evelina in to help the family. The Depression had brought hard times to New York (142)
City, but things were much worse in Puerto Rico. Sending Evelina to live with her aunt was the (160)
best thing to do. (164)

Evelina kissed her little sisters, eight-year-old Lillian and baby Ella, for the last time. (178)
"You will grow so fast, little Ella," Evelina said sadly to her baby sister. "I won't be able to see (198)
you take your first steps." (203)

She kissed the baby again as the ship's shrill whistle blew. It was time to board. Evelina had (221)
to hurry. She hugged her sister Lillian and then mother. "I'll miss my best friend and sister and (239)
you, too, Mama. I'll miss all of you so much and think of you every day." (255)

	Correct	Error
First Try		
Second Try		

READING PASSAGES

Third Grade Level—Skill Sheet 8 (Social Science: Great Depression)

Directions: Say each word. If you finish before the end of the timing, go back to the beginning and start over.

In Spanish Harlem, school had already started. So one morning, just a few days after she arrived, (17)
Evelina found herself seated in a big classroom with a tall ceiling and heavy, ink-stained desks. (33)

At first, it was hard to understand the teachers because they only spoke English. But Evelina was (50)
smart and a very fast learner. Soon she was speaking English well enough to make friends. (66)

Her first friend was a pretty little girl named Sarah. Sarah, who reminded Evelina of Lillian, was (83)
always by her side. She and Evelina ate lunch together at school and walked home together. Sarah (100)
helped Evelina with her English, too. (106)

At school, Evelina was one of the brightest students in class. Her favorite subject was history. She (123)
read constantly. Evelina was often called upon to help the teachers. (134)

Evelina's first year in New York City came and went. She was making friends, learning English, and (151)
doing better and better in school. But not a day passed that she didn't miss her mother and sisters. (170)

Meanwhile, Evelina's household on 117th Street was growing. In order to bring in some additional (185)
income, her aunt rented their extra bedroom. Their tenant's name was Miriam, a young single parent (201)
with a baby boy. Evelina liked Miriam very much and loved the baby. She was always taking care (219)
of baby George when Miriam had to go out. (228)

SEE TO SAY

READING PASSAGES
Third Grade Level—Skill Sheet 9 (Social Science: Great Depression)

Directions: Say each word. If you finish before the end of the timing, go back to the beginning and start over.

	Correct	Error
First Try		
Second Try		

The Great Depression was hurting Spanish Harlem, just as it was hurting the rest of the (16)
United States. Many people were out of work and unable to feed their families or themselves. (32)
Old clothes were repaired, not replaced. Who had money for a new coat or new gloves? (48)

Empty stomachs and worn clothes made February 1935 seem even colder than usual. The (62)
Depression was in its sixth year, and people were struggling just to survive. Even those who (78)
had jobs, like Evelina's aunt and uncle, needed to find extra income to make ends meet. (94)

Evelina could see that many people were hungry. Their children went to school without having (109)
eaten breakfast. In the streets she saw people selling apples for pennies. She saw homeless people (125)
huddled in doorways. She saw people line up by the hundreds in front of soup kitchens waiting (142)
to eat. Yet some of her neighbors refused available food. (152)

Evelina wanted to do something. Her mother had brought her up with a strong sense of right (169)
and wrong. Her mother used to tell her that people who work hard and pay taxes deserve (186)
some help from the government when times are difficult. The government should help those in (203)
need fine jobs. It should, her mother said, make sure everyone can live a decent life. (217)

If her mother was right, why did these people refuse to claim food that they needed and (234)
deserved? Evelina was confused, so she spoke to her aunt and uncle. (246)

SEE TO SAY

READING PASSAGES
Third Grade Level—Skill Sheet 10 (Social Science: Great Depression)

Directions: Say each word. If you finish before the end of the timing, go back to the beginning and start over.

	Correct	Error
First Try		
Second Try		

Despite the hard times of the Depression, Evelina's aunt and uncle had never forgotten about (15)
Evelina's mother and sisters. From the day Evelina had arrived, they had saved any extra money they (32)
could spare for the fares to bring Evelina's family to New York. Evelina had done her best to help, too. (52)

Each morning and each night, she prayed that her family would be reunited. During the day she (69)
searched for empty cans and bottles to cash in for their deposits. She saved every penny of the (87)
deposit money. She kept the money in a sealed jar in the back of a drawer in her bureau. Slowly (107)
the pennies began filling the jar. Too slowly, thought Evelina. (117)

Evelina went to her aunt and uncle. "Tell me," she pleaded, "what else I can do to help get money (137)
for Mama and Lilli and the baby to get here?" (147)

"Some of our neighbors could use the help of an interpreter. Maybe you could earn money that (164)
way," suggested her uncle. "Your English is very good." (173)

Her English was very good indeed. Evelina began to help her neighbors who didn't speak English (189)
by acting as their interpreter. She went with the people to clinics and city agencies to help them fill (208)
out forms and to talk to clerks behind the counters. (218)

Most of the people were poor, but they gave Evelina what ever they could spare. Neighbors began (235)
to rely on Evelina even when they couldn't pay for her help. Evelina never refused. (250)

READING PASSAGES

Third Grade Level—Skill Sheet 11 (Social Science: Great Depression)

Directions: Say each word. If you finish before the end of the timing, go back to the beginning and start over.

	Correct	Error
First Try		
Second Try		

Evelina took the money she had saved, ten dollars, to her aunt and uncle. They were very surprised (18)
and very moved. "Listen," said her uncle, "we were not going to tell you this right away, but." He (37)
hesitated, then smiled. "Your aunt and I will be sending some money to your mother very soon. (54)
Together with the money your mother has saved, there is finally enough for the fares. She and Lillian (72)
and baby Ella will be coming to live with us by May." (84)

On hearing the news, Evelina thought her heart would burst with happiness. She would finally have (100)
her mother and her sisters with her. She ached to see them, touch them, and feel complete with her (119)
family around her once more. (124)

Two months later, just about a year and a half after her own arrival, Evelina once again stood on the (144)
South Brooklyn docks. This time, though, she was filled with joy. She stood at the front of an excited (163)
crowd waiting for the passengers to disembark from the very ship that had brought her to New York. (181)

She searched for her family among the crowd of passengers. The gangplank was down, and people (197)
were streaming off the ship. Then she saw them! Mama, Lillian, and baby Ella! They stepped off (214)
the gangplank and hurried toward Evelina, who was now shouting and waving. (226)

SEE TO SAY

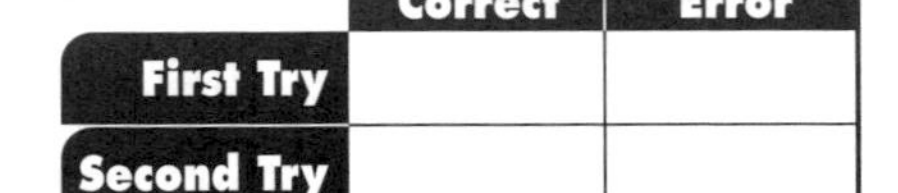

	Correct	Error
First Try		
Second Try		

READING PASSAGES

Third Grade Level—Skill Sheet 12 (Social Science: Great Depression)

Directions: Say each word. If you finish before the end of the timing, go back to the beginning and start over.

By caring about others and taking the initiative, Evelina had helped her neighbors. And she continued (16)
to change things for the better for the rest of her life. (28)

In high school a classmate of Evelina's became ill and was sent to the school infirmary. No one was (47)
on duty in the infirmary. The sick girl sat alone and scared without treatment or help. When Evelina (65)
found out, she decided to do something about it. She persuaded several students to stay out of school in (84)
protest. This small boycott was effective. Soon after, a nurse was in attendance at the school infirmary. (101)

A few years later, Evelina organized a larger boycott—one against neighborhood stores. The store (116)
owners continually refused to hire any people of color to work in their stores. She rallied her (133)
neighbors, and they stopped shopping in those stores. The stores changed their hiring practices. (147)
And it was all for the better. (154)

Later, after she married and had children of her own, she was living in a part of New York City called (175)
the South Bronx. This was one of the city's poorest and most run down areas. Even some people who (194)
lived and worked there called it a "bad neighborhood." (203)

She organized the parents into a group called the United Bronx Parents and they held protests marches. (220)
They called local politicians and television and newspapers. They showed them firsthand how poor (234)
conditions were in the schools of the South Bronx. This led to positive change. Once more Evelina had (252)
made a difference. (255)

SEE TO SAY

READING PASSAGES

Fourth Grade Level—Skill Sheet 1 (Science: Deserts)

Directions: Say each word. If you finish before the end of the timing, go back to the beginning and start over.

	Correct	Error
First Try		
Second Try		

Just before dawn, a kit fox pads quietly across the dry ground. She spies a kangaroo rat beneath a (19)
cactus. The fox springs and catches her pups' next meal! She is lucky. The time for hunting has (37)
nearly ended. Sunbeams are flickering over the landscape as the sun rises. The rattling call of the (54)
cactus wren breaks the silence. The fox heads for her den as another day in the desert begins. (72)

Does the word desert make you think of a hot wasteland of sand? Is it a place where almost nothing (92)
lives or grows? A few deserts are like that. But most have more stones than sand. And many deserts (111)
are full of life. (115)

Deserts are the driest places on Earth. They are found where rain is scarce and the air is very dry. In (136)
western North America, deserts stretch from Idaho south into Mexico. (146)

Deserts are surrounded by other kinds of landscapes. If you travel north, you'll see grasslands and (162)
forests. North of the forests is a cold, treeless plain called the tundra. Tundra, forests, grasslands, (178)
and deserts make up Earth's main land zones. Scientists call these different land zones biomes. (193)

Each biome has a different type of climate. The climate is an area's usual pattern of weather over a (212)
long period of time. (216)

SEE TO SAY

READING PASSAGES
Fourth Grade Level—Skill Sheet 2 (Science: Deserts)

Directions: Say each word. If you finish before the end of the timing, go back to the beginning and start over.

	Correct	Error
First Try		
Second Try		

Deserts have a very dry climate. They do get a little rain, but it doesn't come regularly. One storm (19)
might drench a desert with several inches of rain in just a few hours. It might not rain again for (39)
months—even years. (42)

Some deserts are cold, but most are hot. During the day, hot deserts are the hottest places on Earth. (61)
Clouds are rare in desert skies. There is nothing to block the sun's scorching rays. But when the sun (80)
goes down, deserts cool off quickly. Nighttime temperatures can be freezing cold. (92)

It's hard to imagine that anything could live in such a harsh place. Yet most deserts are home to (111)
many living things. Let's take a walk in the desert and see what life is like here in early summer. (131)

The landscape glows in the morning sun. You're in the middle of a rocky plain full of (148)
strange-looking plants. Many are cactus plants, or cacti. Most cacti don't have leaves. They have (163)
thick, green stems covered with sharp spines. The spines protect cacti from being eaten by desert (179)
animals. They also shade the stems from the sun. (188)

Short and squat or tall and branched, cacti are covered with spines. Some cactus spines are straight. (205)
Others have tips that curve like fishhooks. Barrel cacti look like stubby fingers pushing up through (221)
the soil. (223)

	Correct	Error
First Try		
Second Try		

READING PASSAGES
Fourth Grade Level—Skill Sheet 3 (Science: Deserts)

Directions: Say each word. If you finish before the end of the timing, go back to the beginning and start over.

Cacti come in many shapes and sizes. At your feet are tiny round cacti. They look like pincushions. (18)
Next to them are pancake-shaped prickly pears. Chubby barrel cacti dot the landscape. They grow (33)
about knee-high. Chollas are taller, with many spiny branches. Towering over everything are giant (47)
saguaros. They can grow as tall as a telephone pole. (57)

Bend down and pick up a handful of soil. It's so pebbly and dry it trickles through your fingers. (76)
Desert soil contains many things that plants need to grow. But after a rain, it dries out very fast. (95)
Desert plants must be able to soak up rainwater quickly. They must savor every precious drop. (111)

Many cacti have roots that spread out just under the soil's surface. When it rains, the roots soak (129)
up the water before the soil dries out. The water is stored in a cactus's thick, fleshy stem. A waxy (149)
coating on the outside of the stem keeps the water in. (160)

Cacti aren't the only desert plants. Creosote bushes and mesquite trees grow there, too. Both have (176)
tiny, leathery leaves. Small leaves lose less water in dry desert air than larger leaves would. A (193)
mesquite tree's long roots tunnel deep underground to reach hidden water. (204)

SEE TO SAY

READING PASSAGES
Fourth Grade Level—Skill Sheet 4 (Science: Deserts)

Directions: Say each word. If you finish before the end of the timing, go back to the beginning and start over.

	Correct	Error
First Try		
Second Try		

Many desert animals are nocturnal. They are active only at night, when it is cooler. Nocturnal (16)
desert dwellers spend their days in burrows, dens, and other sheltered places. The kangaroo rat (31)
and the kit fox are nocturnal. They stay underground until the sun goes down. (45)

But some desert animals are active during the day. Insects are on the move everywhere. Columns (61)
of ants march across the ground. Colorful beetles crawl up and down stems. Grasshoppers spring (76)
from leaf to leaf. Insect-eating spiders are busy, too. They spin silken webs among cactus spines. (92)

The sun has climbed higher in the clear blue sky. Can you feel the heat? Desert lizards don't (110)
seem to mind. Their tough, scaly skin seals water inside their bodies and keeps them from drying (127)
out. Lizards rest on rocks, hunt insects, and cling to cactus stems. In one small patch of desert, you (146)
could see tiny skinks, chunky chuckwallas, spiny horned lizards, and lumbering Gila monsters. (159)

Suddenly, something streaks across your path. It's a speedy lizard, and right on its heels is a (176)
roadrunner. Roadrunners can fly. But these desert birds prefer to run after lizards and the other (192)
small animals they hunt. (196)

Roadrunners have long, strong legs. They can run as fast as many lizards can. In fact, this time (214)
the bird is faster. The roadrunner catches the lizard by its tail and swallows it in one gulp. (232)

	Correct	Error
First Try		
Second Try		

READING PASSAGES
Fourth Grade Level—Skill Sheet 5 (Science: Deserts)

Directions: Say each word. If you finish before the end of the timing, go back to the beginning and start over.

Gradually, the sun moves lower in the sky. As shadows grow longer, the temperature starts to (16)
drop. Desert birds begin to sing again. At sunset, coyotes call to each other, barking and yelping. (33)
They join voices in an eerie, wailing song. (41)

The hot desert day is over. The cool night is about to begin. Birds, lizards, and other daytime (59)
animals retreat to snug nests and safe hiding places. There they will sleep the night away. As (76)
darkness falls, the nocturnal animals begin to stir. Snakes slither into the open. They are ready to (93)
track down rats, rabbits, and birds that nest on the ground. Scorpions scuttle around. They search (109)
for crickets, spiders, and small, sleeping lizards. Many-legged centipedes crawl out from nooks (122)
and crannies to hunt insects. Hairy tarantulas creep out of holes in the ground. They look scary. (139)
But they are dangerous only to the insects and other small creatures they eat. (153)

Bats flutter out of caves. They look like dark shadows against the night sky. Some seek the sweet (171)
nectar of cactus flowers. Others hunt for flying insects. (180)

An elf owl whistles softly as it flies out from its saguaro hotel. It glides silently through the (198)
cool night air. The owl dives to the ground to catch a small snake in its sharp claws. (216)

SEE TO SAY

READING PASSAGES
Fourth Grade Level—Skill Sheet 6 (Science: Deserts)

Directions: Say each word. If you finish before the end of the timing, go back to the beginning and start over.

	Correct	Error
First Try		
Second Try		

Soft grunting sounds are coming from a clump of creosote bushes. There's a strong musky odor (16)
in the air, too. Peccaries are near. Peccaries are pig-like animals with coarse, bristly hair. During (32)
the day, they sleep in the shade. But at night, they travel in noisy groups. They poke the dry soil (52)
with their long snouts, eating roots and tender plants. Peccaries don't seem to mind the prickly (68)
pear's sharp spines. (71)

The scent of peccaries can attract large desert hunters. Bobcats and mountain lions hide in the (87)
shadows, waiting for animals to pass by. Then, in a flash, they spring out and pounce on their prey. (106)

As the hours pass, the cool night air turns cold. The temperature may drop 60 degrees or more (124)
between sunset and sunrise. The fur coats of foxes, bobcats, and rats protect them from the cold. (141)
Owls have fluffy feathers to keep them warm. (149)

All night long, the desert is a busy place. It is full of slithering, rustling, whispering sounds as (167)
animals move about. By the light of the stars and the moon, they fly and hop and run and pounce. (187)

Eventually, the rosy glow of dawn lights up the eastern sky. Owls and bats return to their roosts. (205)
Kit foxes and kangaroo rats retreat to underground burrows. Snakes and scorpions go back into (220)
hiding, too. And when the cactus wren calls out at sunrise, the cycle of life in the desert begins (239)
all over again. (242)

READING PASSAGES

Fourth Grade Level—Skill Sheet 7 (Social Science: Immigrants)

Directions: Say each word. If you finish before the end of the timing, go back to the beginning and start over.

	Correct	Error
First Try		
Second Try		

In a Polish village, a seven-year-old girl named Hattie stood at the window of her family's one-room (17)
mud hut. Her stomach gnawed with hunger. (24)

Hattie watched her father bending over his book. His long red beard almost touched the book's (40)
pages. Each time he chanted a verse, the students, who were all boys, looked down at their books (58)
and repeated the verse carefully. Among them strutted a hen and her chicks, pecking at the mud floor. (76)

Hattie's mother sat in a corner of the mud hut peeling potatoes. She put the potatoes into a big iron (96)
pot to steam. Then she began to cut pieces of black bread. (108)

Hattie could smell the potatoes cooking. The smell forced her thoughts back to food. To try to take (126)
her mind off her hunger, she grabbed the end of her thick red braid and squeezed it. She was so (146)
hungry; she almost stuck the braid in her mouth. Her blue eyes started to well with tears. When (164)
could she eat? (167)

She tried to pass the time by tracing pictures in the steam on the glass with one freckled finger. Hattie (187)
couldn't read or write, so she pretended that the pictures were letters. And she wished that she could (205)
learn to read and write like the boys who were her father's students. But learning was believed to be (224)
a boy's occupation among the villagers of Poland. Girls learned to cook. They learned to prepare the (241)
house for visitors. But they were never sent to school. (251)

SEE TO SAY

READING PASSAGES

Fourth Grade Level—Skill Sheet 8 (Social Science: Immigrants)

Directions: Say each word. If you finish before the end of the timing, go back to the beginning and start over.

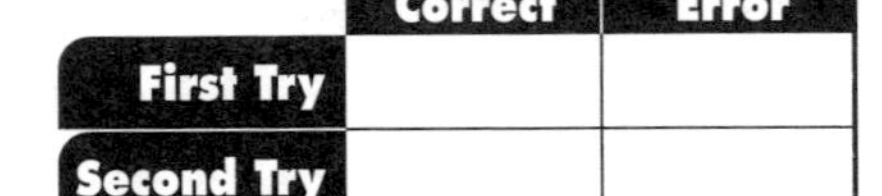

	Correct	Error
First Try		
Second Try		

A few years later, a ship carrying Hattie, her parents, her three sisters, and her three brothers (17)
steamed into New York Harbor. It was the spring of 1890. The anxious family peered over the (34)
ship's railing, searching the crowd on the dock of the Castle Garden immigration station for a (50)
familiar face. A sea of strange faces stared back at them. (61)

Meyer must be somewhere on that dock. But where? His letter had promised that he would be (78)
there to meet the family when their ship came in. They needed his help. Before they could enter (96)
the country, the immigration officials were going to ask them a lot of complicated questions and (112)
would make them take medical exams. Finally Hattie spotted someone who looked a little familiar (127)
across the bridge that connected the Castle Garden immigration station with Manhattan. He did (141)
look a little like her brother, but just a little. He was all dressed up in American-style clothes. (159)
Could that really be the brother she said goodbye to just a few short years before? She doubted it. (178)

Suddenly the man began to wave at her, and at that moment she realized it really was her (196)
brother. But how strange he looked and acted! Though his family didn't know it yet, even his (213)
name had changed. (216)

When he arrived in America, the immigration officials had given him a new name. His real, strange (233)
sounding Polish name had been too difficult for them to pronounce, so they had changed it. (249)

SEE TO SAY

	Correct	Error
First Try		
Second Try		

READING PASSAGES

Fourth Grade Level—Skill Sheet 9 (Social Science: Immigrants)

Directions: Say each word. If you finish before the end of the timing, go back to the beginning and start over.

It took months before Hattie got used to living in their new apartment. As miserable as life in Poland (19)
had been, there had always been plenty of open sky and fresh air. In their new home, it was so dark, (40)
and the air smelled stale. (45)

The smaller of the two rooms was reserved for their father and his books. The only time they saw (64)
their father was at mealtimes. Then he would put down his books and come into the larger room to (83)
eat the meals of carp and garlic or pea soup or fish that had been cooked for him. (101)

In this larger room the family lived. They worked, they slept, they cooked, they ate, they played, they (119)
argued, they washed clothes, and they bathed themselves all in this one room. Beds, tables, washtubs, (135)
wooden chairs, and an iron stove were crowded together, all seeming to shove against Hattie's family (151)
for what little space there was to sit or stand. (161)

Hattie's mother ruled this larger room. Endless work—cooking , scrubbing, sewing, tending the (175)
family—stole her days from early morning darkness to long past the children's bedtime. (189)

Her children helped as much as they could, but almost immediately all but Hattie were sent off to (207)
work. Money seemed just as hard to come by on the Lower East Side as it had been in Poland. (227)

When summer came, the temperature rocketed. The tenement became a furnace. So at night, the (242)
whole family moved outside to the fire escape that looked out on the building opposite. (257)

ONE-MINUTE FLUENCY
SOPRIS WEST SKILL BUILDERS SERIES

SEE TO SAY

READING PASSAGES

Fourth Grade Level—Skill Sheet 10 (Social Science: Immigrants)

Directions: Say each word. If you finish before the end of the timing, go back to the beginning and start over.

	Correct	Error
First Try		
Second Try		

One night, as Hattie trudged home from work, she felt more exhausted than usual. Her feet hurt and her (19)
fingers ached. Her head felt as if it was being squeezed by a steel band. (34)

As she neared her family's tenement, she caught a glimpse of the janitor's daughter through the (50)
basement window. The girl was hunched over a schoolbook, and her forehead was wrinkled into a (66)
scowl. Despite the girl's obvious unhappiness, Hattie watched her with envy. This girl was learning (81)
how to read and write. Quickly, Hattie's brain hatched a plan. Hattie moved close to the window and (99)
called to the little girl, "Hey, what you learning?" (108)

The girl looked up with annoyance. Grumbling, she explained that she was studying synonyms, which (123)
were just words about words. (128)

"I'm crazy about words!" Hattie shouted. Before the girl knew what had happened, Hattie had run into (145)
the basement and grabbed the book from her hand. The words that leapt out to Hattie from the page (164)
seemed like magic symbols. The possibility of reading them all filled her with excitement and hope. (180)
Suddenly her fatigue and her headache were gone. (188)

Hattie handed back the precious book. She took an envelope out of her pocket. Inside it were her week's (207)
wages. Every penny of this money had to go to her mother. Every penny except the extra fifty cents she (227)
had earned for sweeping up the shop. Hattie reached into the envelope and took out a fifty-cent piece. (245)
Would the Janitor's daughter like it? All she had to do was give Hattie ten lessons from her schoolbooks, (264)
at five cents a lesson. (269)

SEE TO SAY

READING PASSAGES

Fourth Grade Level—Skill Sheet 11 (Social Science: Immigrants)

Directions: Say each word. If you finish before the end of the timing, go back to the beginning and start over.

	Correct	Error
First Try		
Second Try		

Years had passed and the world had changed. It was 1918, and World War I, the largest and most (19)
terrible war anyone had ever experienced, had finally come to an end after four long years. Life returned (37)
to normal, but everything seemed different. New ideas were changing the way many Americans thought (52)
about the world around them. (57)

On the streets of the Lower East Side, you could still hear the same cries of pushcart peddlers, or catch (77)
sweatshop workers carrying huge piles of garments on their backs. The first generation of immigrant (92)
children from Eastern Europe had grown up. They were more American than their parents. They were (108)
more aware of what was happening outside the Lower East Side. (119)

Hattie was now a beautiful woman with long auburn hair that she knotted into a simple braid. She had (138)
velvety white skin and broad, open features. In the fourteen years since her graduation from Columbia (154)
she had endured many changes. Now Hattie lived alone in her own apartment, still supporting herself (170)
by working as a cooking teacher. (176)

Three years earlier; she had written a story called "The Free Vacation House." The story was about a (194)
poor immigrant family from the Lower East Side—a family much like that of her sister Annie. (211)

The family is invited to take a charity vacation in the mountains. But there are all kinds of humiliating (230)
rules to remind the family that the vacation is "free." The family must keep from the sight of paying (249)
vacationers. They cannot walk on the grass. They must stay in the background. (262)

SEE TO SAY

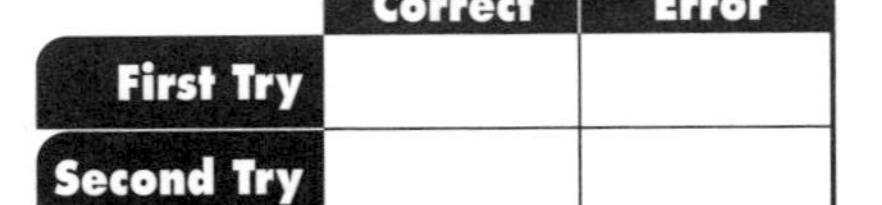

READING PASSAGES
Fourth Grade Level—Skill Sheet 12 (Social Science: Immigrants)

Directions: Say each word. If you finish before the end of the timing, go back to the beginning and start over.

Hattie went on to become one of the best-known American writers of the 1920s. Her success caused a (18)
sensation. Newspapers called her the "Sweatshop Cinderella" and published articles about her "rags to (32)
riches" life. She was invited to speak at universities and literary clubs and even took a tour of Europe. (51)

In 1920 Hollywood bought the movie rights to one of Hattie's books. This brought her a great deal of (70)
money. She was also invited to move to Hollywood to work on scripts. But after just a few weeks in (90)
Hollywood, Hattie moved back to New York. The money, glamour, and fame made her uncomfortable. (105)
She felt she needed to be near the poor neighborhoods that had shaped her in order to keep writing. (124)

Hattie's story is not all that typical of most immigrants who came to the Lower East Side near the turn (144)
of the century. Few became writers. Few even became successful in any career. Most lived like Hattie's (161)
mother and father or like her sister Annie. They spent most of their time working—working in (178)
sweatshops and living in poverty. (183)

For most immigrants, the new lives they built were only slightly better than the ones they left behind (201)
in the Old Country. And some only escaped the tenements by returning to the Old Country. (217)

The many who stayed struggled year after year just to get by. Often it was the children or grandchildren (236)
who first realized the fruits of coming to America. Success like Hattie's was not typical. (251)

SEE TO SAY

	Correct	Error
First Try		
Second Try		

READING PASSAGES

Fifth Grade Level—Skill Sheet 1 (Science: Hurricanes)

Directions: Say each word. If you finish before the end of the timing, go back to the beginning and start over.

In August 1992, tropical storm Andrew grew into a full-fledged hurricane. It became the third strongest (16)
hurricane to hit the United States in the 20th century. Andrew started out as a mass of hot air over (36)
West Africa. Moving across the Atlantic Ocean toward the United States, the weather system gradually (51)
became a tropical storm. Until three days before it hit southern Florida, the storm looked as if it would (70)
remain relatively weak. Unfortunately, very warm water and light winds throughout the atmosphere fed (84)
the storm. Within 48 hours, Andrew's winds increased from 50 to 140 miles per hour. (99)

The National Hurricane Center broadcast reports on radio and TV. They were warning Florida residents (114)
about the possible danger. The Hurricane Center advised people living in low-lying areas along the (129)
southeastern coast to leave their homes and seek shelter inland. Some people listened, but others didn't. (145)

They had prepared for the storm. People waited in one-hour lines at gas stations to fill up their tanks (164)
and two-hour lines at supermarkets to stock up on extra food, water, flashlights, and candles. They had (181)
nailed plywood over their windows. In some cases, they had even hooked portable TVs to car batteries (198)
in case the electricity went out. (204)

When the hurricane slammed into southern Florida about 5 A.M. on August 24, the winds howled like (221)
sirens. Lights went out, telephones went dead. Terrifying crashes and explosions sounded all around. (235)
People stayed put for fear of being hit by debris. Thirty people died, many crushed inside their (252)
own homes. (254)

READING PASSAGES

Fifth Grade Level—Skill Sheet 2 (Science: Hurricanes)

Directions: Say each word. If you finish before the end of the timing, go back to the beginning and start over.

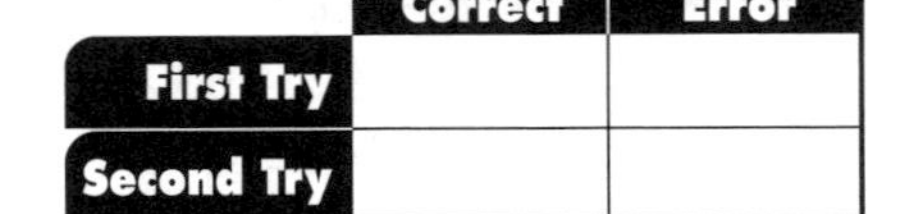

	Correct	Error
First Try		
Second Try		

Hurricanes are the deadliest storms on earth. They start as simple showers and thunderstorms. They (15)
build in size and strength. When storm winds blow 74 miles per hour or greater, a hurricane is born. (34)

No one knows for certain how fast the fastest hurricane winds are. At high speeds hurricane winds (51)
destroy the instruments used to measure them. What we do know is that if hurricane winds were cars, (69)
they would get speeding tickets! The highest recorded wind topped 155 miles per hour—over two (85)
times as fast as the 75 miles per hour speed limit on most U.S. highways. In the strongest hurricanes, (104)
scientists estimate that winds reach approximately 200 miles per hour. (114)

Hurricanes look like giant spinning tops. Although the winds move at high speeds, hurricanes travel (129)
across the surface of the earth at relatively low speeds—usually about 10 to 20 miles per hour. They (148)
can move forward in a straight line, travel in zigzags or loops, or stay in one place. (165)

Hurricanes form in areas around the world where the climate is hot. They develop most frequently in (182)
the tropics, though not right on the equator. (190)

They are most frequent during the hottest seasons of the year, in late summer and early fall. In the (209)
North Atlantic the official hurricane season takes place from June to November. In the Southern (224)
Hemisphere it's the opposite, from December to June. This is because the two hemispheres experience (239)
summer at different times of the year. (246)

SEE TO SAY

READING PASSAGES

Fifth Grade Level—Skill Sheet 3 (Science: Hurricanes)

Directions: Say each word. If you finish before the end of the timing, go back to the beginning and start over.

	Correct	Error
First Try		
Second Try		

Offshore hurricanes produce enormous waves, driving winds, and sheets of rain. But hurricanes cause (14)
the most damage when they come ashore by three means—wind, flooding, and storm surge. (29)

Hurricane winds range from 74 miles per hour to more than 200 miles per hour. They have incredible (47)
force. In one instance Hurricane Andrew carried an 80-foot steel beam weighing several tons the (62)
distance of one city block. High winds are responsible for much of the damage caused to buildings and (80)
other man-made structures. (83)

Hurricanes can also produce tornadoes. They are small, violently spinning windstorms. Tornadoes are (96)
funnel shaped and extend from the ground up to the clouds. Twisters travel across land, hurling large (113)
objects, such as cars and buildings. In 1967, Hurricane Beulah sent 141 tornadoes whirling across Texas. (129)

A typical hurricane brings 6 to 12 inches of rain in a single day. It can flood land hundreds of miles from (151)
the storm center. Hurricane Camille hit the Mississippi River Delta in 1969. Nearly half of the 256 people (169)
killed by it died in floods far from the coast. In 1955 Hurricane Diane did little coastline damage, but its (189)
rains flooded Pennsylvania, New York, and New England. It killed 200 people and caused $300 million (205)
in damage. (207)

When hurricane winds blow, the ocean water is pushed toward shore. As a result, the ocean level can (225)
rise 10 to 20 feet higher than an average high tide. The storm surge is the deadliest part of a hurricane. (246)
It is blamed for nine out of every ten deaths caused by a hurricane. (260)

ONE MINUTE FLUENCY
SOPRIS WEST SKILL BUILDERS SERIES

SEE TO SAY

	Correct	Error
First Try		
Second Try		

READING PASSAGES
Fifth Grade Level—Skill Sheet 4 (Science: Hurricanes)

Directions: Say each word. If you finish before the end of the timing, go back to the beginning and start over.

In August of 1969, a hurricane named Camille slammed into Mississippi, Alabama, and Louisiana, (14)
and eventually affected Virginia and West Virginia. Winds were recorded at speeds of up to 175 miles (31)
per hour. Some scientists suspect they reached more than 200 miles per hour. Unfortunately, the (46)
weather instruments were destroyed in the high-speed winds. Forecasters had expected Camille to hit (60)
the Florida Panhandle. When it became apparent that areas to the west were threatened, warnings were (76)
issued that saved many lives. (81)

Mary Ann was one of the twenty-four people who lived in an apartment building in Christian, (97)
Mississippi. This group did not evacuate when Hurricane Camille hit in 1969. She and her friends (113)
decided not to leave their homes as they had been warned. They thought it would be fun to ride out the (134)
storm and hold a hurricane party instead. (141)

When the storm surge hit, Mary Ann's second-floor apartment flooded within minutes. Her furniture (155)
floated up toward the ceiling. The building creaked and moaned; the windows shattered. Mary Ann (170)
managed to grab a sofa pillow and swim out the window—just in time. Amid the roaring winds, her (189)
three story brick apartment building collapsed behind her. She grabbed other floating debris, but it was (205)
quickly swept away, too. Mary Ann held on to anything that drifted by. Twelve hours later she was (223)
found in a tree top 4 ½ miles from her home. She was taken to the hospital and thankfully, she survived. (244)
Of the other twenty-three people who stayed in her apartment house, only one other person survived. (260)

	Correct	Error
First Try		
Second Try		

READING PASSAGES

Fifth Grade Level—Skill Sheet 5 (Science: Hurricanes)

Directions: Say each word. If you finish before the end of the timing, go back to the beginning and start over.

Predicting the path of a hurricane can be very difficult. As a rule, hurricanes tend to hit southern states (19)
more often than northern ones. Hurricanes require warm ocean water conditions. Consequently, many (32)
New Englanders don't consider hurricanes a threat. Hurricanes can and have slammed into the northern (47)
United States. (49)

In the year 1938, weather experts predicted an offshore hurricane would make landfall in Miami. When (65)
it was reported that the storm was heading out to sea, people heaved a collective sigh of relief and went (85)
back about their lives. In fact, the storm was racing north toward New England at 70 miles per hour. (104)
Winds were whirling well above 100 miles per hour. (113)

By the afternoon of September 21, the sky had turned black and the hurricane hit Long Island full force. (132)
Rain poured and winds roared. Storm waters crashed over the shore, ripping boats from their moorings (148)
and slamming them down on the city streets. Entire houses and cottages were lifted off their foundations (165)
and then floated away. Flood waters trapped people inside their cars, offices, and shops. (179)

Eight hours after it first hit land, the storm died out over Canada. It left death and destruction in its (199)
wake. More than 600 people had died and 63,000 were left homeless. (211)

The Hurricane of 1938 is one of the most famous of the century because of its severity and the fact that it (233)
was so unexpected. It spurred scientists to develop better ways to track hurricanes and to predict the paths (251)
they might take. (254)

SEE TO SAY

	Correct	Error
First Try		
Second Try		

READING PASSAGES
Fifth Grade Level—Skill Sheet 6 (Science: Hurricanes)

Directions: Say each word. If you finish before the end of the timing, go back to the beginning and start over.

Even after the storm passes, conditions outside still may be dangerous. Be careful and be aware of (17)
hazards. Many lives can be saved if people stay calm and follow the advice of forecasters and (34)
local officials. (36)

No one would wish for a hurricane. They cause too much suffering and damage. And yet, hurricanes do (54)
have positive effects on the earth's weather. They are nature's way of bringing much-needed rain to drier (71)
parts of the world. Japan, for example, gets a quarter of its rain from typhoons. Hurricanes also help move (90)
warm air from the equator to cooler parts of the world. (101)

One of the most positive aftereffects of a hurricane, or any natural disaster, is the way relief efforts boost (120)
community spirit. It brings people of all ages, races, and religions together. After Hurricane Andrew, (135)
churches, charities, and concerned citizens across the country responded with an incredible outpouring of (149)
supplies. They gave groceries, clothing, baby food, diapers, money, towels, bed linens, and other everyday (164)
supplies. School children, including pre-schoolers, recycled soda cans and sent favorite books and toys. (178)
They emptied their piggy banks to send cash to those in need. World-famous singers and comedians (194)
organized their own relief efforts. They donated money from their concerts. Businesses distributed free (208)
medical supplies and construction materials. They gave advice to those whose lives were devastated. (222)

As one survivor of Hurricane Andrew put it, "Hurricane Andrew put things in perspective." It made (238)
thousands of people in Florida, Louisiana, and across the country grateful for the things too many of us (256)
take for granted—food, water, shelter, and family. (264)

SEE TO SAY

	Correct	Error
First Try		
Second Try		

READING PASSAGES

Fifth Grade Level—Skill Sheet 7 (Social Science: American Indians)

Directions: Say each word. If you finish before the end of the timing, go back to the beginning and start over.

It was a fresh spring afternoon in 1807, and just about everyone in the Shawnee village at Greenville, (18)
Ohio, was outdoors. Some women were farming corn near the creek while others stirred steaming cook (34)
pots in the village. Most of the men were in the woods, felling saplings for new wigwams. Everywhere, (52)
children were underfoot. (55)

Inside one wigwam, though, a group of men sat in a tight circle, talking in low voices. A shaft of bright (76)
sunlight fell through the doorway, lighting up their faces. They were all dressed alike, in simple (92)
warrior's buckskins, but one was clearly the leader. When he spoke, the others listened. When he flashed (109)
his white teeth in a smile, they smiled, too. They were devoted to him and he was their chief, Tecumseh. (129)

Not quite forty years old, Tecumseh was now a man in the prime of life. He had grown from an athletic (150)
boy into a powerful, muscular man. He had changed in some ways. His face had hardened and when he (169)
got angry, his temper could be volcanic. But he still had the same clear hazel eyes, the same grave (188)
expression. A keen intelligence shone from those eyes, and a dignity that kept him from losing his (205)
temper very often. His shock of black hair was now adorned with a single eagle feather, the mark of (224)
a chief. (226)

Today, in his circle of friends, Tecumseh was neither angry nor particularly dignified. He was laughing (242)
when a young brave entered the wigwam. "Anthony Shane is here," he told Tecumseh. "He brings a (259)
message." Would Tecumseh see him? Of course he would. Tecumseh had known Shane since they were (275)
boys together in Chillicothe. Shane's father was a white trader, but his mother was a Shawnee. (291)

SEE TO SAY

READING PASSAGES

Fifth Grade Level—Skill Sheet 8 (Social Science: American Indians)

Directions: Say each word. If you finish before the end of the timing, go back to the beginning and start over.

	Correct	Error
First Try		
Second Try		

After the council ended, Shane had hastily mounted his horse and set off for Fort Wayne to bring Wells (19)
Tecumseh's answer. The stars were out by the time he got there. Shane saw the lights of the fort first, (39)
like candles in the distance. Soon, snatches of sound—laughter, a barking dog, a jingling harness— (55)
reached his ears on the night breeze. As he approached the stockade, he called out to the guard and the (75)
gate was dragged back. With a shake of the reins, he trotted into Fort Wayne, a United States military (94)
outpost in what was still in 1807, Indian land. (103)

Shane knew Wells would be angry when he heard Tecumseh's answer to his letter, and he was right. (121)
Wells was alarmed at what was going on at Greenville. All spring, bands of Indians had passed Fort (139)
Wayne on their way there. Supposedly they were pilgrims going to hear that Shawnee medicine man, (155)
the one they called the Prophet, preach his new religion. Maybe so, thought Wells. He'd seen families (172)
on the way to Greenville, not just warriors. But he didn't believe it. All those Indians gathering in one (191)
place made him nervous. (195)

Wells had also been listening to rumors. One rumor had it that war belts were being passed among the (214)
tribes from the Gulf of Mexico all the way to the Great Lakes, carried by Shawnee messengers. Another (232)
rumor said that the British up in Canada were giving the Indians guns and ammunition. Wells believed (249)
it. He wouldn't trust a British Indian agent as far as he could throw him. If the Prophet was planning a (270)
war, Wells would bet the British were behind it. (279)

	Correct	Error
First Try		
Second Try		

READING PASSAGES
Fifth Grade Level—Skill Sheet 9 (Social Science: American Indians)

Directions: Say each word. If you finish before the end of the timing, go back to the beginning and start over.

Not long after the Fort Wayne Council ended, the weather turned cold. Bitter winds tore through the trees, (18)
stripping leaves from the branches and dancing them ruthlessly about. Under a leaden sky, the air smelled (35)
of snow. (37)

At Prophetstown, Tecumseh sat in his wigwam, staring moodily into the fire. He was thinking about the Fort (55)
Wayne treaty, going over and over it in his head. He'd been sitting here when the runner had first brought the (76)
news. He had listened, and when he understood what had happened, his handsome face twisted with fury. (93)
They must die. (96)

The Fort Wayne Treaty seemed to have caught Tecumseh by surprise. He'd been away most of the summer, (114)
visiting the Sacs and Foxes who lived along the Mississippi River. In village after village, warriors shouted in (132)
angry agreement when he called on them to join him in standing against the Long Knives. By the time he got (153)
back in August, it was too late to stop the Fort Wayne Council from taking place. (169)

So he'd sent spies to the council to keep him informed of what went on. He flushed with anger all over again (191)
thinking about it. He knew those old village chiefs were weak and corrupt. But the younger ones, the warriors, (210)
why had they gone along with it? He'd counted on them to stop the treaty from going through. But no—more (231)
than a thousand warriors had all just watched their chiefs sign away their land forever! Couldn't they see that (250)
this was the road to destruction? (256)

Winter had set in. There wasn't much Tecumseh could do about the treaty right now except council and plan (275)
and store up his anger. He'd discovered that his following among the tribes was not yet as strong as he'd hoped. (296)

READING PASSAGES

Fifth Grade Level—Skill Sheet 10 (Social Science: American Indians)

Directions: Say each word. If you finish before the end of the timing, go back to the beginning and start over.

	Correct	Error
First Try		
Second Try		

The next morning, when Tecumseh's temper had cooled, he sent the governor an apology, which (15)
Harrison accepted. They talked a great deal more before the council was through, but neither (30)
side budged. (32)

Harrison refused to give back any of the land acquired by the Fort Wayne Treaty. He claimed that the (51)
treaty had been negotiated fairly. Tecumseh insisted that it hadn't been and that the land still belonged (68)
to the Indians. If the government tried to have it surveyed, he warned, bloodshed would result. And if (86)
the land wasn't returned, the chiefs who had signed the treaty would be killed and he, Harrison, "will (104)
have a hand in killing them." The old government chiefs no longer spoke for the people, Tecumseh (121)
said. The warriors were running things now, and he was their chief. "I am alone the acknowledged head (139)
of all the Indians," he said. (145)

How then, Harrison interrupted, would the tribes receive their yearly payments? Usually the money and (160)
goods were given to the village chiefs to distribute. (169)

"Brother," Tecumseh said, "When you speak to me of yearly payments, I look at the land and pity the (188)
women and children. I am authorized to say that they will not receive them, Brother. They want to (206)
save that piece of land. We do not wish you to take it. It is small enough for our purposes. If you do take (230)
it, you must blame yourself as the cause of trouble between us and the tribes who sold it to you. I want (252)
the present boundary line to continue. Should you cross it, I assure you it will be productive of (270)
bad consequences." (272)

READING PASSAGES

Fifth Grade Level—Skill Sheet 11 (Social Science: American Indians)

Directions: Say each word. If you finish before the end of the timing, go back to the beginning and start over.

	Correct	Error
First Try		
Second Try		

The weeks passed, summer turned to fall, and the fighting Tecumseh predicted didn't come to pass. On (17)
the surface, everything was peaceful. But there was a feeling of uneasiness in the autumn air, as distinct (35)
as the tang of wood smoke in the wind. Everybody started making sure which side everybody else was (53)
on, just in case. Things stayed that way during the winter. Heavy snows and bitter cold kept people at (72)
home, gathered around their fires. In Prophetstown snow drifted deep around the wigwams, but everyone (87)
inside was warm and well fed. The Great Spirit had been generous and had sent a bountiful corn harvest. (106)
The British had been generous, too. Tecumseh had gone to Canada again that fall, to ask the British for (125)
help. The British Indian agent there had sent a pack train with supplies. So no one at Prophetstown (143)
went hungry. (145)

The spring came, and the tension that had been lurking beneath the surface sprang to life. Reports came (163)
of Potawatomi and Kickapoo raids on white settlements in Illinois. All along the Big Muddy river, (179)
settlers abandoned their homesteads. From the Fort Wayne Treaty lands came the news that one of the (196)
Miami tribes had frightened off the surveyors who'd begun surveying the land. The Indians hadn't hurt (212)
them, just scared them half to death, but it was a bad sign, Harrison thought. Very bad. The tribe was (232)
usually the most peaceful of tribes. Tecumseh's influence must be growing. (243)

ONE MINUTE FLUENCY
SOPRIS WEST SKILL BUILDERS SERIES

SEE TO SAY

	Correct	Error
First Try		
Second Try		

READING PASSAGES

Fifth Grade Level—Skill Sheet 12 (Social Science: American Indians)

Directions: Say each word. If you finish before the end of the timing, go back to the beginning and start over.

It was a weary band of travelers that rode out of the leafless forest that cold January day in 1812. Their (21)
horses were thin and walked with their heads down. As they started across the snow-covered plain, the (38)
icy wind whipped their faces and stung their eyes. The riders clutched their blankets closer. They were (55)
almost there. (57)

At the head of this little band rode Tecumseh, returning with his followers to what was once (74)
Prophetstown. Now it was nothing but a heap of cold, dead ashes. They reached the village outskirts (91)
and paused. There were the charred remains of the council house, sticking up through the snow. They (108)
walked their horses down a smooth, snowy slope where rows of wigwams once stood. No one said (125)
much. Finally, at a word from Tecumseh, they urged their horses on, eastward. He's seen enough. (141)

Tecumseh's tour of the southern tribes had failed. The handful of Creek warriors who rode with him now (159)
were all he could persuade to join him. He'd done his best. He'd been on the move for six months. He'd (180)
smoked the pipe of peace at one council fire after another, with Creeks, Choctas, Chickasaws, and Osages. (197)
He'd spoken to great crowds of warriors, spoken brilliantly and passionately. He's spoken the truth. But (213)
no one believed it. (217)

Tecumseh was sure—as sure as he was of anything—that the Indian tribes could only survive if they (236)
united. Separately, they were doomed. Of this he was certain. But he simply couldn't convince the (252)
southern tribes. They'd been enemies of the northern tribes for so long they just couldn't change. (268)

SEE TO SAY

READING PASSAGES

Sixth Grade Level—Skill Sheet 1 (Science: Rain Forest)

Directions: Say each word. If you finish before the end of the timing, go back to the beginning and start over.

	Correct	Error
First Try		
Second Try		

The Amazon River starts with melting snow from the Andes Mountains and has arms reaching through (16)
nine countries to drain mist and rain from the world's largest jungle into the Atlantic Ocean. (32)

It's big. It's the longest river in the world, sometimes deep enough to cover a ten-story building and, (50)
during the rainy season, up to twenty miles wide. (59)

It's beyond big. One of its islands is larger than Vermont and Connecticut combined. (73)

Over two-thirds of the world's freshwater is found within its basin. In fact, the water pouring from the (91)
Amazon into the Atlantic each day would satisfy New York City's freshwater needs for nine years. (107)

A look at life on the passing shore shows that the Amazon is not only its people's highway, but also (127)
their supermarket, their bathtub and washing machine, their kitchen sink and swimming hole. Men (141)
fish from dugout canoes. Women wash clothes and children are washing up and splashing around (156)
for fun. (158)

Years ago, you could have cruised for miles without seeing many houses on shore. Today, more and (175)
more people live along the Amazon and its tributaries. Traditionally, parents had a dozen or more (191)
children, although often only two to four survived to adulthood. Medical care is still scarce, but the (208)
small amount now available helps more children live long enough to have children of their own. In (225)
addition, many Peruvians, unable to find work in the cities, have moved to make a new start in the (244)
jungle along the Amazon River. (249)

READING PASSAGES
Sixth Grade Level—Skill Sheet 2 (Science: Rain Forest)

Directions: Say each word. If you finish before the end of the timing, go back to the beginning and start over.

	Correct	Error
First Try		
Second Try		

The jungle canopy is one of the earth's last unexplored frontiers. Scientists who had studied species (16)
within reach already knew that tropical rain forests are our planet's richest ecosystem. Until recently (31)
they had no idea that, over their heads, an amazing number of unknown plants and animals was living (49)
and dying without ever coming down to earth. (57)

One entomologist, for example, sprayed several rain forest trees to strip them of all their insects. (73)
Approximately 80 percent—4 out of 5—of the insects he found were new species. (88)

You can step out on the only canopy walkway in the Amazon. It starts from a platform built around the (108)
trunk of a 150-foot shimbillo tree. The narrow bridge slants upward to the second giant tree. It zigzags (126)
from one huge tree to the next, up and up again. You get a bird's-eye view of the canopy on the last (148)
platform, which is 118 feet above the ground. (156)

Fed by the tremendous energy of the tropical sun, the canopy is a factory. Ninety percent of the (174)
jungle's photosynthesis takes place, using the sunlight to create food for its plants. Here, eiphytes, (189)
plants that live on trees without harming them, park themselves in the light. Lianas, or vines, hitch a (207)
ride toward the sun. More than fifty different plant species can attach themselves to one tree. These (224)
plants flower and fruit, providing food for insects, birds, and larger animals—that, in turn, are food (241)
for different insects, birds, and larger animals. (248)

SEE TO SAY

READING PASSAGES

Sixth Grade Level—Skill Sheet 3 (Science: Rain Forest)

Directions: Say each word. If you finish before the end of the timing, go back to the beginning and start over.

	Correct	Error
First Try		
Second Try		

Each layer of the rain forest captures light and heat from above while trapping humidity below. As a (18)
result, each layer has its own unique environment inhabited by different kinds of life. (32)

The canopy, the rain forest's dense ceiling, is made of trees over sixty-five feet high. These trees grow (50)
straight and tall, putting out branches once they reach the sun. Popping through the canopy here and (67)
there is the emergent layer, trees 130 feet or higher. Fully exposed to sun and wind, this layer endures (86)
temperatures of 90 degrees or more. But they have only about 60 percent humidity. (100)

The understory, from near ground level to the canopy, consists of shrubs, smaller trees, and young (116)
canopy trees pushing toward the light. Many of its plants and trees have larger leaves than those living (134)
in the canopy. This way they can absorb as much of the dim light as possible. (150)

Only 1 to 2 percent of the sun's light ever reaches the rain forest floor. Its few plants have thin, very (171)
large leaves to absorb what light is available. Its average humidity of 90 percent is perfect for the fungi (190)
and bacteria. The bacteria team up with termites and earthworms to decompose, break down, the dead (206)
plants and animals that drop there. The forest, thirsty for nourishment, quickly reabsorbs the nutrients (221)
from them. Shallow tree roots take up these nutrients. Some insects lay eggs on dead animals to provide (239)
their offspring with a ready food supply. So few nutrients are left in the soil that the rain forest has been (260)
called the "wet desert." (264)

SEE TO SAY

	Correct	Error
First Try		
Second Try		

READING PASSAGES
Sixth Grade Level—Skill Sheet 4 (Science: Rain Forest)

Directions: Say each word. If you finish before the end of the timing, go back to the beginning and start over.

People throughout the Amazon are chopping down the rain forest. They are chopping down the rain (16)
forest to sell its lumber. They are chopping it down to farm, although, in many areas, the soil is too (36)
poor to produce crops for more than a few years. They are chopping it down for cattle pastures, but, (55)
again, the soil is so poor that each square yard only produces enough beef for three Quarter Pounders (73)
before it's abandoned. If today's rate of destruction continues, the world's tropical rain forests could (88)
be gone by the year 2030. (94)

The world needs the rain forest to help clean the air we breathe and make the medicines that keep (113)
us well. But the people who live in rain forests have needs, too. (126)

H. Morgan Smith spent several years with the Choco Indians in the rain forest in Panama. For the past (145)
forty years, he has taught others how to stay alive in the jungle with little more than a machete and, of (166)
course, the most important survival tool, common sense. (174)

If you understand your environment, you can survive. Then the environment can survive also. If you (180)
know what is dangerous, you can relax and enjoy what's beautiful. He shows what is dangerous—a (197)
dumbcane plant, that if bitten, could swell your tongue until you suffocate. Some of the jungle's (223)
medicine chest—bryophytes, mosslike plants that are used for soothing wounds, and ants with huge (238)
jaws that you can force to bite both sides of a bad cut. When you twist their bodies off, the ants' (259)
mandibles remain, acting like stitches to keep the gash closed. (269)

	Correct	Error
First Try		
Second Try		

READING PASSAGES
Sixth Grade Level—Skill Sheet 5 (Science: Rain Forest)

Directions: Say each word. If you finish before the end of the timing, go back to the beginning and start over.

Symbiotic relationships also are important in the rain forest. For example, the cecropia tree teams up (16)
with Azteca ants to form a symbiotic relationship or partnership in which each member benefits. The (32)
cecropia's hollow trunk gives the ants a place to live. The tree also feeds the ants by producing a starchy (52)
food at the base of its leaf stalks. In return, the ants patrol the cecropia. They sting leaf-eating insects to (72)
drive them off, throw sprouting epiphytes overboard, and cut the tendrils of vines before they can attach. (89)

The rain forest is full of such obliging partnerships. The sloth, for example, gives algae a home and (107)
consequently takes on a greenish tint, helpful camouflage in the treetops. (118)

Actually, no jungle plant or animal lives a separate life. Each has adapted to take advantage of certain (136)
features of the jungle. The hummingbird has a long beak that can poke into trumpet-shaped flowers for (153)
nectar. Each plant or animal has adapted to perform special tasks for others. For example, the (169)
hummingbird carries pollen from flower to flower in its search for food. These associations build upon (185)
one another to create the life of the rain forest (or any ecosystem, for that matter). (201)

A bush is not a separate thing. It gives shade to others plants, gets pollinated by birds, and provides for (221)
the fungi underneath, and so on. (227)

SEE TO SAY

	Correct	Error
First Try		
Second Try		

READING PASSAGES

Sixth Grade Level—Skill Sheet 6 (Science: Rain Forest)

Directions: Say each word. If you finish before the end of the timing, go back to the beginning and start over.

The rain forest affects the weather around the world. It absorbs huge amounts of energy from the sun, (18)
but also manages to give a lot of it back. When rain fall is pumped back into the air through evaporation, (39)
it carries heat along with it. When trees give off moisture from the surface of their leaves, heat (57)
accompanies that water, too. Winds then push the moisture and the warmth to colder parts of the globe. (75)

The rain forest is also a good weapon against global warming. Plants take carbon dioxide, a gas that adds (94)
to the greenhouse warming effect, from the air. In return, they release oxygen. (107)

The United States and Europe used to be covered with great forests. They were chopped down to build (125)
farms, cities, and factories. Now the people in rain forest countries want lives as comfortable as ours. (142)

If rain forests benefit the entire world, perhaps the entire world should help support them. Some experts (159)
suggest finding less destructive ways to harvest rain forest lumber. Others suggest bringing renewable (173)
crops—Brazil nuts, nuts from the tagua palm to make buttons, unusual fruits such as guanabana, copaiba (190)
oil for hair conditioners—into the world market. There we can all help by buying them. Still others say (209)
we should support organizations that help pay off tropical countries' debts if they agree to protect rain (226)
forest land. (228)

	Correct	Error
First Try		
Second Try		

READING PASSAGES

Sixth Grade Level—Skill Sheet 7 (Social Science: Integration)

Directions: Say each word. If you finish before the end of the timing, go back to the beginning and start over.

Wednesday, September 4, 1957, was going to be another warm, dry sunny day in Little Rock, Arkansas. (17)
The sky was cloudless, and the temperature was already in the seventies by seven o'clock in the morning. (35)
At 4405 West 18th Street, fifteen-year-old Elizabeth Eckford was getting ready for her first day at Little (52)
Rock Central High School. The small house echoed with the morning sounds of water running the (68)
bathroom sink and shower. Doors and drawers were opening and closing. The half-awake voices of the (84)
Eckford family were greeting each other good morning. (92)

Mrs. Birdie Eckford was already in the kitchen, getting the family breakfast ready. (105)

In the living room, Elizabeth was ironing the black-and-white dress she and her mother had made just (122)
for this day. It was hard to keep the iron moving slowly and carefully over the checkered skirt. She (141)
wanted the dress to be perfect, but her mind was racing with excitement and worry. (156)

In just a couple of hours, she would be going to Central High, the biggest and best high school in (176)
Arkansas. Some people even said it was one of the best schools in the whole United States. Most of the (196)
students who graduated from Central went on to college. Elizabeth wanted to go to college. She'd be (213)
able to take classes at Central that weren't offered at other high schools. (226)

But Central was an all-white school. And Elizabeth would be one of nine black students, the first of (244)
their race, to go to Central. Here was a reason to be worried. (257)

SEE TO SAY

	Correct	Error
First Try		
Second Try		

READING PASSAGES
Sixth Grade Level—Skill Sheet 8 (Social Science: Integration)

Directions: Say each word. If you finish before the end of the timing, go back to the beginning and start over.

The bus rumbled and lurched down the street, heading east toward Central High. It was a short ride. (18)
Elizabeth sat calmly, a small smile on her lips. She was looking forward to seeing the other eight (36)
teenagers again. Carlotta Walls and Gloria Ray were the youngest, at fourteen. Melba Patillo, Jefferson (51)
Thomas, and Terrance Roberts were the same age as she, fifteen. Minnijean Brown, Thelma (65)
Mothershed, and Ernest Green were sixteen. They had all spent many mornings and afternoons (79)
together at Mrs. Daisy Bate's house during August. (87)

Mrs. Bates was a leader in the black community of Little Rock. She was normally a shy, quiet woman (106)
who enjoyed gardening and making pottery. But she had a bold and strong side to her personality, too. (124)
She had learned how to fly a plane and she helped her husband run a newspaper, *The Arkansas State* (143)
Press. Slender and only five feet three inches tall, Mrs. Bates was actually smaller than some of the (161)
teenagers. During the summer, however, she had become their coach—a tough trainer. But she was (177)
one who cared and listened. The teenagers needed to be ready for some of the problems they'd face at (196)
Central once school started. (200)

Mrs. Bates helped them to understand that they had a right to go to Central. The Supreme Court had (219)
made it clear that they could not be kept from going to a school because of the color of their skin. But (241)
once in the school, they were on their own. (250)

	Correct	Error
First Try		
Second Try		

READING PASSAGES

Sixth Grade Level—Skill Sheet 9 (Social Science: Integration)

Directions: Say each word. If you finish before the end of the timing, go back to the beginning and start over.

On Friday, September 20, Judge Davies ruled that Governor Faubus had indeed disobeyed the Supreme (15)
Court order that schools be integrated. The judge ordered the governor to stop using the National Guard (32)
to keep the students out of Central. (39)

On television that night, Governor Faubus gave his response to the judge's order. Looking very (54)
businesslike in his dark suit, he said, "I have tried to follow a course that would preserve and maintain (73)
the peace and order in Little Rock and in the state." He continued in a steady, calm voice that barely (93)
masked his anger. "Now that a Federal court has chosen to substitute its judgment for mine as to how (112)
the peace and order should be preserved, I must temporarily at least abide. Therefore, I have issued (129)
orders that the National Guard stationed in Little Rock be removed." (140)

Winding up his speech, he asked the black students to voluntarily stay away from Central "until such (157)
time as there is assurance that their right to integrate can be accomplished in a peaceful manner." (174)

Mrs. Bates was not fooled by the governor's words. She knew that if it were left to him, black students (194)
would never be allowed into Central. She wasn't going to wait. (205)

"These students are definitely going to enter Central High School," she said. "They have been enrolled (221)
and officially accepted. That is the only school open to them now." She was just not sure if they would (241)
enter the next Monday, or a day or two later. (251)

SEE TO SAY

READING PASSAGES
Sixth Grade Level—Skill Sheet 10 (Social Science: Integration)

Directions: Say each word. If you finish before the end of the timing, go back to the beginning and start over.

	Correct	Error
First Try		
Second Try		

In Washington, D.C., President Eisenhower was growing more and more irritated with the situation in (15)
Little Rock. Since its beginning, he'd hoped Governor Faubus would obey the Supreme Court order (30)
and prove to be a leader in helping integration occur peacefully in the South. He'd even met with the (49)
governor, who had promised that he'd tell the National Guard to protect the nine teenagers as they (66)
entered Central. Instead, Faubus had ordered the guardsmen to leave Central altogether. Then he went (81)
off to a conference in Georgia, allowing the mob to riot freely and take control of Little Rock. President (100)
Eisenhower was furious. (103)

The evening of September 23, as the mob began attacking people, President Eisenhower decided it was (119)
necessary to get tough. He issued an executive order calling for everyone who was preventing the (135)
students from entering and remaining in Central to "cease and desist." (146)

"I will use the full power of the United States," he warned, "to prevent any obstruction of the law and (166)
carry out the orders of the Federal Court." (174)

Mrs. Bates heard the President's order, but she didn't think the order by itself was enough protection (191)
for the teenagers. She told them to stay home the next day, Tuesday, September 24. (206)

She did the right thing. The people paid no attention to President Eisenhower's order. In their minds, (223)
the President of the United States had no right to tell the state of Arkansas what to do. They remained (243)
outside the school until it was clear that the teenagers were not showing up that day. (259)

SEE TO SAY

	Correct	Error
First Try		
Second Try		

READING PASSAGES

Sixth Grade Level—Skill Sheet 11 (Social Science: Integration)

Directions: Say each word. If you finish before the end of the timing, go back to the beginning and start over.

School had begun as usual for most of the white students at Central. At 8:45, the United States flag was (20)
raised. The bugle sounded the "call to colors." And the students and teachers placed their right hands (37)
over their hearts and recited the Pledge of Allegiance. But everyone knew this was not just another (54)
morning at Central High School. (59)

At a nine o'clock assembly, General Edwin A. Walker, the commander of the soldiers, spoke to the (76)
white students. He explained the 1954 Supreme Court decision—that skin color could no longer be (92)
the reason for sending children to separate schools. The President had ordered the Army and the (108)
National Guard to carry out the Court's orders, he said. "As an officer of the United States Army," (126)
he announced, "I have been chosen to command these forces and to execute the President's orders." (142)

The tall, no-nonsense commander recognized the audience as "law-abiding citizens," and said they had (156)
nothing to fear. However, he warned "That those who interfere or disrupt the proper administration of (172)
the school will be removed by the soldiers and turned over to the local people." (187)

While General Walker spoke, a mob gathered across the street from the school. It was much smaller (204)
than the previous day's mob but just as angry and stubborn. They ignored Major James Morris's orders (221)
to go home, so Major Morris radioed for help. Within minutes, a squad of soldiers arrived and moved (239)
steadily toward the mob, bayonets lowered and pointed straight ahead. (249)

READING PASSAGES
Sixth Grade Level—Skill Sheet 12 (Social Science: Integration)

Directions: Say each word. If you finish before the end of the timing, go back to the beginning and start over.

	Correct	Error
First Try		
Second Try		

Eight of the nine students made it through the entire school year. After school each day, they met with (19)
Mrs. Bates at her home or talked to her on the phone. If the students were like nonviolent soldiers at war, (40)
Mrs. Bates was their commander in chief. She couldn't be in school with them because she was neither (58)
one of their parents nor a teacher. But in their daily talks, she helped them keep up their courage. She (78)
reminded them of how important it was to stay at Central High School. It was important for their own (97)
education and for that of many other black students who would be going to white schools in the future. (116)

Mrs. Bates listened carefully to the students and kept records of everything that happened to them. (132)
When the students' worried parents called her, she calmed them and assured them that the teenagers (148)
would be okay. She phoned the school and scolded the officials for not protecting the students or for (166)
not treating them fairly. At one point she even called the Pentagon in Washington, D.C., to talk to the (185)
general in charge of the guards at Central. She told him she didn't like the way the guards ignored (204)
attacks on the students. After her call, the general sent in more troops from the 101st Airborne Division. (222)
These troops were more fearsome to the segregationists, and there were fewer bold attacks. (236)

On May 27, 1958, Ernest Green—the only senior among the Little Rock nine—graduated from Central (253)
High School. It had been a hard year for him. No one cheered when he walked across the stage. "I didn't (274)
care," Ernest said later. "I accomplished what I'd come there for." (285)

SEE TO SAY

	Correct	Error
First Try		
Second Try		

READING PASSAGES

Seventh Grade Level—Skill Sheet 1 (Science: Volcanoes)

Directions: Say each word. If you finish before the end of the timing, go back to the beginning and start over.

Some mountain ranges owe their birth to volcanic action. Uplifting along the edge of a tectonic plate, (17)
the Rocky Mountains and the Andes contain sharp-topped extinct volcanoes, quiet dormant volcanoes, (30)
and peaks that still smolder with the potential of eruption. The Cascade Range, extending from (45)
California to Washington, has at least fourteen snow-capped peaks that could suddenly erupt, as Mount (60)
St. Helens did in 1980. (65)

Volcanoes come in many shapes and sizes. Helgafell, in Iceland, is only 725 feet tall. Mount (81)
Kilimanjaro in Africa, a snow-capped dormant volcano, is 19,340 feet tall. Cotopaxi, in Ecuador, is (96)
an active volcano almost 20,000 feet tall. And the world's tallest mountain isn't Mount Everest—it's (112)
Mauna Loa! This active Hawaiian volcano rises more than 30,000 feet from the deep seafloor of the (129)
Pacific Ocean, with only 13,680 feet of the volcano sticking out above sea level. (143)

The depths of the world's oceans hide most of our planet's volcanoes—nearly 20,000 of them, (159)
called seamounts. They form along fissures in the seafloor near the edges of tectonic plates and over (176)
hot spots where plumes of magma rise like fountains from exceptionally hot regions in the earth's (192)
mantle. Silent and unseen in their submarine world, seamounts constantly build upward from the (206)
ocean floor. Because of the depth of the ocean, many seamounts rival the height of volcanoes on the (224)
earth's surface. Eventually they pop through the surface of the ocean and we stop calling them (240)
seamounts. They become islands. (244)

TSEE TO SAY

	Correct	Error
First Try		
Second Try		

READING PASSAGES
Seventh Grade Level—Skill Sheet 2 (Science: Volcanoes)

Directions: Say each word. If you finish before the end of the timing, go back to the beginning and start over.

As gas-laden magma rises through the pipes inside of a volcano, it becomes bubbly. When this frothy mix (18)
spills out on the earth's surface, we call it lava. Depending on the amount and size of bubbles in the lava, (39)
and the size and shape of the lava as it falls, it can be classified under many different names. (58)

Unlike the ash that comes from burning wood, volcanic ash is made of sharp particles of fragmented (75)
lava, like scouring powder. This fine dust easily floats on air currents. When thrown high into the (92)
atmosphere as a volcanic plume during an eruption, the dust can travel vast distances. In less than three (110)
days, the ash cloud from the 1991 eruption of Mount Pinatubo in the Philippines drifted more than 5,000 (128)
miles, raining down on the east coast of Africa. Volcanic ash, or dust, includes any particles less than (146)
2 millimeters, less than 1 inch, across. (153)

Scoria occurs when clots of lava cool in midair. Depending on the size of the scoria, it can end up as tiny (175)
cinders or lapilla. Lapilli are pieces of solidified lava, ranging from the size of a peppercorn to the size (194)
of a peach—2 to 634 millimeters or about an inch to 2.5 inches across. (209)

Pumice looks like a rocky sponge when it hardens, but it also starts out as lava. As magma rises from (229)
chambers deep within the earth, it reaches a point where its gas content becomes bubbly. The more the (247)
bubbly magma rises, the foamier it gets—like the froth coming out of a shaken-up bottle of soda pop. (266)
When the volcano erupts, the extremely foamy portion of the magma solidifies into pumice in midair. (282)
It is the only rock that can float. (290)

	Correct	Error
First Try		
Second Try		

READING PASSAGES

Seventh Grade Level—Skill Sheet 3 (Science: Volcanoes)

Directions: Say each word. If you finish before the end of the timing, go back to the beginning and start over.

Tapping deep into a magma chamber, a volcano grows by spitting, spattering, and spewing lava and solid rocks. (18)
This accumulation of debris builds a cone around the volcano's main vent. While the main vent carries the force (37)
of each eruption, side vents sometimes also spew lava, building up the sides of the volcano. Many of the world's (57)
largest volcanoes have composite cones—a cumulative combination of layers of ash and cinders, lava flows, and (74)
spattered lava. (76)

Inside the cone, the crater is the cup-shaped depression in the middle, surrounding a vent. A crater is relatively (95)
small, and is created when the volcano blasts material out of the vent. A caldera, on the other hand, happens (115)
when the cone collapses into the magma chamber below. Compared to a crater, a caldera is huge—like an (134)
upside-down volcano. (136)

Calderas sometimes contain other formations dependent on a magma chamber: boiling springs, fumaroles, and (150)
lava lakes. Crater lakes form when a caldera fills with water. The deepest lake in North America is inside a (170)
caldera—Crater Lake, Oregon. The lake is 2,000 feet deep and 5.6 miles in diameter. (185)

Spatter cones grow when the volcano spits out lots of clots of hot lava. These spatter around the vent and cool. (206)
The cone grows higher as more spattered clots pile up on top of old, cooled clots. (222)

During an eruption, cinder cones form as ash settles around the vent. During an active eruption, a cinder cone (241)
can grow hundreds of feet high in just a few days. One such rapidly growing volcano in Mexico popped up in (262)
a cornfield in 1943. It grew 33 feet in one day, 450 feet in its first week, and over 1,000 feet in two months! (286)

READING PASSAGES

Seventh Grade Level—Skill Sheet 4 (Science: Volcanoes)

Directions: Say each word. If you finish before the end of the timing, go back to the beginning and start over.

	Correct	Error
First Try		
Second Try		

Fumaroles are vents in the earth's surface that sputter volcanic gases and hot steam. They are most often (18)
found on and around volcanoes, and in conjunction with geysers. A pool of magma can be lying beneath (36)
a layer of bedrock, as it does in Yellowstone National Park. As vapors rise from the magma pool and (55)
pass through the water table, they turn the water to steam, which has a thousand times more volume than (74)
water. The fumarole then vents the steam and the vapors at the surface. (87)

Vapors from fumaroles may contain dissolved minerals transported from deep underground. Chemicals (99)
in the vapors stain the rocks around fumaroles with colorful patterns. Deposits of stinky yellow sulfur, (115)
bright white ammonium chloride, yellow ferrous chloride, and tiny amounts of metals such as iron, zinc, (131)
lead, and tin all build up around fumaroles. White calcium carbonate, clear quartz, and yellow and red (148)
sodium aluminum sulfates add more touches of color. (156)

Fumaroles provide warm spots where wildlife gathers. At Yellowstone, bison often cluster around the (170)
steamy vents in the middle of the winter. The warm air keeps snow at bay for a small radius around (190)
the vent, allowing deer, bison, and elk to browse for plants even when the snow is deep elsewhere in (209)
the park. (211)

Rocks do a great job of holding and transmitting heat from magma. When hot rocks warm up pools of (230)
water underground, the water pushes its way upward through fissures and fractures, dissolving minerals (244)
from the surrounding rocks. The result is a pool of water called a hot spring. (259)

	Correct	Error
First Try		
Second Try		

READING PASSAGES

Seventh Grade Level—Skill Sheet 5 (Science: Volcanoes)

Directions: Say each word. If you finish before the end of the timing, go back to the beginning and start over.

Boiling springs are an intermediate stage between hot springs and geysers. Geysers are the rarest of (16)
all the earth's hot formations. Only eight hundred or so are found on the entire planet. Like fumaroles, (34)
geysers don't require a volcano nearby, just the proper heat and plumbing under the earth's surface. (50)
The unique vents spit up steam and water on a regular schedule. Old Faithful, in Yellowstone National (67)
Park, is the world's best-known geyser, throwing 5,000 gallons of water up to 150 feet in the air. It (86)
erupts every 75 to 90 minutes—not as often as it used to, but patterns of geysers tend to change. There (107)
are more than 500 known geysers in Yellowstone National Park, more than anywhere else in the world. (124)
Coming in second is the Kronotsky Nature Preserve on Russia's Kamchatka Peninsula, with almost (138)
200 geysers, some as small as 1 inch tall. Other countries with major geyser fields include Iceland, (155)
Chile, and New Zealand. (159)

The word "geyser" comes from an Icelandic verb meaning to erupt. In its heyday, the Great Geysir (176)
burst over 200 feet into the air. Today, it takes a little priming with laundry soap to encourage the (195)
Great Geysir to explode (the soap encourages the superheated water to boil). (207)

There are two types of geysers, fountain geysers rise from within a surface pool of boiling water. (224)
Columnar geysers pop out of a dry sinter cone, like a small volcano. At Yellowstone some of the (242)
sinter cones look like giant beehives. Colors in the hot pools vary from clear and brilliant blue to (260)
yellows and reds caused by heat-loving algae, and ink black water muddied by suspended particles (275)
of iron. (277)

SEE TO SAY

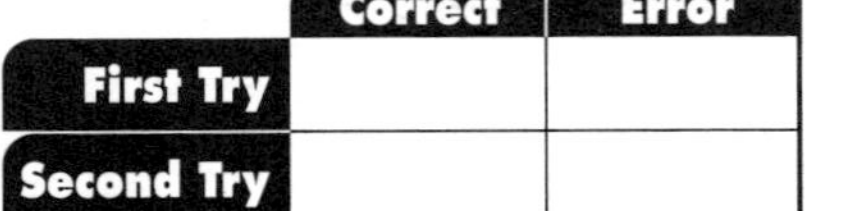

	Correct	Error
First Try		
Second Try		

READING PASSAGES
Seventh Grade Level—Skill Sheet 6 (Science: Volcanoes)

Directions: Say each word. If you finish before the end of the timing, go back to the beginning and start over.

Mud pots are hot springs with very little water. The consistency of the mud is dependent on the amount of water. (21)
Mud pots can be soupy or almost dry. Minerals—mostly iron pyrite—color mud pots gray, white, black, or (40)
cream-colored. (41)

Mud pots can be any size, from a tiny hole in the ground to a funnel shape up to 33 feet in diameter and 16.5 (66)
feet deep. The outward explosions of mud create bizarre patterns on the surface of a mud pot, like concentric (85)
rings and stiff knobs. (89)

Thanks to steam in the water, mud pots bubble and boil. If the gases build up in a viscous mix of mud, a mud (113)
pot can belch and spatter its surroundings with boiling mud. Mud volcanoes happen when a mud pot gets (131)
hyperactive, spitting huge globs of mud into the sky. The blobs of mud form a cone or mound, forming the (151)
mud volcano. At the Mushpots site in Wyoming's Yellowstone Park, one large mud volcano churned out (167)
globs of mud as big as a cabin. It spewed mud up to 100 feet into the air. (185)

Paint pots are mud pots with style. Colored by additional minerals in the hot water, they glisten in odd shades: (205)
blue, orange, red, pink, and yellow. Pink and red paint pots get their color from iron oxide. Sulfur minerals (224)
color yellow and orange mud pots. (230)

Hot water dripping from the spray of geysers or running in a stream from a hot spring contain a lot of dissolved (252)
minerals. If the mineral laden water flows over surfaces, it leaves the minerals behind, forming an ever-growing (269)
deposit. These deposits create terraces of stone cover with travertine—flowstone formations called terraces. (283)

SEE TO SAY

	Correct	Error
First Try		
Second Try		

READING PASSAGES
Seventh Grade Level—Skill Sheet 7
(Social Science: Japanese Internment)

Directions: Say each word. If you finish before the end of the timing, go back to the beginning and start over.

Karen Korematsu watched her friend Maya Okada nervously approach the front of the class. Their social (16)
studies teacher, Mr. Wishnoff, had asked the students to give oral reports about some aspect of World War II. (35)
Maya was to present the last report on this spring afternoon in 1967. (48)

Sunlight streamed through the dusty Venetian blinds, filling the classroom with a warm, sleepy haze. Students (64)
tried to keep their attention focused on Maya, but their eyes and minds wandered. After listening to presentations (82)
all period, they were feeling bored and restless. Some gazed idly at the large maps of the United States and world (103)
hung on one wall of the classroom. In another hour, school would be out, and they could enjoy the rest of the (125)
sunny day. (127)

Like most of her classmates, Karen was looking forward to the end of the period, but it wasn't because she was (148)
bored. In fact, she was feeling tense as she watched Maya make her way to the front of the class. Karen didn't (170)
like talking about World War II. She and Maya were the only Japanese Americans in the class, and their (189)
classmates often made fun of them whenever the topic of World War II came up. (204)

Standing in front of the class in her white blouse and freshly ironed skirt, Maya announced in a clear voice that (225)
her report would be about what happened to Japanese Americans living in the United States during World (242)
War II. (244)

Maya explained that after the Japanese bombed Pearl Harbor, many Americans blamed Japanese Americans for (259)
the attack and accused them of acting as spies for the Japanese government. Life became hard for Japanese (277)
Americans, especially for those living on the Pacific Coast. (286)

SEE TO SAY

	Correct	Error
First Try		
Second Try		

READING PASSAGES
Seventh Grade Level—Skill Sheet 8
(Social Science: Japanese Internment)

Directions: Say each word. If you finish before the end of the timing, go back to the beginning and start over.

All student eyes were focused on Maya as she reported that more than 112,000 Japanese Americans were (17)
imprisoned during the war. They were the only group of American citizens singled out in this way, she said. (36)
Even though the United States also went to war against Germany and Italy, President Roosevelt did not allow (54)
German Americans or Italian Americans to be forced into internment camps. (65)

The internment camps were like prisons, Maya explained. There were ten camps, and armed soldiers stood (81)
guard to make sure no one escaped. Japanese-American families had to live in cramped barracks as if they (99)
were prisoners of war. (103)

Several Japanese Americans refused to obey President Roosevelt's order to report to the camps, Maya went (119)
on, including a man from California named Korematsu. Korematsu believed the government had no right to (135)
force him from his home because of his Japanese heritage. He took his case against Roosevelt's order all the (154)
way to the Supreme Court. (159)

Karen gasped when she heard her family name. "It couldn't be my father," she thought, "not in a million (178)
years. Maybe it's one of my uncles." (185)

Then she heard Maya actually say her father's name: "Fred Korematsu." Karen could feel all 34 students in (203)
the classroom staring at her, waiting for her to explain the connection between herself and the man. "Is that (222)
your father? Is that your father?" everyone, including the teacher seemed to ask at once. (237)

Karen didn't know how to respond. She felt confused, angry, and embarrassed. She was mad at Maya for (255)
not having told her the topic of her report. How could Maya have presented all that information to the class (275)
without warning her beforehand? (279)

SEE TO SAY

	Correct	Error
First Try		
Second Try		

READING PASSAGES
Seventh Grade Level—Skill Sheet 9
(Social Science: Japanese Internment)

Directions: Say each word. If you finish before the end of the timing, go back to the beginning and start over.

Fred Korematsu was a Japanese-American student born and raised in Oakland, California. However, after the bombing (16)
of Pearl Harbor in December 1941, his life changed dramatically. (26)

Early on the morning of May 2, 1942, many people were still in bed, enjoying the luxury of a Saturday off from work. (49)
Fred's parents, though, were already hard at work in their greenhouses, preparing their roses for the Mother's Day (67)
holiday just two weeks away. (72)

As they worked, Army jeeps once again came rumbling through the community. Soldiers began posting official notices (89)
on telephone poles around the Oakland area. This time, though, the worst had come. This time, the innocent-looking (107)
sheets of white paper announced that "All persons of Japanese ancestry" were to evacuate their homes immediately. (124)
"Dispose of your homes and property. Wind up your business," the posters instructed. "One sea bag of bedding, two (143)
suitcases of clothing allowed per person." On the following Saturday, May 9, they were to report to authorities with (162)
their belongings, prepared to move into "assembly centers." (170)

Many Japanese Americans were numb with shock as they read the notice. Some spoke angrily of the injustice that (189)
they were powerless to stop. Others cried in distress. (198)

One week to wrap up a lifetime! Where should they begin? What should they pack to bring with them? Should they (219)
take heavy wool sweaters or light cotton clothing? The answer depended on where they were going—but that was (238)
something no one knew. No one could answer that question either. It was a maddening dilemma, and their future lives (258)
might well depend on what they put inside their two suitcases and one sea bag, but there was no way to know what (281)
things they might need. (285)

While his family busily packed and prepared to leave the nursery, Fred thought about what he should do. If he evacuated (306)
and went to the assembly center with his family, he would leave his fiancé behind—and they did not want to separate. (328)
On the other hand, if he didn't follow the evacuation orders, he could be arrested as a criminal. (346)

SEE TO SAY

	Correct	Error
First Try		
Second Try		

READING PASSAGES
Seventh Grade Level—Skill Sheet 10
(Social Science: Women's Rights)

Directions: Say each word. If you finish before the end of the timing, go back to the beginning and start over.

On July 14, 1848, an announcement appeared in the *Seneca County Courier*. A convention "to discuss the social, (18)
civil, and religious condition and rights of women" was to be held the next week at the Methodist Church. (37)
Women, it said, were "earnestly invited to attend." (45)

Five days later, the roads into Seneca Falls were clogged with carriages. The church was a sea of bonnets, with (65)
quite a number of bare male heads among them and people had come from miles around, and the church was (85)
filled to bursting. (88)

On a raised wooden platform at the front of the church sat a very nervous Elizabeth Cady Stanton. Eight years (108)
had passed since she and Mrs. Mott had first talked about doing this; it was eight busy years filled with children (129)
and housekeeping. But at last it was happening and she and Mrs. Mott were finally holding that convention. (147)

Talking about it had been one thing and even putting the announcement in the paper had been easy. But now (167)
she, Elizabeth Cady Stanton, actually had to stand up in front of all those people—men, too—and talk! She had (188)
never felt so shy in all her life. (196)

Oh, it was all right for Mrs. Mott because she was a Quaker preacher and was used to speaking before an (217)
audience. But Elizabeth had never done such a thing since public speaking was another one of those things that (236)
"nice" women didn't do. It was considered unfeminine, and in 1848, unfeminine was about the worst thing a (254)
woman could be. Well, at least Lucretia's husband would preside. None of the women, not even Mrs. Mott, felt (273)
equal to that. (276)

SEE TO SAY

	Correct	Error
First Try		
Second Try		

READING PASSAGES
Seventh Grade Level—Skill Sheet 11
(Social Science: Women's Rights)

Directions: Say each word. If you finish before the end of the timing, go back to the beginning and start over.

February 14, 1854, was a very special day in the history of the New York Legislature. For the first time, (20)
a woman was to have a hearing before it, to be sure most of the members already had their minds made (41)
up on this "woman" question. Nothing could convince them that married women should have their own (57)
money, or that women should vote, or that women should have equal rights of any sort. (73)

Still they sat back, crossed their legs, and got ready to listen, for wasn't this Mrs. Henry Stanton, the wife (93)
of one of their own legislators from some years back? There she was now, entering the senate chamber; (111)
very ladylike she looked in black silk with a white lace collar and a diamond pin. Uncommonly dignified (129)
the way she held her head up and didn't appear nervous at all. (142)

Mrs. Stanton stepped to the podium and quiet fell over the room. Taking one long look around she began (161)
with a flourish, in the grand nineteenth century manner. "The tyrant, Custom" she declared in a clear; (178)
ringing voice, "has been summoned before the bar of Common Sense." (189)

Now what did that mean and did her audience understand her? They did all right; they knew that by (208)
Custom, she meant all the traditions that put men over women, rich over poor, white over black, (225)
somebody over somebody else. (229)

These traditions, she was saying, were like a monster. They had ruled far too many people's lives for far (248)
too long. (250)

	Correct	Error
First Try		
Second Try		

READING PASSAGES
Seventh Grade Level—Skill Sheet 12
(Social Science: Women's Rights)

Directions: Say each word. If you finish before the end of the timing, go back to the beginning and start over.

The work that Susan B. Anthony and Mrs. Henry Stanton did together in the 1850s was just the (18)
beginning. Each passing year found them working just as hard as ever for women's rights. There were (35)
setbacks, and they made mistakes, but they never, ever gave up. (46)

When the Civil War came in 1861, women's rights faded from most people's minds—even from the (63)
minds of many women's rights leaders. The war was all consuming. Susan B. Anthony and Mrs. Stanton (80)
founded the Women's Loyal League, a group that raised money for the Union side. Mrs. Stanton thought (97)
that if women put their effort into winning the war and freeing the slaves, then later on, when the war (117)
ended, abolitionists and Union supporters would help women win the vote. (128)

She was wrong, though. When the war ended, the Fifteenth Amendment to the Constitution was ratified. (144)
It defined a citizen as a male, and guaranteed the right to vote and hold office to all males, regardless of (165)
race. So black men won the right to vote finally, but women of all races still couldn't vote. (183)

The worst of it was, in Susan and Mrs. Stanton's eyes, that in the fight over the amendment, the (202)
abolitionists turned their backs on women. Frederick Douglass, William Lloyd Garrison, Wendell (214)
Phillips—all their staunchest allies over the years—refused to support an amendment that would (229)
include race and sex. Even some prominent women refused to support such an amendment. They were (245)
afraid they couldn't win and they thought it was more important for black men to have their rights— (263)
a sure thing—than to try to win equal rights for everyone and lose. (277)

Appendix

Equal Interval Graph

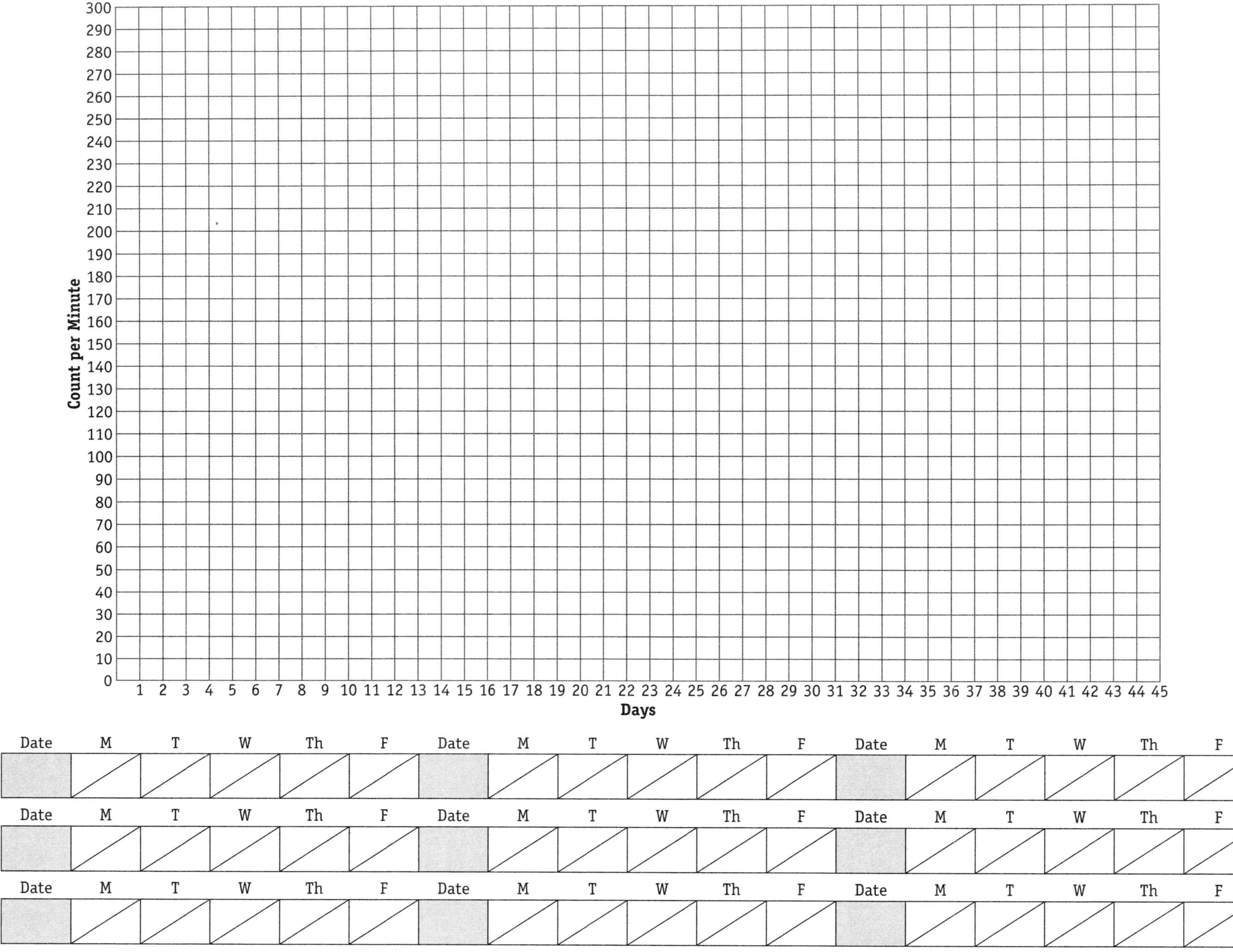

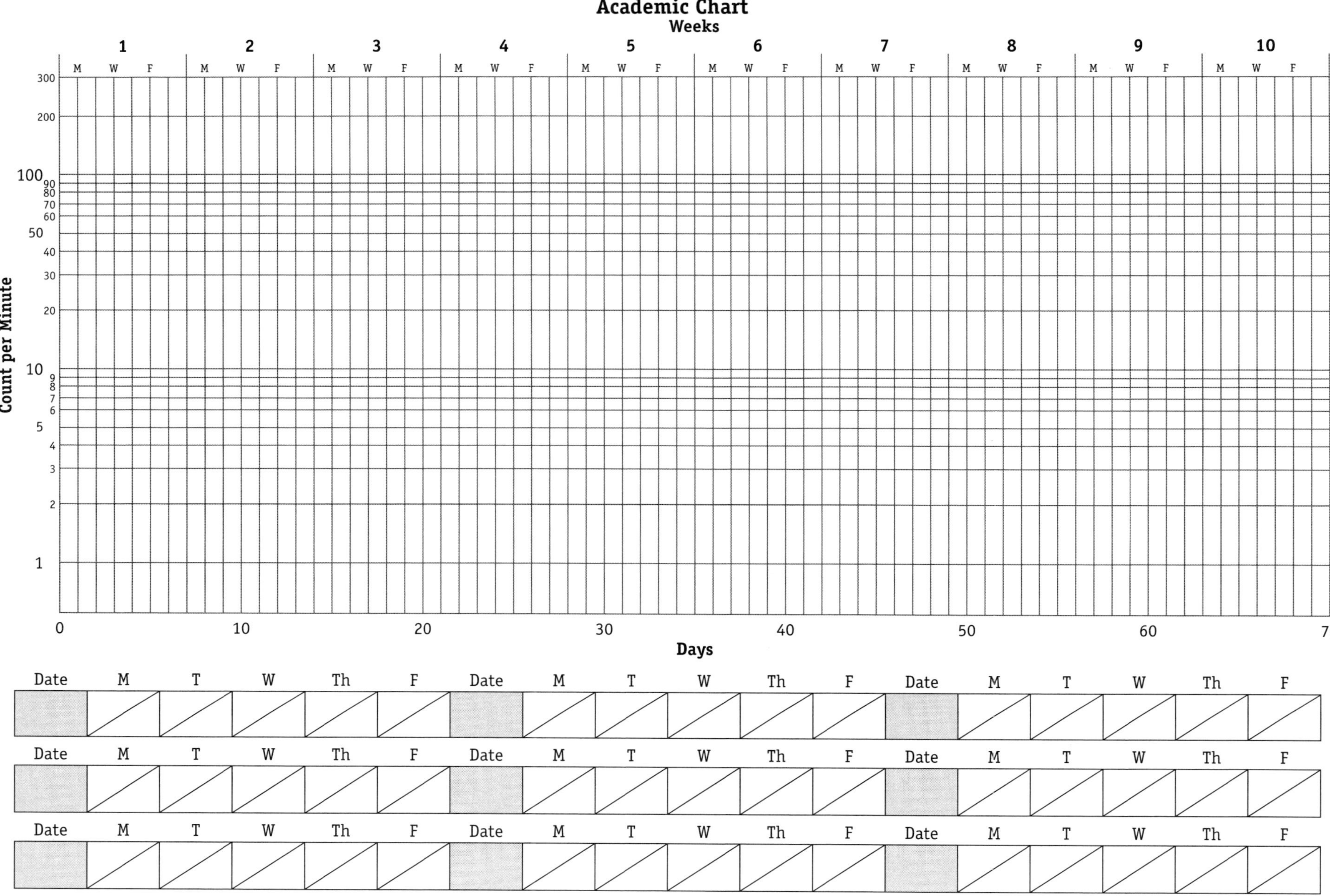
Academic Chart
Weeks
1 2 3 4 5 6 7 8 9 10
M W F
Count per Minute
300 200 100 90 80 70 60 50 40 30 20 10 9 8 7 6 5 4 3 2 1
0 10 20 30 40 50 60 70
Days
Date M T W Th F Date M T W Th F Date M T W Th F
Date M T W Th F Date M T W Th F Date M T W Th F
Date M T W Th F Date M T W Th F Date M T W Th F